MY ANCESTOR SETTLED IN
THE BRITISH WEST INDIES

(with Bermuda, British Guiana
and British Honduras)

by John Titford

GW00454920

SOCIETY OF GENEALOGISTS ENTERPRISES LTD

Published by
Society of Genealogists Enterprises Limited
14 Charterhouse Buildings, Goswell Road
London EC1M 7BA

© The Society of Genealogists Enterprises 2011.

ISBN: 978-1-907199-08-0

British Library Cataloguing in Publication Data
A CIP Catalogue record for this book is available from the British Library.

The Society of Genealogists Enterprises Limited is a wholly owned
subsidiary of the Society of Genealogists, a registered charity, no 233701.

About the Author

John Titford is a professional genealogist, a freelance writer and lecturer and an antiquarian bookseller. He has written a number of books and articles on accents and dialects, cinema studies and family history, and is the author/editor of the latest edition of the *Penguin Dictionary of British Surnames.*

In 1983 he was awarded First Prize by the Institute of Heraldic and Genealogical Studies in a competition to find the best-written family history. *The Titford Family 1547-1947* was subsequently published by Phillimore's in 1989.

He belongs to a number of Family History Societies, is a Trustee and Chairman of Examiners for the Institute of Heraldic and Genealogical Studies and former Vice-Chairman and Chairman of the Board of Assessors for the Association of Genealogists and Researchers in Archives (AGRA).

He has been Chairman of the Education Sub-Committee of the Federation of Family History Societies, a member of the Executive Committee of the Society of Genealogists, chairman of the Society's Publications Committee and General Editor for the 'My Ancestor was...' series of publications. He was elected a Fellow of the Society in 2004 and a Fellow of the Society of Antiquaries in 2011.

In what spare time he has, he plays guitar, melodeon and concertina, is a great lover of American blues and English folk music, sings, with his wife Heather, in the 'Rolling Stock Company' and the Duffield West Gallery Choir, based in Derbyshire, and is a magistrate.

Cover - The splendidly named Inspector Uailean Hamish McUistean Gooden-Chisholm of the Trinidad Constabulary in the driving seat of his official car, alongside another officer. This picture was taken in about 1900. Mr Gooden-Chisholm, son of a plantation owner, died in Inverness, Scotland, in 1929, aged 35.

CONTENTS

A word of explanation

It is fitting and appropriate that Caribbean history is now being written and re-written in such a way as to pay tribute, not to the colonizers of past times, but to those who were colonized, or who were forced to labour ceaselessly for the benefit of their colonial masters.

Yet this book concerns itself with those colonizers themselves, be they rich and powerful, of middling wealth only, or poor and exploited. Here the focus is on those who went *to* the West Indies, not to those who formed part of the late twentieth century diaspora of those who travelled *away from* the region, moving east from the Caribbean to Britain in search of work or of a new home.

Never let it be said that making genealogical investigations into British families who settled in the West Indies is an easy task. The problem is not so much that detailed records were not created: it is what has happened to them subsequently which has so often been nothing short of a disaster for those who treasure archives and the stories they can reveal.

Story after sad story reveals itself as we move from island to island: archives have so often been shamefully neglected, left to rot in an unfriendly climate in unsuitable storage areas, chewed up by rodents, attacked by insects, destroyed during fires, hurricanes, earthquakes or at times of civil strife. Matters were bad enough during colonial days, but have sometimes not improved in more recent years, grievous losses having occurred as if lessons have not been learned. Newly-independent nations in the Caribbean have clearly had more pressing matters to occupy their time and resources than the need to preserve records of a departed colonial power, though one sometimes wishes that archive material which could not be safely housed on the islands might have been transported to the Mother Country or elsewhere for safe keeping. In the case of Guyana, for instance, we have something like a worst-case scenario: the Guyana / British Guiana Genealogical Society, which has made sterling efforts to provide a wide range of genealogical material on its website, seems to be both bewildered and frustrated by the state of affairs in a country where archive holdings are uncatalogued and generally inaccessible, and where, for example, records of birth, marriage and death may be consulted - but only by callers in person, and only on a Friday… The Society has this to say: 'When the British left the then Colony named British Guiana, vital records (births, marriages, and deaths) were left in-country. Since independence, Guyana has experienced severe economic depression and civil strife, excluding any interest or ability to preserve or make available the historical and vital records'. The Society's website tries to redress the balance, but so much damage has already been done, and not many years ago a well-

v

known British genealogist who visited Georgetown was horrified to watch unique documents being wafted out of the archive office window by a strong breeze...

For all that, matters are now improving in many instances, and I must say that when I have written to various archive offices in the West Indies with an enquiry concerning their records, I have always had a most courteous, helpful and professional response.

There is a certain inconsistency in the treatment given to each territory featured in this book; in some cases there has been almost too much to say (Barbados, Jamaica), and in other cases too little (Caymans, Turks and Caicos). Where relevant information regarding archive holdings has been thin on the ground, I have tried to eke it out with other material - as I have done, for example, in the chapters on Anguilla and British Guiana, where I have included a thick forest of names of individuals. I have gone into a lot of detail regarding records held in Trinidad and in Tobago, for example; this is because there is very little such information available elsewhere, and also because, having commissioned a researcher to let me have a detailed report on what material was available, I didn't want to waste any of it!

To write about genealogical research in the West Indies is to aim at a moving target: archive holdings may be augmented or reduced, be catalogued or left in a chaotic mess; the repositories where records are held may change, as may their addresses; websites come and go, URLs are often altered or lost without trace, and new sites are appearing almost daily. *Nil desperandum*: a search engine will often lead the researcher in the right direction. If in doubt, 'Google it', is my advice. In this book I have tried to be as accurate and as up-to-date as possible, but things will assuredly change over time.

Finally: I have included Bermuda in this book, though I am well aware that it is situated in the Atlantic, not in the Caribbean; for administrative purposes it was always considered to be part of the West Indies by the Colonial Office in London - and that, shall we say, is good enough for me... Similarly, Guyana (British Guiana) and Belize (British Honduras) are also dealt with here; they certainly belong to the Caribbean region in its broadest sense - and if they don't fit here, they fit nowhere?

Acknowledgments

The golden rule when it comes to Acknowledgments is to keep a note of individuals who have helped you as you go along, lest you forget to mention them. This I have signally failed to do in this case, alas, largely because much of the material in this book was initially destined to be used for a series of articles in *Family Tree Magazine* from the late 1990s onwards, and a book was not then in prospect. So here I am happy to make a more-than-conventional apology to those kind souls I may have omitted to mention here.

My most grateful thanks - not for the first time - go to my wife Heather, who loves to visit West Indian islands as much as I do, and who has been a tower of strength, as ever.

I must also thank the members of the Publications Working Party at the Society of Genealogists (of which working party, it must be admitted, I am a member…) for agreeing to support this publishing venture, and am pleased to acknowledge my debt to Else Churchill, to Graham Collett and to other members of staff at the Society who have made its production possible. In particular, my heartfelt thanks go to Nicholas Newington-Irving for having undertaken the not-inconsiderable task of indexing the book - a labour of love which he has carried out with his customary skill and enthusiasm.

I am most grateful to my friend Jim Lynch of Toronto for all he has done, and continues to do, to help those who are researching West Indian ancestry, and Anita Lisbey and Emory King (an indefatigable enthusiast), both of Belize, have also been a great help. Rob Thompson, formerly at the Society of Genealogists and later a Caribbean representative for MacMillan publishing, has been most supportive, as has Nicholas Battle of Countryside Books, my friend Sandi Hewlett from Philadelphia and Nathan W. Murphy of the Family History Library in Salt Lake City.

At one stage the renowned genealogist and indexer Cliff Webb produced a typescript relating to British islands overseas with a view to publication; I was lucky enough to have acquired a copy of his text, compiled with the thoroughness for which he is famed, and have found it most useful as a complement to my own findings.

Many archivists in the region have replied promptly and courteously to my enquiries about their holdings, and I thank them for their professionalism in that regard.

Others have trod this path before me, of course, and in particular I must say how useful I have found it to have books by Guy Grannum at my side when compiling this work of my own.

And to all those of you I have forgotten: thanks, guys!

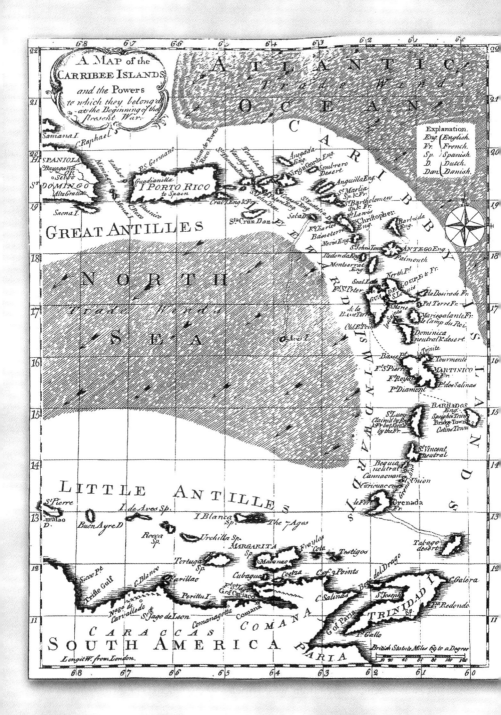

The empire on which the sun eventually set

That rag-tag collection of countries across the globe that made up the old British Empire: was it acquired in a fit of forgetfulness, as some have said? In fact the story is more complicated than that, and we can rarely say that Britain lacked motive of one sort or another as it added more and more places to its imperial portfolio. Some colonies had a strategic importance, but in any case it must have been sweet indeed to act at times like a dog in the manger - to annex territory, whether you really wanted it or not, just to prevent old enemies from getting their hands on it. In other instances the home country was not at all keen to welcome this or the other applicant or supplicant into the imperial club: Fiji, for example, had to pester the authorities in London on countless occasions before being granted its membership card.

The most essential colonies had a lot more to offer, however - they could act as a market for goods produced in the home country, and above all they could be stripped of their natural resources or could provide products which the colonial power was eager to acquire. Foremost amongst such products, strange to say, were non-essential luxuries. Europeans travelled east for spices and for silks, but went west in search of tobacco and sugar - which is one of the factors that helps to explain the critical importance of North America and of the West Indies in the history of the British empire.

Europeans are not best suited, either in terms of physique or temperament, to hard labour in tropical climates, and the original impressed white workers in the tobacco and sugar plantations were soon replaced by an unimaginably vast number of slaves from West Africa and elsewhere. The British had not invented slavery, and were made aware of its utility in the Caribbean by the Portuguese colonists from Brazil, but the gruesome and inexcusable trade in 'black ivory' would leave an all-but indelible stain on Britain's colonial story which still threatens to overshadow its more positive aspects, of which there are more than a few.

That empire has now been reduced to a mere rump, consisting of fourteen so-called British Overseas Territories (formerly known as Crown Colonies or British Dependent Territories), of which no fewer than five (Anguilla, British Virgin Islands, Cayman Islands, Montserrat, Turks and Caicos Islands) are in the West Indies, together with Bermuda, which is so often associated in the public mind with the islands of the Caribbean.

History and geography

We may think of the British West Indies today as God's gift to travel agents' brochures - as a charming earthly paradise in which sun-soaked and palm tree-fringed beaches are lapped by the glittering blue ocean - but to colonists of earlier generations these islands merited much more serious consideration, being not just a playground but also, at times, a battleground, as the English, the Dutch, the French, the Spanish and the Portuguese struggled to extend their global influence. More often than not the islands were used as bargaining counters in peace treaties. In the year 1763, for example, during negotiations leading to a treaty with the French, the British authorities thought long and hard as to whether it might be better to hand back the whole of Canada in exchange for the one single Caribbean island of Guadeloupe. At times the island colonies, strategically important and providers of sugar and other exports, seemed more vital to the British than the mainland settlements of North America; Barbados and Jamaica were valued more than Massachusetts or Virginia. Indeed, the very concept of 'North America' in earlier centuries would usually have included the West Indian dimension as well as the original thirteen colonies. Had not Admiral Nelson received erroneous information regarding the location of the French fleet under Villeneuve when he was anchored in Carlisle Bay, Barbados (he proceeded south to Trinidad instead of north to Antigua), one of the world's great sea battles would have taken place, not off Cape Trafalgar, but in West Indian waters. In short, we should never underestimate the importance of the islands of the West Indies, these apparently trivial yet geographically-critical and wealth-creating off-shoots of empire, in world history.

The West Indies consist of a chain of islands stretching in a curve from Florida to the northern coast of South America - from the Bahamas in the north-west to Trinidad, off the coast of Venezuela, in the south-east Cuba, with an area of 44,178 miles, is by far the largest island, while some of the smaller islets are only a few acres in extent, and in colonial days some islands of minimal size or importance were treated as sub-dependencies of dependencies, as it were.

It might be useful to define and to clarify a number of terms associated with the area at the outset:

West Indies. Named by Columbus in 1492, who believed he had arrived at India. The West Indies include the Bahamas, the Greater Antilles (Cuba, Hispaniola, Puerto Rico and Jamaica) and the Lesser Antilles, sometimes called the Caribbee Islands.

Antilles. Synonymous with the West Indies; before the European navigators had discovered the New World, they used the term 'Antilla' to designate a mythical land between the Canaries and India. After Columbus determined that this land was in fact a group of islands, the plural 'antilles' was used.

Caribbean Sea. Named after the hostile Carib Indians whom Columbus found on the islands of the Lesser Antilles and the Venezuelan coast.

Leeward and Windward Islands. Early cartographers had referred to the more protected Greater Antilles as the 'Islas de Sottovento' (islands under the wind) and to the Lesser Antilles as 'Islas de Barlovento' (islands over the wind), but in time the term 'Leeward Islands' came to mean those formerly British Islands that lie north of St Lucia - Antigua, St Kitts, Nevis, Anguilla, Montserrat and the British Virgin Islands - while the 'Windward Islands' consist of the once-British islands of St Lucia, Dominica, the Grenadines, St Vincent and Grenada, situated between the Leeward Islands and Venezuela, within the same geographical area as Barbados, Trinidad and Tobago, and the French island of Martinique.

Until 1671 the Leeward Islands had been part of the general government of the Caribbean Islands, but in that year Antigua, St Kitts, Montserrat, the Virgin Islands and Nevis were separated from Barbados and the Windward Islands and put under their own Governor-in-Chief. In 1816 the Leeward Islands were divided into two divisions, the first consisting of Antigua and Montserrat, and the second of St Kitts, Nevis, Anguilla and the Virgin Islands. In 1833 they were reunited under one Governor General, with Dominica being added, and in 1871 a federal colony of the Leeward Islands was constituted. Dominica was transferred to the Windward Islands in 1940.

In 1763 the 'Southern Caribbee' islands of Grenada, Dominica, St Vincent and Tobago were united under one Governor. Dominica was separated from this group in 1771, as was St Vincent in 1776; Tobago was ceded to France in 1783. In 1833

St Vincent, Grenada, Barbados and Tobago were brought under a single Governor-in-Chief (though each retained its own institutions and had a local administrator or Lieutenant Governor), to be joined by St Lucia five years later. The political entity known officially as the Windward Islands came into existence on 17th March 1885, comprising four individual colonies (the existing grouping, with Barbados omitted) with a common Governor-in-Chief. Tobago was withdrawn and attached to Trinidad in 1888, and Dominica, formerly part of the Leeward Islands, was transferred to the Windwards in 1940. Each of the islands achieved a degree of self-rule in 1960, and the post of Governor-in-Chief was abolished.

Spanish Main. This expression is sometimes applied to the entire Caribbean area, though more properly it refers to the mainland of the South American countries bordering on the Caribbean sea - that is, Venezuela and Colombia - and also Panama.

Not all place names in the West Indies are pronounced in the way that we might expect: so Antigua is 'Anteega'; Nevis is 'Neevis'; Anguilla is 'Angwilla', Grenada is 'Grenayda', Dominica is 'Domineeka' (not to be confused with the Dominican Republic) and the Leeward Islands are sometimes 'Looard'.

The tropical climate of the West Indian islands and the fertility of the soil proved an attractive prospect for the early Spanish voyagers and settlers who were, in any case, only too pleased to extend the areas of influence of their home country and to enslave the indigenous Indian population to work for them in building an empire. In the event, Spain's predominance in Europe would decline as rapidly as it had risen, and during the seventeenth century it would be the English, the French and the Dutch who fought for possession of the islands in the sun. It wasn't long before the lack of a workforce capable of planting, tending, harvesting and processing large quantities of sugar and tobacco led to the importation of indentured white labourers, and then of black slaves from West Africa - an inhuman practice learned by the British from their Portuguese and Dutch counterparts. These black slaves in the West Indies and elsewhere were settlers of the Old Empire by constraint rather than by choice. Not that all those who were transported ever reached their destination; it has been estimated that during the three centuries of the slave trade over a million individuals died at sea on their journey to the Americas. For all that, over a million and a half slaves were successfully transported to the British West Indies. Eventually, on an island such as Antigua, blacks would outnumber whites by as many as ten to one; hardly surprisingly, the descendants of black slaves still form a large part of the population of the islands as a whole, alongside those with British, Dutch, Spanish, Portuguese, Danish, Swedish and French ancestry. The resultant racial mix is both broad and complex.

The British in the West Indies

The first British colony in North America was that of Newfoundland, settled as early as 1583, followed by Bermuda in 1609-12. It was following the great success of Virginian tobacco that the English looked for new lands upon which to grow this profitable crop, with the result that a settlement was established on St Kitts in 1623, followed by Barbados four years later. A number of islands came into and out of British hands as the years went by. A summary of the situation follows:

Barbados (settled 1627), Antigua (settled 1632) and the Bahamas (settled 1666) were continuously under British rule from the time of their first settlement.

St Kitts (settled 1623), Nevis (settled 1628) and Montserrat (settled 1632) were in French hands from 1782 to 1783, but otherwise always British.

Grenada and St Vincent were taken from the French in 1762, were in British hands from that date to 1779, in French possession from 1779 to 1783, and from 1783 continuously British.

Dominica was taken from the French in 1761, was British until 1778, French from 1778 to 1783, British from 1783.

St Lucia, taken from the French in 1762, was British from 1762 to 1763, from 1778 to 1783, from 1794 to 1795, from 1796 to 1802, and from 1803 onwards.

Tobago became a British colony in 1762, before which time it had enjoyed a neutral status; it was a colony from 1762 to 1781, from 1793 to 1802 and from 1803 onwards.

Trinidad was taken from Spain in 1797.

Jamaica (originally Spanish) and the Caymans were conquered in 1655 and the British Virgin Islands in 1672; Anguilla was settled in 1650, Barbuda in 1661-2 and the Turks Islands in 1678.

Of Islands which passed out of British control, Guadeloupe was taken from the French in 1759, was restored in 1763, was held by Britain briefly in 1794, and at greater length from 1810 to 1825; Martinique was in British possession from 1762 to 1763, from 1794 to 1802 and from 1809 to 1815; Curaçao, taken from the Dutch, was in British hands during part of 1798 and from 1807 to 1814; St Eustatius (also taken from the Dutch) was British during a part of 1781.

North America, including the West Indies, was a favourite destination for emigrants from Britain; it is estimated that about 540,000 people left England between 1630 and 1700, of whom about 380,000 went to the Americas. Voluntary settlers, many of whom came from wealthy backgrounds in England or were the impoverished sons of parents of high social status, lived alongside transported criminals and indentured servants, who would serve seven to ten years on the plantations and would then be granted a few acres of land of their own. Some settlers hoped to make a fortune and return home; others were content just to survive the ravages of disease and the monotony of daily toil and to live to see better days.

CHAPTER ONE

Genealogical sources for settlers in the British West Indies: a general survey

1. MANUSCRIPT SOURCES HELD IN THE WEST INDIES

In principle, and if records have been generated and have survived, genealogical research in the West Indies relies upon sources similar to those which are used within Britain itself, namely: parish registers, civil registers of birth, marriage and death, census returns, tax returns, legal records, deeds, military records, criminal records, newspapers and correspondence, both official and private. Most people living in the West Indies had their wills proved in local church courts (or, later, in civil courts), but wills of British subjects dying abroad or at sea with estates back in England or Wales were proved in the Prerogative Court of Canterbury (or in the Principal Probate Registry in London, from 1858). From the late seventeenth century onwards many wills of seamen on merchant vessels, and some on ships of the Royal Navy (to circa 1750), appear in the records of the Commissary Court of London at the London Metropolitan Archives, and the original wills of seamen in the Royal Navy from 1786 to 1882 are in class ADM48 at The National Archives in London.

Many of the vital records of interest to the student of West Indian family history are held on the islands themselves, and I have tried to identify relevant repositories, such as archive offices, museums, and public or

historical society libraries, in each chapter of this book. Sad to say, much archive material has not survived the ravages of war, hurricanes, earthquakes, fires, climate, insect damage and a general lack of care. So in 1930 the records of the Vice-Admiralty Court of Jamaica were found to be heaped together 'in a huge mound, of which only the edges could be examined', and one nineteenth-century Governor of Barbados is known to have thrown large quantities of documents into the sea... More often than not it is no easy task to determine exactly which records have survived, and if so, precisely where they are now held. Archive material of all sorts may have been resited, recatalogued, destroyed or mislaid. Luckily the internet can help to clarify the situation in some instances, and there are useful printed archive listings (some now out-of-date, alas) for the Leeward and Windward Islands, Jamaica, Barbados, the Bahamas and elsewhere. Yet even when the researcher has been lucky or tenacious enough to locate records which may be of interest, frustration may lie in wait: as Anthony Camp remarked in an article entitled 'Some West Indian sources in England' (*Family Tree Magazine*, November 1987), '...it seems impossible to find anyone there who will undertake competent searches at reasonable fees.' One can only hope that such a situation will improve; a personal visit to a West Indian archive office could be a most rewarding experience (alongside a holiday, naturally), and if a local researcher is sought, it is certainly worthwhile using the internet to determine the current state of affairs.

2. MANUSCRIPT SOURCES HELD IN BRITISH REPOSITORIES

A guide to manuscript sources for the history of Latin America and the Caribbean in the British Isles by P Walne (1973) gives details of holdings in the British Isles county-by-county, and includes private as well as public records, all fully indexed. Particularly voluminous are the archives held by The National Archives, the British Library, the Bodleian Library and the National Library of Scotland. This is not a work intended for family historians, but you will find certain items of genealogical value featured here; so among the entries for Bedfordshire, for example, are eighteenth and nineteenth century accounts, family settlements, wills and other documents relating to the estates of the Payne family in St Vincent, St Kitts and Nevis, together with various papers relating to Jamaica and a memorial to the Roman Catholic inhabitants of Grenada in 1771.

A very significant collection of manuscript sources for the West Indies is housed in The National Archives in London; a helpful list of several of these may be found in *Tracing your ancestors in The National Archives* by Amanda Bevan (2006), and a detailed survey of the major classes of relevant documents appears in *Tracing your West Indian ancestors* by Guy Grannum (2002). For a really comprehensive listing of what is available, look at the TNA catalogue at www.nationalarchives.gov.uk/catalogue/search.asp. Of particular importance for the West Indies as a whole are the records of the Colonial Office, which was established in 1854, though the CO series includes records of its predecessors from the sixteenth century onwards (until 1782 responsibility for colonial matters was split between the Board of Trade and Plantations and the Secretaries of State). CO records include the following: original correspondence; entry books; acts; sessional papers; government gazettes; miscellanea; blue books of statistics; Naval Office returns and newspapers. Finding a reference to a particular person in most of these records will rarely be an easy task, as few of them are indexed, but original correspondence will often include inhabitants' lists and much else, while gazettes contain a good deal of information of interest to family historians, such as birth, marriage and death notices, obituaries, public appointments and a variety of name lists. TNA also holds various records of slaves, of slave-owners and of colonial regiments raised in the West Indies; you should refer to Grannum's book for details and examples.

Colonial Office records in TNA for the Leeward Islands, the Windward Islands and 'West Indies, General' will by definition contain material relevant to the islands within these groupings, as will certain records held there for former colonial powers in the region (Denmark, France, the Netherlands, Spain, Sweden, the USA). After 1967 relevant records were generated by the Foreign and Commonwealth Office, not by the Colonial Office. Additionally, some records, especially those relating to military affairs, can exist before Britain became the controlling power - so see certain records of the War Office.

The Land and Emigration Commission, established in 1833, promoted emigration by providing free passage and grants of land. The Emigration Entry Books, 1814-71 (CO 385) and the Land and Emigration Commission Papers, 1833-71 (CO 386) give the name of emigrants.

The Society of Genealogists in London has an excellent collection of books and manuscripts of West Indian interest, including the forty three volumes of manuscripts compiled by Mrs Vernona T C Smith, who died in 1902. Mrs Smith had worked alongside the indefatigable V L Oliver (whose printed works we will consider below), and her manuscripts include extracts from Colonial Office papers, Close Rolls and wills proved in the Prerogative Court of Canterbury; most of the volumes of her work are indexed in the Society's Great Card Index. Oliver himself died in 1942; his own papers on various West Indian families were sorted by surname and entered in the Society's document collection.

The library of the Royal Commonwealth Society, now housed within Cambridge University Library, has a significant collection of archive material relating to the West Indies, including fifteen boxes of manuscript, typescript and printed material which comprise the Nicholas Darnell Davis collection. Davis had a life-long interest in the history and genealogy of the West Indies, and was the author of *The cavaliers and roundheads of Barbados, 1650-1652* (1887). *The manuscript catalogue of the library of the Royal Commonwealth Society*, edited by Donald H Simpson in 1975, includes a short summary of the Davis collection, but the library itself has a more detailed manuscript listing.

A number of parish registers and other records relating to the West Indies have been microfilmed by the Church of Jesus Christ of Latter-Day Saints and details of holdings may be found at: www.familysearch.org/eng/Library/FHLC/frameset_fhlc.asp. Films can usually be viewed by arrangement at LDS Church Family History Centres. Some, for Jamaica and other islands, are kept permanently at the London LDS Family History Centre in Exhibition Road. Listings of such material for Bermuda, Barbados and the Bahamas also appear in *The Library: a guide to the LDS Family History Library* by J Cerny and W Elliott (1988), pp. 693-702. Voluminous vital records relating to settlers in the West Indies may be found in the International Genealogical Index (now within FamilySearch) and related databases at www.familysearch.org/ (or at its forerunner, www.familysearch.org/eng/)

3. PRINTED BOOKS

In the present book, each individual chapter includes a list of suggestions for further reading. The works featured below are of more general relevance. There is no shortage of printed works relating to genealogical sources for the West Indies, and with luck the efforts of authors and editors will have saved the researcher the frustration of having to trawl through original documents with no certainty of success. Intrepid researchers will find that some of the printed works featured here have been (or no doubt will be) made available on the internet, or by way of a CD-ROM edition.

Published works on holdings in The National Archives
(formerly the Public Record Office)

Various West Indian holdings at TNA are featured in printed calendars, transcripts and other works, including the following:

Acts of the Privy Council of England. Colonial series 1613-1783. 6 vols. 1908-12.
Banton, M *Administering the Empire, 1801-1968: a guide to the records of the*

Colonial Office in the national archives of the UK. 2008.
Calendar of State Papers, Colonial (1574-1660): America and the West Indies (1661-1739). 40 vols. 1860-1993.
Journals of the Board of Trade and Plantations 1704-1782. 14 vols. 1920-38.
List of Colonial Office records. Vol 36 of *PRO Lists and Indexes.* 1911.
Ragatz, L J *A guide to the Official Correspondence of the Governors of the British West Indies colonies with the Secretary of State, 1763-1833.* 1923.
Thurston, A. *Sources for colonial studies in the Public Record Office: Records of the Colonial Office, Dominions Office, Commonwealth Relations Office and Commonwealth Office.* 1995.

Published works by Vere Langford Oliver

The tireless genealogical endeavours of V L Oliver, ably assisted by Mrs Vernona T C Smith, resulted in the publication of a number of printed works of inestimable value to anyone interested in the history of West Indian settler families. In 1927, having already written a definitive three-volume history of Antigua and a work on the monumental inscriptions of Barbados, Oliver produced *The monumental inscriptions of the British West Indies*, based upon inscriptions personally transcribed by him in Antigua, Dominica, Montserrat, Nevis, St Kitts, Grenada, St Lucia, Tobago, Trinidad, Demerara and the Bahamas. An earlier work with a similar title, *Monumental inscriptions of the British West Indies from the earliest date* by J H Lawrence-Archer, had appeared in 1875.

It could be argued that Oliver's greatest achievement was the publication of *Caribbeana: being miscellaneous papers relating to the history, genealogy, topography and antiquities of the British West Indies*. This appeared in quarterly parts from 1910 to 1920, making five full volumes, together with an incomplete sixth volume and two supplements (*The registers of St Thomas, Middle Island, St Kitts* and *West Indian bookplates* in two parts). It ran as a journal over more years than Oliver would have liked, owing to the intervention of the First World War, but includes at least some material for nearly all the islands of the West Indies. Few enough libraries hold a full set of this work, but the Society of Genealogists has all the published volumes, supplemented by a typescript index to the incomplete volume six. In 2000 Jim Lynch of Toronto undertook to reprint *Caribbeana* in its entirety in a very limited edition, complete with a freshly-compiled index to volume six and a facsimile set of accumulated indexes for ease of reference. Each volume contains a preface by John Titford, giving a brief outline of Oliver's career.

Caribbeana should surprise and delight the reader: it is packed with calendars and transcriptions of parish registers, wills, deeds and correspondence; it includes pedigrees, extracts from newspapers, extensive notes on families and a host of illustrations. Fully indexed, it is easy to consult and fascinating to browse through. Its main series of pedigrees is indexed in J B Whitmore's *Genealogical Guide* (1953).

Published works on emigration to the West Indies

A substantial number of published works relating to emigrants to North America and the West Indies have appeared over the years. A selection (many of which can be found at the Society of Genealogists) follows:

Passenger and immigration lists: a guide to published records of immigrants who came to the New World between the sixteenth and the mid-twentieth centuries by W Filby [with various co-editors], published by Gale of Detroit. There are three original volumes, 1981, continued by regular supplements. The core volumes and earlier supplements are also available on CD-ROM and are also on Ancestry.com. Use Filby's book with its alphabetical listings of millions of individuals as a master index which will refer you to other printed works. Each volume contains its own bibliography, but there is a complementary publication: *Passenger and immigration lists bibliography, 1538-1900, being a guide to published lists of arrivals in the United States and Canada* (Second Edition, 1988).

Of the many printed works indexed by Filby, perhaps the most useful and comprehensive are those produced by the English genealogist, P W Coldham. The crowning glory of all his work is *The complete book of emigrants* (four volumes, 1607-1776, published 1988-93), together with *The complete book of emigrants in bondage, 1614-1775* (1988, with a *Supplement*, 1992) and *More emigrants in bondage* (2002). These compilations, taken from various English (but not Irish, Welsh, Scottish or American) records render several of Coldham's earlier works (and those by various other authors) redundant, and update and augment Hotten (see below). *Emigrants* and *Emigrants in bondage* are now available together on one CD-ROM, with the great advantage that a search can be made on place names. In this way the full impact of Coldham's research becomes abundantly clear. Here you will find thousands of references to individuals with West Indian connections:

16 May 1631: Probate of PCC will of John Bourne of Dagenham, Essex (of Nevis), died overseas.

25 August 1683: Apprenticed in London, Francis East to Phillip Redwood, 4 years Tobago.

9 January 1629: Henry Jones, brought in from Bread Street as a vagrant, says he was born in Berkshire and is willing to go to St Christopher's, apprenticed for 7 years to George

Best, Citizen and Grocer of London.

17 February 1632: John Howlet, a vagrant boy who has been here before [Bridewell], to go to Barbados.

Not only that, but several entries throw fascinating light upon the history of the colonies themselves:

16 March 1639. The King orders that no attempts be made to allure inhabitants from St Christopher's, Barbados, Nevis, Montserrat or Antigua which were granted to the late Earl of Carlisle.

26 September 1655. Instructions for Daniel Godkin now bound to New England regarding the removal of people from Nevis to Jamaica. The inhabitants of New England are to be instructed that the English Army took possession of Jamaica on 16 May 1655; they are to be told of the goodness of the place and those who fear the Lord to be offered encouragement to remove there. Those in New England driven from their native land to a barren wilderness for conscience' sake may remove to a land of plenty. Every man above the age of 10 who removes to Jamaica will be granted 20 acres of land and every other male or female 10 acres.

Two of Coldham's further works, *American wills and administrations in the Prerogative Court of Canterbury 1610-1857* (1989) and *American wills proved in London 1611-1775* (1992), contain West Indian references and have place indexes, and nearly every page of *Child Apprentices in America from Christ's Hospital, London, 1617-1778* (1990) has details of young children apprenticed to the Caribbean islands:

Richard Davies, baptised 28 January 1752, son of Rev. Thomas Davies, admitted from Ystraddyfodwg, Glamorgan; 30 June 1767 with the consent of his mother Ann Davies to James Brebner Esq. of Antigua, merchant.

Coldham's *English adventurers and emigrants 1609-1660: Abstracts of examinations in the High Court of Admiralty with reference to Colonial America* (1984) is packed with detail of people who journeyed to the West Indies or Bermuda, even if they did not actually settle there. So in the case of The Lord Protector vs. John White, Nehemiah Bourne and others in 1658, Moyses Butler, a 25 year old merchant, deposed that he was factor of the *White Rock* of London, which sailed from there in December 1657 with state provisions intended for Barbados and Jamaica. The ship went from Barbados to New England to load masts and two chests of money at Piscataway and departed for London on 22 July 1658. On 22 August she met with two Spanish ships which she fought for five or six hours before being lost and driven ashore in Cornwall.

Similarly-detailed entries appear in *High Court of Admiralty Examinations 1637-1638* by D O Shilton and R Holworthy (1932). In the case of Howe and others vs. Thomas Pead and John Worsam (January 1637-8), Abraham Paule of Exeter, merchant, aged 28, and Christian Brookehaven of Barbados, merchant, aged 27, depose that when Joseph Jordan came home master of the *Amity* from Barbados to London, they were both passengers on board. Paule laded seventeen bags of cotton-wool for the account of John Barringer of London, merchant, but on the homeward voyage the ship proved very leaky, and for three weeks the company (including the passengers) had to pump and bale out water night and day. It was generally feared that the ship would founder, but eventually she put into Plymouth and had the leaks stopped. In the meanwhile, hardly surprisingly, the lading had been 'much damnified by water'.

A little-known but fascinating work by George Sherwood, an early stalwart of the Society of Genealogists, entitled *Dramatis Personae: new discoveries in biography and genealogy*, published in weekly parts from 8th January 1916, contains a smattering of items of American and West Indian interest. Compared to the voyage of the *Peggy* of New York in 1766, during which James Campbell, a mariner, died raving mad and David Flat, a foremast man, found that it had fallen to his lot to be killed and eaten, the experience of the crew of a ship sailing to Guinea and Jamaica featured in a case in the Court of Delegates for 1705 seems tame enough. John Ingle, the master, took in negroes at Guinea and delivered them at Antigua; meanwhile James Sherwood, a boatswain, was put into irons for four or five days and John Richards, a foremast man, was beaten by Ingle with a cat-o'-nine-tails made of cod line in very barbarous and inhuman manner. Edward Wildman, John Richmond and John Wappin had gone on shore at Guinea and stayed away a week without leave; the master wished to return to Guinea from Antigua, but the sailors demanded to be taken back to London according to agreement, whereupon he refused to pay them.

A well-known book by J C Hotten, *The original lists of persons of quality, emigrants, religious exiles, political rebels, serving men sold for a term of years, apprentices, children stolen, maidens pressed and others who went from Great Britain to the American plantations, 1600-1700, with their ages, the localities where they formerly lived in the mother country, the names of the ships in which they embarked and other interesting particulars*, which takes its information from 'manuscripts preserved in the State Paper Department of her Majesty's Public Record Office, London', has been published in various editions from 1874 onwards. Hotten's work can also be searched on the Ancestry.co.uk website, where it has been given the title of *Persons of quality original lists*. Here you will find a significant number of references to individuals in the West Indies and Bermuda

('The Somer Islands'), together with seventeenth century parish register abstracts, lists of inhabitants for Barbados and details of tickets granted to emigrants leaving Barbados, 1678-9, bound for New England, Carolina, Virginia, New York, Antigua, Jamaica, Newfoundland and elsewhere.

Hotten also features names of rebels transported to Barbados and other plantations following the unsuccessful Monmouth Rebellion in 1685, for further details of which see *The Monmouth rebels 1685* by W McD Wigfield (1985), which contains informative entries such as the following:

> Whicker, John, father of Benjamin [also transported] of Colyton, yeoman...tried at Dorchester, transported for Nipho on the Betty from Weymouth, Nov.25, to Barbados; sold to Charles Thomas & Co; escaped with Dr.Pitman and returned to London. He wrote part of Pitman's Relation. He had been presented at Exeter and misreported at large.

Hotten's work was continued by J C Brandow in *Omitted chapters from Hotten's original lists, etc.* (1983), which features census returns, parish registers and militia rolls from Barbados, 1679/80.

The Association Oath Rolls of the British Plantations [New York, Virginia, etc.] AD 1696 by W Gandy (1922) gives only the names of individuals with a place, but can be a useful location aid; it includes lists for Barbados, Antigua, Nevis, Montserrat, Antigua, St Kitts and Bermuda.

H F Waters' monumental work, *Genealogical gleanings in England: abstracts of wills relating to early American families, with genealogical notes and pedigrees constructed from the wills and from other records* (reprinted in two volumes, 1981) contains many West Indian references, and is indexed by place. Here you can find, for example, reference to the 1708 will of John Perrie, late of Antigua, now of St James, Westminster, one-time Provost Marshall General of St Christopher, Nevis, Montserrat and Antigua.

Coldham, Hotten and others made extensive use of archival material held by the former Public Record Office in compiling their books on emigration to North America. It is always open to you to refer to the original records if you so wish, and in any case you might find certain published TNA/PRO calendars of interest, principally those of Treasury Books and Papers.

Published works: West Indies, including emigration:

Andrews, C M and Davenport, F G *Guide to manuscript materials for United States history to 1783 in the British Museum, etc.* 1908. Includes, useful material on the Bahamas, etc.

Baker, E C *A guide to records in the Leeward Islands.* 1965.

Baker, E C *A guide to records in the Windward Islands.* 1968.

[Each of these two volumes gives a very comprehensive account of archive material which was then available locally in the islands concerned. A history of the archives is followed by an account of the records covering the island groups as a whole and an in-depth account of government, legal, ecclesiastical, agricultural, commercial and private records for each island separately, including parish, non-conformist and Roman Catholic registers and probate records. These are arranged by repository, both public and private, and newspapers and gazettes are included. Some reference is made to records in English repositories such as those held by the former Public Record Office, the Methodist Missionary Society, the Moravian Union, the National Maritime Museum and the Post Office].

Bell, H C & Parker, D W *Guide to British West Indies archive materials in London and the islands.* 1926. Covers records held at that period both in England and on the islands themselves.

Besse, J *A collection of the sufferings of the people called Quakers...1650 to 1689.* 2 vols. 1753. See vol 2, pages 278-391, for references to Barbados, Nevis, Bermuda, Antigua and Jamaica. Volume 2 has been reprinted with a new introduction and a newly-compiled index of people and places by Michael Gandy, 2001.

British Imperial Calendar (1810-1972), continued as *The Civil Service Year Book.* For the names of senior civil servants posted abroad.

The British overseas : a guide to records of their births, baptisms, marriages, deaths and burials available in the United Kingdom. Guildhall Library Research Guide #2. 3rd edition, 1995. Note: a significant amount of archive material relating to the West Indies has been, or is being, transferred from Guildhall Library to London Metropolitan Archives.

Burns, A *History of the British West Indies.* 1965.

Caribbean historical and genealogical journal. TCI Genealogical Resources, PO Box 15839, San Luis Obispo, California 93406, USA. From 1993.

Catalogue of the West India Reference Library [National Library of Jamaica]. 6 volumes, 1980.

Coke, T *History of the West Indies...especially of the missions which have been established in that archipelago by the Society late in connection with Rev.John Wesley.* 1808, reprinted 1969.

Coldham, P W *Emigrants in chains.* Baltimore, USA. 1992.

Coldham, P W *The Bristol registers of servants sent to foreign plantations 1654-1686*. 1988.

Colonial Office List. From 1862.

Commonwealth Relations Office List. From 1953.

Cundall, F *Bibliography of the West Indies (excluding Jamaica).* 1909.

Dobson, D. This author has produced many titles featuring Scottish emigrants who settled in North America and the West Indies, including *Scots in the West Indies, 1707-1857* (1998) and *The original Scots colonists of Early America: Caribbean supplement 1611-1707* (1999). His *Directory of Scottish settlers in North America 1625-1825* was published in 6 volumes, 1984-1986, and various of his publications have been made available on CD-ROM.

Edwards, B *The history, civil and commercial, of the British colonies in the West Indies*. 5th edition, 5 vols, 1819. Reprinted 1966.

Ezratty, H A *500 years in the Jewish Caribbean: the Spanish & Portuguese Jews in the West Indies*. 2002.

Ferguson, S 'West Indian medical graduates of Edinburgh to 1800'. *Journal of the history of medicine and allied sciences*, Volume 29, no.1 1974.

Fisher, E F S *List of officers who have held local charge of naval stores, etc or have had an administrative responsibility for them, from 1514 A D to 1965, together with some historical notes on the growth and function of the dockyards, bases, etc listed.* c 1969. An unusual and rather obscure book; there are name-lists for Jamaica, Barbados, Antigua, St Lucia, Bermuda and Trinidad.

Gatfield, G *Guide to printed books and manuscripts relating to English and foreign heraldry and genealogy*. 1892. Contains a short list of books and manuscripts in the British Museum relevant to the West Indies, page 227.

General Register Office: *Abstract of arrangements respecting registration of births, marriages and deaths in the United Kingdom and the other countries of the British Commonwealth of Nations, and in the Irish Republic*. 1952. Very dated, but still useful. I know of nothing else that gives as much detail as to what each individual British Caribbean island recorded as part of its registration process.

Green Book of the West Indies. First published in London, 1909.

Grieb, K J (ed) *Research guide to Central America and the Caribbean*. 1985.

Giuseppi, M S *Naturalization of foreign protestants in the American and West Indies colonies*. 1921, reprinted 1964.

Henige, D P *Colonial Governors from the fifteenth century to the present: a comprehensive list* 1970.

Higman, B W (ed) *General history of the Caribbean*. 2011.

Hilton, R *A bibliography of Latin America and the Caribbean: the Hilton Library*. 1980.

Hough, S J and P R O *The Beinecke Lesser Antilles Collection at Hamilton College*. 1994.

Ingram, K E *Manuscript sources for the history of the West Indies*. 2000.

Ingram, K E *Manuscripts relating to Commonwealth Caribbean countries in United States and Canadian repositories*. 1975.

Ingram, K E *Sources for West Indian studies: a supplementary listing, with particular reference to manuscript sources*. 1983.

Keen, R *A survey of the archives of selected missionary societies*. 1968.

Kemp, T J *International vital records handbook*. 5th edition 2009. (This is extremely useful for the exact address of local registration offices. It also has links to websites, coverage of LDS records and costs of certificates.)

Kershaw, R *Emigrants and expats: a guide to sources on UK emigration and residents overseas*. 2002.

Kuczynski, R R *Demographic survey of the British Colonial Empire*. Volume 3: West Indian and American Territories. 1953.

Lucas, C P *A historical geography of the British colonies: Volume 2: The West Indies*. 2nd edition, 1905.

Manross, W W *The Fulham Papers in the Lambeth Palace Library: American colonial section calendar and indexes*. 1965.

Parry, J H, Sherlock, P & Maingot, A *A short history of the West Indies*. 4th.edition, 1987.

Penfold, P A *Maps and plans in the Public Record Office: volume 2: America and the West Indies*. 1974.

Ragatz, L J *A guide for the study of British Caribbean history 1763-1834*. 1970.

Red Book of the West Indies. First appeared in the early twentieth century. The edition of 1922 is the one most commonly met with.

Sabin, J *A dictionary of books relating to America*. 29 volumes, 1868-1936.

Sibree, J *London Missionary Society: A register of missionaries, deputations, etc, from 1796 to 1923*. 4th edition, 1923.

Stewart, J *The British Empire: an encyclopedia of the Crown's holdings, 1493 through 1995*. 1996.

Street's Indian and Colonial Mercantile Directory, etc. Editions from the 1860s onwards.

Titford, J 'Settlers of the Old Empire: The West Indies: manuscript sources', 2 parts, *Family Tree Magazine,* November 1998 and January 1999.

Tyson, G F *A guide to manuscript sources in United States and West Indian depositories relating to the British West Indies during the era of the American Revolution*. 1978.

The Year Book of the Bermudas, the Bahamas, British Guiana, British Honduras and the British West Indies. Various editions, containing lists of officials and the names of various professionals such as lawyers, clergymen, doctors and dentists.

The following book dealers specialise in out-of-print and rare books on the West Indies:

G.& R.Leapman. 37 Hogarth Court, High Street, Bushey, Herts. WD23 1BT.
Pennymead Books. 1 Brewerton Street, Knaresborough, North Yorks. HG5 8AZ.

Many newspapers published in the West Indies or in the UK will contain information which can be exceptionally useful for family historians. Some such publications are held in repositories in the Caribbean, but the greatest single collection is that held by the British Library in London. Several former colonies produced printed handbooks, gazettes and directories, sometimes illustrated and frequently full of names. Gazettes, for example, sometimes include lists of wills proved and letters of administration granted. A good collection of these is held by the Society of Genealogists in London.

THE BAPTIST MISSIONARY SOCIETY
(FOUNDED 1792)

HAS MISSION STATIONS in India (Bengal and the North-West Provinces), Ceylon, China (the Provinces of Shansi and Shantung), Japan, Palestine, Africa (the Lower and Upper Congo River), the West Indies (Jamaica, the Bahamas, Caicos, Turks Islands, San Domingo, and Trinidad), and Europe (Brittany, Italy, and Norway).

The Baptist Missionary Society. From the Missionary Year Book, 1889.

Many Christian missionary societies were active in the Caribbean and in Central and South America; their archives, together with the large number of printed books relating to their activities, may throw up interesting material for the genealogist. The principal societies were as follows: the Church Missionary Society (Anglican), the London Missionary Society (interdenominational, evangelical), the Baptist Missionary Society, the Methodist Missionary Society, the Society for the Propagation of the Gospel in Foreign Parts, the Colonial Missionary Society (Congregationalist). The Roman Catholic Church and the Moravians/United Brethren were also particularly active in the mission field. The online MUNDUS database (www.mundus.ac.uk) provides a gateway to missionary collections websites. This is a very simple way of locating information about the archives and resources that exist relating to missionary societies - including all mentioned here.

The ardent genealogist can find grist to his or her mill in a wide range of places, some of them unexpected. As K J Grieb says, in *Research Guide to Central America and the Caribbean*. (1985, page 184): 'Specific investigations could well carry the historian into collections not listed here, because, like gold, historical evidence is where you find it'. So a lucky touch of serendipity might lead the researcher to references such as the following:

London Gazette. 1837. p1199. 3 Feb 1837. District of Demerara and Essequebo. Provost-Marshall requests that George Robertson, Andrew Rankin and Alexander

Shaw, all residents there, and James Robertson and Anna Christina Johnstone (née Buse), now in Europe, executors and executrix of the will of James Johnstone, deceased [his estates named] will their claims...

(The next item in the *London Gazette*, dated 1 March 1837, deals with a sugar plantation in British Guiana).

The parish registers of St George the Martyr, Queen Square, Holborn, London (1922):

Baptised, 27 January 1727: Anne a negro female servt of Edmond Kelly Esq late of Jamaica.

Baptised, 14 October 1730: Mary Young aged 18 native of Jamaica; Juliana Lee aged 30 native of Guinea; Rosanna Quossey aged 6 native of Jamaica; Jamaica Wills aged 3 native of Guinea - Servants to Major Askcough.

Calendar of wills proved in the Consistory Court of Carlisle:

Thomas Atkinson of Jamaica, Admon 1766.

Robert Watson of Demerara, South America. Will, 1831...

Many pedigrees and historical accounts of families with West Indian connexions can be found in manuscript or in print, as you would discover if you were to stumble across a five-generation pedigree of the family of Bushell of Frodham, Bishopsgate and Barbados in - of all unlikely places - *Transactions of the Congregational Historical Society,* volume five (1913-1915), pages 378/379. A more obvious publication in which to discover an account of West Indian families is *A genealogical and heraldic history of the colonial gentry* by Sir Bernard Burke, 2 volumes, 1891, reprinted in one volume, 1970. Here you will find, for example, pedigrees of the family of Blake (Sir Henry Arthur Blake was Governor-in-Chief of Jamaica) and of Espeut (long settled in Jamaica). You can search for surnames featured in *Colonial gentry* by looking in *Burke's family index* (1976).

Several monumental inscriptions in parish churches, cathedrals and abbeys throughout Britain feature former inhabitants of the West Indies. Bath Abbey, for instance, is particularly rich in such memorial plaques, including one dedicated to John Gordon, M D, of the island of St Croix, West Indies, who died in 1807, the year in which the British took this island from the Danes. This tablet, featured in *Caribbeana*, (volume one, page 77) may still be seen in the Abbey.

WEBSITES:

General

For generalised internet searches relating to West Indian families, individuals, places, record offices and the like, use an established search engine, or narrow down your search, if appropriate, by looking at genealogy sites made accessible by way of links on a site such as the ever-reliable Cyndi's list: **www.cyndislist.com/**

West Indies general

Web sites which relate to specific places within the West Indies are listed at the end of each chapter in this book. Here is a selection of sites which are concerned with the West Indies as a whole:

www.candoo.com/surnames/index.html
Caribbean Surname Index: a discussion forum

www.candoo.com/genresources/index.html
Caribbean Genealogy Research: details of Country Resources, and a link to Cynthia Rosers, who is prepared to carry out research in the entire Caribbean area.

http://groups.google.com/group/soc.genealogy.west-indies/topics
West Indies news group

www.candoo.com/genresources/index.html#CARIBBEAN-L
Explains how to subscribe to a CARIBBEAN-L Discussion List, copied to the soc.genealogy.west-indies newsgroup, messages from which will appear with great frequency if you search for specific topics using a search engine.

www.rootsweb.ancestry.com/~caribgw/
The CaribbeanGenWeb Project, which describes itself in the following terms: 'An on-line data repository for queries, family histories, and source records as well as being a resource center to identify other on-line databases and resources to assist researchers. It is the regional branch of the WorldGenWeb Project'.

www.movinghere.org.uk/galleries/roots/caribbean/lifeevents/
usefuladdresses.htm
Useful addresses for West Indian genealogy, courtesy of Guy Grannum.

www.books.ai/index.html
Don Mitchell's West Indian Bibliography.

www.tombstones.bb/
Tombstones database, also including some burial records. Compiled using data collected from actual headstones and monumental plaques, as well as from published works by Vere Langford Oliver and E M Shilstone. At present the Antiguan survey mostly covers inscriptions dated before 1901, and the Barbados survey from before 1951, but the site is being added to over time.

http://surhelp.rootsweb.ancestry.com/wg/car.html
CaribbeanGenWeb: Surname helper.

www.rootsweb.ancestry.com/~atgwgw/resources/resourcelist.html
Caribbean family history: resources for study.

www.empiremuseum.co.uk/
The British Empire and Commonwealth Museum, Temple Meads, Bristol.

Nathan W. Murphy, who works in the Family History Library in Salt Lake City as a United States and Canada Reference Consultant, has been locating online versions of published books relating to the West Indies - of which there are a great number - at both free and for-fee sites. Here are a few of the sites he has located which carry this and other material:

www.worldvitalrecords.com/
World Vital Records. Subscription site.

www.archive.org/
Archive Books. Free.

www.british-history.ac.uk/
British History Online. Free.

www.ancestry.com/
Ancestry.com. Subscription site.

http://search.ancestry.com/search/default.aspx?cat=40
Ancestry.com. Immigration and travel. Subscription site.

https://www.familysearch.org/
FamilySearch. Free.

www.genealogical.com/
Genealogical.com. Free name search. Subscription site.

https://wiki.familysearch.org/en/Barbados_Genealogy
FamilySearch: Barbados genealogy. Free.

www.virtualjamestown.org/indentures/search_indentures.html
VirtualJamestown. Free.

www.immigrantservants.com/search/surname.php?letter=T
Immigrant servants database. Free.

For a broader overview of digitised genealogical books world-wide, see:
http://pricegen.com/english_genealogy.html.

The National Archives, London

Useful information concerning genealogical resources for West Indian research held at TNA can be found as follows:

www.nationalarchives.gov.uk/records/research-guides/transportation-america-west-indies.htm
TNA Guide: 'Transportation to America and the West Indies 1615-1776'. It has been estimated that 50,000 men, women and children were transported to America and the West Indies during this period. Most were poor, and many came from the London area. Most such emigration took place between 1615 and 1660, generally for no more than ten years, but between 1834 and 1853 some 9,000 convicts from Britain were sent to help build the naval and military station at Ireland Island, Bermuda.

www.nationalarchives.gov.uk/records/research-guides/calendar-state-papers-colonial.htm
TNA Guide: 'America and West Indies: Calendar of State Papers Colonial 1574-1739'.

www.nationalarchives.gov.uk/records/research-guides/american-west-indian-colonies.htm
TNA Guide: 'American and West Indian colonies before 1782'.

www.nationalarchives.gov.uk/records/research-guides/british-colonies-and-dominions.htm
TNA Guide: 'British colonies and dominions'.

www.nationalarchives.gov.uk/records/research-guides/emigration.htm
TNA Guide: 'Emigration'.

It is now possible to carry out a PCC will search on The National Archives website (www.nationalarchives.gov.ukldocumentsonlinel/) and to enter the name of a specific West Indies location in the 'place' box.

CHAPTER TWO

The West Indies: unsettled settlers: pirates and buccaneers

Not all individuals who left their mark on the history of the West Indies were settlers as such. As early as 1494, Pope Alexander VI had formally divided up the New World between Spain and Portugal - a ruling which would be ignored by most English and other voyagers, who either established themselves as settlers regardless, or chose piracy and the plundering of ships on the so-called Spanish Main as an alternative. Somewhere between the pirates and the settlers lay the infamous buccaneers, who were deemed by many to be fighting a Holy War against European Catholicism. The situation is admirably summarised by Virginia Radcliffe in *The Caribbean Heritage* (Walker & Co., New York, 1976):

'They were called privateers, smugglers, buccaneers, zeerovers, filibusters, freebooters, corsairs or pirates. Whether they were inside the law or in defiance of it depended on whose law you were talking about. If a man and his ship held a commission from an island Governor or his European sovereign to prey upon Spanish colonies and shipping, his king called him a privateer, but the Spanish called him a pirate. If he was English, Dutch or Danish he was probably even worse: he was a 'corsario Luterano', a Protestant (Lutheran) pirate...The activities of this wide-ranging fraternity began in the early 1500s and continued for more than three centuries...It was an individualistic, dog-eat-dog, loosely put-together tribe of disenfranchised bondsmen, hunters, opportunist soldiers and sailors, Huguenots, refugees, runaway slaves, criminals, mutineers, gentlemen, a few women and on occasion, island Governors.'

The buccaneers were more unsettled than settled as they roamed the seas in search of booty. Mainly English or French, they preyed primarily on Spanish shipping and settlements and reached their hey-day during the second half of the seventeenth century. Myth has been kind to them: countless visitors of all ages who have taken the 'Pirates of the Caribbean' rides at one of the Disney parks have been thrilled and fascinated by the swashbuckling experience, which starts off with the stirring strains of 'Yo, Ho, Yo, Ho, a pirate's life for me...'

The reality of it all, sad to relate, was not so romantic. Buccaneers would commonly steal a ship, collect together a band of desperadoes, then use any means - including torture - to rob the Spaniards on Hispaniola of their cattle. Taking the spoils back to their own little island of Tortuga, they would cure the beef by drying it in the sun - a process known as 'buchanning', which gave them their name. These men operated on a 'no prey, no pay' contract, and would usually divide up any spoils between themselves equally; generally they treated each other honorably, and the rest of the world with various degrees of cruelty.

Governments had an equivocal relationship with the buccaneers; they were often hired by the French Governors of Tortuga and by the English of Jamaica, and it was only towards the end of the seventeenth century that the authorities decided that they had outstayed their welcome.

There is no shortage of literature on buccaneers and pirates. *The Buccaneers of America: a true account of the most remarkable assaults committed of late years upon the coast of the West Indies by the buccaneers of Jamaica and Tortuga, both English and French* was written in Dutch by John Esquemelin, himself a buccaneer. The first English translation of his work dates from 1684, and in more recent years Dover and Penguin editions appeared in 1967 and 1969 respectively. Various not-so-worthy worthies mentioned in *Buccaneers* include Captains Edward (or Edmund) Cook, John Coxon, Peter Harris, Cornelius Essex, Bournano (or De Bernanos), Richard Sawkins, Robert Allison (or Alleston), John Rose (or Row), Bartholomew Sharp and Mackett (or Maggott). The journal of Basil Ringrose, who accompanied the buccaneers and was eventually killed by the Spaniards in Mexico in 1686, was published as a second volume of Esquemelin's work in 1685. *Family Tree Magazine* (December 1997, page 47) carries an account of Paul G Pratt's search for his ancestral roots in the West Indies, aided by an edition of Esquemelin's book.

Howard Pyle's *The Buccaneers and Marooners of America: being an account of the famous adventures and daring deeds of certain notorious freebooters of the Spanish Main*, published in 1905, incorporates but expands Esquemelin's work and features several more notorious pirates and buccaneers.

Meanwhile, enthusiastic researchers of pirates and their nefarious colleagues should also refer to *The Pirates' Who's Who: giving particulars of the lives & deaths of the pirates & buccaneers* by Philip Gosse (1924), which consists of an alphabetical listing of biographies of pirates famous and obscure, most of whom had at least some dealings with the West Indies.

Rogues featured in the aforementioned books who hailed from the British Isles include the following:

Sir Henry Morgan, the eponymous hero of the present-day brand of rum. Son of Robert Morgan, a well-to-do yeoman, he was born at Llanrhymmy in Monmouthshire in 1635 and began his career as an indentured servant in Barbados. He eventually escaped to Jamaica, the island where his uncle, Colonel Edward Morgan, had once been Lieutenant Governor and where Morgan himself would eventually hold the same post, transforming the town of Port Royal into a pirate capital. Morgan was stripped of office in Jamaica in 1683, and died in Port Royal five years later, being buried at St Catherine's Church on 26 August 1688. Port Royal was destroyed by an earthquake in 1692, and the pirates retired briefly to the Bahamas; their activities had finally come to an end by the 1730s.

Blackbeard the Pirate.

Bristol-born Edward Teach, alias Blackbeard, a notorious pirate. During his final hand-to-hand combat he was wounded twenty-five times before he died.

Captain Edward Teach, alias Blackbeard, was born in Bristol; having distinguished himself as a privateer operating out of Jamaica during the War of the Spanish Succession, he finally took to being a pirate once Captain Benjamin Hornygold had put him in command of a prize sloop in the latter part of 1716. Blackbeard, a tall powerful man with a fierce expression, had a long black beard which grew from below his eyes and hung down to a great length; this he would plait into many tails, each one tied with a coloured ribbon and turned back over his ears. When going into action, he wore a sling on his shoulders with three pairs of pistols, and stuck lighted matches under the brim of his hat. Little wonder that the mere mention of his name would strike terror into the hearts of many a community from Newfoundland to Trinidad. A splendid illustration of Blackbeard, complete with flaming matches, may be seen in *The British in the Caribbean* by Cyril Hamshere (1972), following page 80. Blackbeard was eventually killed during an engagement off the coast of North America in 1718, following a savage hand-to-hand struggle with a plucky naval officer, Lieutenant Robert Maynard of the sloop *Ranger*, who wounded the awesome pirate in twenty five places before he finally fell. Touches of Rasputin? Other pirates killed alongside Blackbeard that day were: Philip Morton, gunner; Garret Gibbons, boatswain; Owen Roberts, carpenter; Thomas Miller, quartermaster; John Husk; Joseph Curtice; Joseph Brooks and Nathaniel Jackson. Others, later hanged in Virginia, were: John Carnes; another Joseph Brooks; James Blake; John Gills; Thomas Gates; James White; Richard Stiles; Caesar; Joseph Philips; James Robbins; John Martin; Edward Salter; Stephen Daniel and Richard Greensail. Israel Hands was pardoned and Samuel Odel was acquitted.

Captain William Kidd, alias Robert Kidd or Kid, was born in Greenock, Scotland, in about the year 1655, the son of Rev John Kidd. He arrived at Nevis in the West Indies in August 1689 as the commander of a privateer of sixteen guns, and by 1696 was in London, accepting a commission from King William III to apprehend certain pirates - particularly Thomas Tew of Rhode island, Thomas Wake, William Maze of New York, John Ireland and 'all other Pirates, Free-Booters, and Sea Rovers of what Nature soever'. Two years later, Kidd would become the scapegoat for the various aristocratic patrons who had funded this enterprise. In 1701 he was charged at the Old Bailey with piracy, alongside Nicholas Churchill, James How, Robert Lumley, William Jenkins, Gabriel Loff, Hugh Parrot, Richard Barlicorn, Abel Owens and Darby Mullins (a Londonderry man who had been sold to a planter in the West Indies when orphaned at the age of 18) - despite the fact that the two ships he was accused of seizing were lawful prizes. All were found guilty except Lumley, Jenkins and Barlicorn. Kidd was also found guilty of murdering a gunner, William Moore, by striking him with a wooden bucket bound with iron hoops - even though Moore was a mutineer at the time. Kidd was hanged at Wapping on 23rd May, 1701, the innocent victim of the machinations of others who had financed his piratical excursions. His reputation was soon spread far and wide by the ballad-mongers.

The pirate Captain Bartholomew Roberts, whose motto was: 'A short life and a merry one'.

Captain Bartholomew Roberts, a 'tall black man' born near Haverfordwest in 1682, was so successful that he is said to have taken over 400 vessels. A total abstainer who only drank tea, he would have no women aboard his ships, permitted no gambling, was a strict Sabbatarian and did his best to stop his crew from drinking alcohol. He met his end off the coast of Guinea, struck down by grape-shot on 10th February, 1722. His body, fully dressed, with his arms and ornaments, was thrown overboard according to repeated requests made during his lifetime. His motto had always been 'A short life and a merry one'.

Captain John Avery, alias Henry Every, alias Captain Bridgeman (nicknamed 'Long Ben' or the 'Arch Pirate'), was born near Plymouth in about 1665. After a colourful career, he eventually settled in Bideford, assumed a false name, and died a pauper.

Other members of the pirate fraternity include:

John Alexander, a Scottish buccaneer, drowned on 9th May, 1681; Captain Thomas Anstis, shot whilst asleep in his hammock in 1722; Captain Dixey Bull, born in London of a respectable family, the first pirate on the New England coast during the 1630s; Henry Chandler, alias Rammetham Rise, born in Devonshire, the son of a man who kept a chandler's shop in Southwark, hanged in the 1620s; Captain Condent, alias Congdon or Conden, born in Plymouth, an early eighteenth century pirate, but later a successful merchant in France; Captain Richard Coyle, born at Exeter, tried at the Old Bailey and hanged in 1738; Captain Edward (or John) Davis, buccaneer and pirate, who flourished from 1683 to 1702; Doctor Thomas Dover (1660-1742), privateer commander, inventor of 'Dover's Powders' and rescuer of Alexander Selkirk (the original for Defoe's Robinson Crusoe), whose sister Magdalen Dover married Charles Titford, leaseholder of the Swan Inn at Charing Cross in London, in 1674; Captain John Gow, alias Smith, alias Goffe, born in Thurso, Scotland, whose short career ended when he was hanged (at the second attempt) in Wapping in June 1725, alongside fellow Scotsmen William Melvin and Robert Teague; Captain Richard Holland, an Irishman, who commanded a Spanish pirate vessel in the West Indies in 1724; William May, a mariner from London, one of Captain Avery's crew, who was hanged at London in 1696; John Power, born in the West of England, hanged in London on 10th.March, 1768; Captain Lawrence Prowse, from Devon, a terror to the Spaniards, condemned to death during the reign of King James I, but released following a public outcry; John Upton, a boatswain, born in 1679 in Deptford of honest parents, turned pirate in order to pay off a number of creditors following the death of his wife, and was eventually tried and hanged in London in 1729; Captain Brigstock Weaver, of Hereford, took many ships in the West Indies and off Newfoundland, and was eventually hanged in London in 1723.

Major Stede Bonnet, alias Captain Thomas, alias Edwards, a retired Army Major, was hanged at Charleston, South Carolina, in 1718, along with various of his crew, including: John Thomas (of Wales), James Wilson (of Dublin), Thomas Carman (of Maidstone, Kent), Henry Virgin and Thomas Price (both of Bristol), Edward Robinson (of Newcastle Upon Tyne), George Ross alias Rose (of Glasgow), William Eddy and Neal Patterson (both of Aberdeen), Daniel Perry (of Guernsey), John Ridge, James Robbins and James Mullet alias Millet (all of London). Thomas Nicholls, alias Nicholas, of London, was found not guilty on the same occasion.

Various members of Captain Charles Harris's crew were hanged at Newport, Rhode Island, in July 1723, including: Thomas Hazel of Westminster (aged fifty - one of the longest-lived pirates on record), John Bright, Charles Church, Thomas Huggit,

William Jones, Stephen Mundon and Joseph Sound (all of London), James Brinkley (of Suffolk), John Tompkins (of Gloucestershire), William Shutfield (of Lancaster), Peter Kneeves (of Exeter), Abraham Lacy (of Devonshire), Edward Lawson (of the Isle of Man), Owen Rice (of South Wales), Thomas Linsler (of Lancashire), Edward Eaton (of Wrexham), John Fitzgerald (of Limerick), William Read (of Londonderry) and John Brown (of Durham). Dr John Hincher, graduate of Edinburgh University, was acquitted on the same occasion, while John Brown of Liverpool narrowly escaped a similar fate by virtue of the fact that he was only seventeen years of age.

As to women pirates, we have: Anne Bonny from County Cork, daughter of an attorney, who seems to have escaped hanging by pleading ill-health in Jamaica in 1720; Mrs Maria Cobham, married to Captain Cobham, late of Poole, Dorset; Mary Read, born in London of obscure parentage, brought up as a boy, turned pirate, and died in prison in Jamaica in November 1720 whilst under sentence of death.

Here, then, are a number of individuals from the British Isles who made their home in the West Indies and elsewhere, but were rarely settlers in any one place. More often than not, their home was on board ship, and we may make an informed guess that many if not most were too occupied with their looting activities to have produced legitimate progeny. You may have a pirate or a buccaneer amongst your ancestors - but it might prove no easy task to establish the fact beyond reasonable doubt.

FURTHER READING:

The bibliography of books on pirates and buccaneers is very extensive; a few of the better-known works are listed below:

Abbott, J S C *Captain William Kidd and others of the buccaneers.* 1874.
Alleyne, W *Caribbean Pirates.* 1986.
Black, C V *Pirates of the West Indies.* 1989.
Cordingly, D *Pirates: terror on the high seas - from the Caribbean to the South China Sea.* 1998.
Gosse, P *The history of piracy.* 1932.
Lapouge, G *Pirates and buccaneers.* 2002.
Rogozinski, J *The Wordsworth Dictionary of Pirates.* 1997.

Captain Charles Johnson was the author of several early eighteenth century works on pirates and other rascals. Later publications based in whole or part upon his originals include:

Anonymous. *Lives, exploits and cruelties of the most celebrated pirates and sea robbers*. Manchester. 1847.

Douglas, T. *Lives and exploits of the most celebrated pirates and sea robbers*. Newcastle-upon-Tyne. 1841.

Ellms, C. *The Pirates' Own Book*. Boston, USA. 1837. The latest edition of this much-reprinted work was published under the title *The Pirates* by Gramercy Books of New York in 1996.

'Captain Scarfield' by Howard Pyle, 1921. From Howard Pyle's Book of Pirates: Fiction, Fact & Fancy Concerning the Buccaneers & Marooners of the Spanish Main. Public domain image.

CHAPTER THREE
Anguilla

LOCATION

Anguilla is the most northerly of the Leeward Islands, lying between the Caribbean Sea and the Atlantic Ocean, 60 miles north-west of St Kitts. It is a long, low and narrow island of limestone and coral, sixteen miles in length and varying in breadth from three to one and a half miles, with a total area of 35 square miles. There is no tropical growth, just low shrub, and there are no rivers or mountains - the highest point being a mere 213 feet. 'Anguilla' means 'little snake' - a reference to the shape of the island, not to any prevalence of snakes there. The capital of Anguilla is situated in The Valley, which is home to the island's main administrative offices. Anguilla's dependencies consist of Scrub Island, Sandy Island, Dog Island, Sombrero, Anguillita and Prickly Pear.

HISTORY

When Columbus's travels took him near Anguilla in 1493, it was inhabited by Arawaks, an Amerindian people who called the island Malliouhana. The English first colonised the island in 1650, probably at Road Bay or in the area around Cauls Pond. Life was not easy for the new settlers; in 1656 a raiding party of Caribs from Martinique killed almost all the men and enslaved the women and children; ten years later a contingent of 300

Frenchmen attacked the island, driving its inhabitants into the woods, and in 1688 other islanders made their escape to Antigua in the face of a joint Irish and French attack. Undaunted, English settlers returned to Anguilla. Further skirmishes with the French followed; Governor Hodge and the 150-strong militia repulsed De la Touche and his men in 1745, and the disciplined French force which invaded the island in 1796 was only driven out after fierce fighting on land and sea.

The Leeward Islands Administration, of which Anguilla formed a part, was disbanded in 1816. Nine years later a new legislative union of St Kitts and Anguilla dissolved the latter's own council and replaced it with a system known as the 'Vestry', the island being divided into three divisions known as Road, Valley and Spring for the purpose of elections. The strong protests which followed were to no avail, and the 3000 inhabitants of Anguilla found themselves living under a political system which they felt was to their detriment.

Social and economic conditions on the island deteriorated during the 1830s and 1840s; slavery came to an end in 1838, by which time most of the white sugar planters had sold their land to their ex-slaves and returned to England or migrated to North America. The distressed state of the remaining peasantry of Anguilla forced many of them to move to Demerara in British Guiana or to other islands such as Dominica, Antigua and Trinidad; those who remained ensured the survival of Anguilla as a separate society, though many were barely able to eke out a living.

The Leeward Islands Federation was created in 1871, and in the following year the inhabitants of Anguilla petitioned Queen Victoria, saying that there was no island 'so little known or cared for, and none more oppressed'. Not only did this plea go unheeded, but matters were made worse in 1882 with the merger of St Kitts and Nevis, when the freeholders of Anguilla were even denied the right to send a single representative to the new House of Assembly in St Kitts. As the century ended, the population of Anguilla was beset by famine; 3500 of its 4400 inhabitants (one hundred or so of them whites) were living on government assistance.

Matters improved only slightly during the first decades of the twentieth century; the cotton industry was wiped out by the boll weevil, and a number of Anguillan men and boys took refuge in the Dominican Republic, where they found work in the sugar cane fields. The hostility felt towards St Kitts continued to grow, and it was only after a popular revolution of 1967 and a number of failed initiatives that Anguilla became a separate British Dependent Territory on 19 December 1980. Many years of persistence by a doggedly independent people had paid off; 399 years after the foundation of its first colony of Newfoundland, Britain had acquired its latest and its last Dependent Territory. For a modern-day traveller's account of Anguilla, see *Outposts* by Simon Winchester (1985).

Anguilla has had its fair share of hurricanes; the island was devastated in 1822, and subsequent visitations occurred in 1898, 1922, 1950, 1955, 1960, 1979, 1984 and 1995.

ECONOMY

Tobacco had been the island's first cash crop, followed by cotton, but the early eighteenth century saw the introduction of sugar production, slaves from Africa being imported to work on the estates. Many such slaves came from the Gold Coast, as their Fanti names indicate - Quashi, Quacou, Quow, Quamin, Membah and Cumbah. The shallow soil of Anguilla was never ideally suited to the cultivation of sugar, however, and the island would eventually export cotton, indigo, fustic and mahogany as well as sugar and rum. A salt industry was developed during the eighteenth century, becoming a much-needed source of revenue and of employment.

PEOPLE

• Volume three of V L Oliver's *Caribbeana* (pages 255-256) contains a transcription of an important name list for Anguilla, taken from an original in the former Public Record Office: 'Leeward Islands: List of the inhabitants of Anguilla referred to in Genl. Hamilton's letter of 3 Oct.1716. Rec'd 24 Nov.1716. Read 3 April 1717'.

[Columns after each person's name indicate the number of people in his or her household under the following headings: men; women; children; negroes; working negroes].

Men's Names:
Capt. George Leonard; Capt.Abraham Howell; Arthur Hodge; Jno Rogers; Dars Downing, wid.; Isac Thiboue; Isac Aderly; Chas Kagen; Peter Rogers ; Jno Chapman; Ellil Conner, wid.; Paul Rowan; Timoy Conner; Josh Newton; Peter Downing; Jerh Spencer; Cathr Downing, wid.; Deborah Gumbes, wid.; Wm Chalivell; Jno Pain; John Haragin; Jerih Martin; Geo.Leonard; Sarah Leonard, wid.; Barll Howell; Thos Flanders; Rich.Downing; David Darick; Charles Kagan; Cornes Harragen; Briant Markdonaha; And.Tellies; Saml Floid; Wm Gumbes; Edwd Leake; Doriy P..., wid.; Thos Loyde; Jno Richards; Thos.Howell; Danl Briant; John Leake; Abram Arundell; Wm Roberts; John Bryant; Richard Robarts; Thos Leake; Rowl Williams; Ann Williams, wid.; Micll Rowan; Barell Rogers; Jon Leake; Jan Leake; Jno Welch; Wm Farrington; Alice Flight, wid.; Richd Arthur; Richd Richardson; Thos Rumny; Wm Long; Darby Carty; Wm Howell; Abednigo Pickren; Edwd Coakley; Jno.Rumny; Jno.Downing; Grace Leonard; Jno Morgan; Jno Powell; Peter Frare; Saml Fincent; Thos Hughs; Robt Lockrom; Thos Rumny; Thos Coakley; Edwd Coakley; Jno Thomas; James Richardson; Thomas Richardson; Jal Howell; Thos Hodge; Chris.Hodge; Peter Hodge; Benj.Rogers; Henry Hodge; Suah Manning; Olir Downing; Wm Bale; Thos Rogers; Berell Rogers; Jerih Richardson; Neheh Richardson;

Edwd Welch; Ann Arrendell; Mary Watson; Jone Gladden; Benj.Arrendell; Thos Hencock; Saml Kentish; Jno.Richadsorn; Abra.Wingood; Henry Leonard.

- The Wesleyan Methodist Missionary Society on Anguilla was established in 1813. by John Hodge, a 'free coloured man'.

ANNALS OF ANGUILLA,

British West Indies.

1650 – 1923

BY

S. B. JONES, M.B.E., M.A. (Durh.),
L.R.C.P., L.R.C.S. (Ed.)

SOMETIME MEDICAL OFFICER
AND MAGISTRATE,

ANGUILLA, B.W.I.

The title page of one of the few books to feature the island of Anguilla: Annals of Anguilla, British West Indies 1650-1923 by S B Jones, printed by the Progressive Printery, Ltd, St Kitts, in 1937.

There are few enough printed works which include material of interest to those researching family history in Anguilla, so we should be grateful for the existence of *Anguilla: tranquil isle of the Caribbean* by B Cart and C Petty (1997), which includes a coloured photograph of a tombstone on the Anguillan island of Sombrero, once famous for its phosphate mining (...Memory/ of/ ...ms WILLIAMS/...of the late/ Dr.Benjamin Davies/ of Regent Park College/ London/ one of the company/ of revisers of the /bible/ and brother-in-law/ of M Tutton/ Swansea/ Born 1st January/ 1846/ Died 2nd.January/ 1876) and for a small book of earlier date entitled *Annals of Anguilla*, written by S B Jones, former medical officer and magistrate on the island, which was printed by the Progressive Printery, Ltd., St Kitts, in 1937. This scarce publication includes at least some references to names of individuals, and its illustrations include photographs of the tomb of Governor John Richardson in Sandy Hill Churchyard ('Here lieth the body of John Richardson, Esq., who was born the 16th day of March 1679, and departed this life 25th December 1742') and of the church of St Mary-in-the-Valley and of the Methodist Chapel, The Road.

The first appendix to Jones's book contains a transcript of the will of Governor John Richardson, 'planter', in which the following individuals are mentioned: wife, Joan Richardson; grandsons John and William Richardson, 'sons of my son John Richardson of the island of St Martin, deceased'; son William Richardson; daughter Jamima Hardtman; daughter Dorcas Howell; daughter Mary Wingood, deceased; daughter Elizabeth King, deceased; father, John Richardson, senior, deceased, of Antigua; grandson Abraham Howell; grand-daughter Rebeckah Howell; grandson John Hardtman; grandson John King; son in law Abraham Howell; daughter in law Elizabeth Powell; Mrs Catharine Red (given a legacy of 'one negroe man boy and one negroe wench fit to be put to the wash tub') and her son Samuel Red; cousin John Ruan; esteemed friend Arthur Hodge, Esq.; (lands of:) Arrowsmith, William Farrington, senior, Joseph Burnett.

Richardson made his will on 'this ninth day of January in the year of our Lord One Thousand Seven Hundred and thirty nine forty' - an interesting method of indicating Old Style and New Style dating. Witnesses were John Ruan, John Farrington and Edward Coakley. A codicil followed in March, 1741/2, witnessed by Jonathan Flemming, Edward Coakley and Samuel Red, and makes reference to the following additional individuals: William and Elizabeth Hodge (from whom land was purchased); grand-daughters Mary and Anne Richardson, daughters of son John, deceased; grandsons Abraham and William Wingood.

It fell to Edward Coakley to travel to Antigua to obtain probate of Richardson's will from Sir William Matthews, 'Captain General and Governor in Chief in and over all His Majesty's Leeward Charibbee Islands in America, Chancillor, Vice Admiral & Ordinary of the same' in February 1742/3, swearing that he had seen the deceased 'Sign Seal publish and declare the above Written Will and also the Codicil thereto annexed' and that at the time Richardson was 'of sound and disposing mind and Memory and understanding to the best of this deponent's Judgement'.

Another fascinating appendix to Jones's book features a transcript of a 'Report on the Population, Culture, Revenue &c of the late French part of the Island of Saint Martin' dated 1815. Saint Martin lies south of Anguilla; originally settled by the English, it came under the joint ownership of the French and Dutch (an unusual arrangement which persists to the present day), despite the fact that most of its inhabitants were English. In 1795, at the time of the French Republic, many English settlers were seized and sent to Guadeloupe, others fled of their own accord, and a few remained on Saint Martin, only to find their property confiscated or sequestrated. The report contains a useful list of proprietors of sugar estates, indicating the total size of each estate, the acreage of it given over to sugar cane, and an indication as to whether it was sequestered in 1795:

District of Marigot: John P.Jennings; Heirs of Durat; Chr.Blyden (then Davis); Michael Hannah; Heirs of Maillard; Mary Gibbes; J.J.Cremony (then Gumbes); John Hodge, junior; Ann Ververe. District of Columbier: Heirs of Ahman; Louis Ducan; Benjamin Gumbes; Samer S.Howell; Van Heyningen; Ann Dormoy; Nicholas Heyliger; Heirs of Richardson; Heirs of Wilson.

District of Grande Case: Philip O'Rielly; Andrew Mildrum; Anthony Smith; John Hodge (second).

District of Orleans: P.M.Gunn (then Lake); Benjamin Hodge, senior; Heirs of Flanders; Abraham Arrindell; Heirs of R.Richardson; Benjamin Richardson (then Desmont); Heirs of Cannigeter.

In these Districts there are two Cotton Estates the property of Col.Druault and Thomas Lacroisade, besides the stock estates of Col.Gumbes, Doctor Hodge, John Hodge (senior), Anthony Smith, Mr.Duzong, Dr.Chittick, Mrs.Chambard, Jacques Matthieu, Mrs.Winfield, Mr.Enialbert, Mrs.Calvert, Hazel, Bell and Richardson, upon which are raised Cattle and Stock of all kinds.'

In 1815 the English settlers petitioned the Prince Regent in England, imploring him to annex Saint Martin to the British Crown - or at least to allow it to be governed by the House of Orange. Anything was preferable to control being exercised by Guadeloupe, they said, 'whose customs are totally dissimilar to our own'. Their pleas fell on deaf ears, alas.

Jones also provides some population statistics for Anguilla taken from censuses. Here are the figures for the year 1819:

Whites: 89 men, 142 women, 73 boys, 61 girls; Free coloured and blacks: 60 men, 109 women, 90 boys, 68 girls; Slaves: 527 men, 760 women, 546 boys, 555 girls. Women outnumber men in each grouping of the adult population. The decennial census figures from 1881 to 1921 are as follows: 1881: 1452 males, 1767 females; 1891: 1653 males, 2046 females; 1901: 1687 males, 2203 females; 1911: 1562 males, 2513 females; 1921: 1447 males, 2783 females.

RECORDS (UK REPOSITORIES)

The National Archives, London
Various Colonial Office records for the Leeward Islands and for St Kitts and Nevis in the Public Record Office contain material relative to Anguilla. Two significant name lists for Anguilla itself exist for the years 1716 (CO 152/11,f.56) and 1717 (CO152/12, no.67 [iv]). See *Caribbeana*, above.

RECORDS (LOCALLY-HELD)

Archive material for Anguilla is held by the Anguilla Library Service, The Valley, Anguilla, and a few items of Anguillan interest are with the National Archives, Government Headquarters, Church Street, P O Box 186, Basseterre, St Kitts.
There is no up-to-date listing of archives held on Anguilla, though the government has been engaged in discussions with an American University with a view to a survey of holdings being made.

Churches
In *A guide to records in the Leeward Islands* (1965), E C Baker lists a number of Anglican church records then held by St Mary with St Augustine: baptisms from

1826, marriages from 1832, burials from 1852, with some gaps. The present St Mary's church was completed in 1967, replacing an earlier wooden structure, and St Augustine at East End was built in 1890 on the site of an old sugar cane estate. The first Bethel Methodist Church at South Hill was built in 1828 and the Ebenezer Church in the Valley two years later, but Baker remarked in 1965 that no Methodist records were then retained on Anguilla. In general terms the Anglicans took a particular interest in the eastern half of the island, while the Methodists were strongest in the western half; Baptist, Roman Catholic and Seventh Day Adventist churches have been established in more recent years.

Civil registration
Registration of births and deaths on Anguilla began in 1901, and marriages were required to be registered from 1925; the relevant records are now held at the office of the Registrar of births, deaths and marriages, Judicial Department, The Valley.

Censuses
The first nineteenth-century census to include Anguilla dates from 1871; in 1891 the population of the island numbered 3,699. Some census returns are available at the Anguilla Library Service, The Valley.

Miscellaneous records
Baker also lists a number of miscellaneous records for Anguilla which were then held on the island. The Registrar's Office held various deeds, land records and Magistrates' Court records, mainly for the nineteenth or twentieth centuries, and a will and probate register commencing in 1871. Other twentieth-century archives were housed in the Customs and Excise Office, the Public Health Centre, the Agricultural Department, the Cottage Hospital and the Public Library.

SECONDARY SOURCES: PRINTED WORKS, etc.

Probate records
Caribbeana by V.L.Oliver contains various calendars and transcripts of wills relative to Anguilla and other West Indian islands, including wills proved and administrations granted in the Prerogative Court of Canterbury.

FURTHER READING

Titford, J 'Settlers of the Old Empire: The West Indies: Anguilla', *Family Tree Magazine,* June 2000.

And see books by B Cart and C Petty and by S B Jones, above.

WEBSITES

**http://search.ancestry.com/cgi-bin/sse.dll?gskw=BVI+Anguilla&ti=0&ti.si
=0&rank=0&hc=25&gss=mb&db=mb&application=public&filter=0&utype=
Admin**
Anguilla Query Board

www.candoo.com/genresources/stknevang.htm
Includes a Listing of LDS Church microfilm records of St Kitts, Nevis and Anguilla civil registration and parochial records.

www.britishislesgenweb.org/anguilla/
CaribbeanGenWeb: Anguilla Genealogy Project. With Bulletin Boards and a Mailing List.

http://boards.msn.ancestry.com/localities.caribbean.bvi.anguilla/mb.ashx
Anguilla ancestry message board.

www.familysearch.org/eng/Library/FHLC/frameset_fhlc.asp
The LDS Family History Library catalog. Search on 'Anguilla' for a collection of material, some of it on microfilm: St Mary's parish registers (1826-1974), Civil Registration records for St Kitts, Nevis and Anguilla (1859-1932), birth, marriage and death registers, chancery records, register of deeds (1826-1930), indentures, including mortgages, wills, etc, dowers, land and property records, estate appraisals, leases, probate records.

The International Genealogical Index (now within FamilySearch) and related records should also be searched for individuals from Anguilla.

CHAPTER FOUR
Antigua

LOCATION

Antigua is an oval-shaped island with a total area of 108 square miles (the largest in the Leeward Islands), situated forty miles east of Nevis and twenty-seven miles north-east of Montserrat. It is the principal island of a group of three, its junior dependencies being Barbuda and Redonda. The name is pronounced 'Anteega', not as if it rhymes with 'how big you are', as Brian Dyde has charmingly observed. The capital, St John's, is situated on the west side of the island, and other principal towns include Falmouth (the first place settled by the English), Parham and English Harbour.

HISTORY

When Columbus sighted Antigua in 1493, he named the island after a church in Seville, Santa Maria La Antigua.

When a party of Spaniards under Don Antonio Serrano considered making a settlement there in 1520, they were driven away by a lack of water (the island having no rivers - only a few fresh water springs), as was D'Esnambuc, the captain of a French privateer, in 1629. For all that, three years later a group of English settlers from St Kitts, led by Edward, son of

English Harbour, Antigua. Photograph by John Titford.

Sir Thomas Warner, took the island over as a colony. Yet by 1640 only about thirty families were living there, and they found themselves having to repel a concerted Carib attack in that year.

Antigua was to become a fiercely Royalist settlement, and was included with Virginia, Barbados and the Bermudas in the Imperial Act of October 1650 which prohibited trade with these colonies on account of their rebellious attitude towards the home government - a defiant stance which had been encouraged by Lord Francis Willoughby, who was forced to relinquish the Governorship of Antigua in 1652 but was reinstated after the Restoration and returned with a large number of colonists in 1663. Three years later a force of French troops, accompanied by a number of Irish and Caribs, landed at Five Islands Bay and took possession of Antigua. Their victory was short-lived; the next year the island was ceded to England by the Treaty of Breda, and Lord Francis Willoughby's brother, Lord William Willoughby of Parham, became Governor.

A few years after the cession of Antigua there had been only five hundred black people living there; the white population was increased in 1689 following an influx of emigrants from Anguilla who sought protection from the French and the Indians, and settlers on Antigua were encouraged and required by law to take on a certain number of indentured white servants - a system which operated and was developed and amended over many years. For all that, by 1729 the population balance had shifted dramatically following the importation of slaves from Africa: there were then 26,000 or so inhabitants, 22,000 of whom were black. The white population was all too conscious of the fact that it was in a significant minority on the island, and when slave insurrections broke out in 1728 and 1736, they were put down with appalling severity. By 1774 there were 37,808 slaves, 1,230 free people of colour and 2,590 whites. When slave emancipation eventually took place in 1834, Antigua chose not to adopt the transitional 'apprenticeship' system favoured elsewhere.

With its fine natural harbours, Antigua was recognised very early as a place of strategic importance for the navy; the dockyard at English Harbour was begun in 1725, and the island served as an important base during the wars with Napoleon. Nelson operated from Antigua during the period 1786-88.

Antigua came under the overall grouping of the Leeward Islands, on and off, from 1671 to 1871, and was the administrative centre of the Leeward Islands Federation from then until 1956. It had assumed Crown Colony status on 22 March 1898, and achieved its independence within the Commonwealth in November 1981.

ECONOMY

The cultivation of tobacco gave Antigua a sound enough economic base in the early years; sugar eventually took over as the main crop, but two hundred years after the first damaging visitation by sugar ants in 1771, a drop in prices heralded its demise. Since then tourism has played an increasingly major role in the island's economy.

PEOPLE

- During the Carib insurrection of 1640, Mrs Warner, the Governor's wife, was carried off together with her two children. In the years that followed a similar fate befell many other women, including Mrs Cardin, Mrs Taylor, Mrs Chrew and Mrs Lynch, all of whom were taken with their children, never to be seen again, and also Mrs Lee, wife of Captain Lee, who was detained as a prisoner for three years on Dominica after the Caribs had murdered her husband.

- Sir Christopher Codrington established the first large sugar estate in 1674, and leased Barbuda to raise provisions for his plantations.

- Slaves on Antigua were not alone in resorting to violence during hard times: in 1710 the tyrannical and unsavoury Governor of the Leeward Islands, the American-born Colonel Daniel Parke, was literally torn to pieces by an angry mob in Antigua during a popular riot led by Captain John Pigott, Captain Painter, Andrew Murray, Francis Carlisle, Mr Tomlinson and others, which ended with Government House being burned to the ground. Rev James Field, rector of St John's, took the side of the people, while Rev Mr.Baxter, rector of Parham, sided with Parke.

- The first Moravian missionary in Antigua, Samuel Isles, arrived in 1756, to be followed later by Joseph Newby and Samuel Watson. By 1792 there were eleven such missionaries on the island, and it has been said that the influence of the Moravian faith did much to calm the wilder spirits on the island.

- Methodism was first introduced in 1760 by Hon Nathaniel Gilbert, speaker of the House of Assembly, who came from a distinguished family in the west of England. Eighteen years later John Baxter, a one-time shipwright at Chatham Dockyard, arrived in English Harbour and ministered until his death in 1805, having overseen the building of a chapel at St John's which opened its doors in 1783. In the event it was in Antigua that the Methodist Missionary Society had its foundation; in 1786 the Methodist Conference designated William Warrener (born in 1750, reputedly in the East Riding of Yorkshire) to work amongst the slaves there, and in the same year the Methodist Dr Thomas Coke, a native of Brecon in South Wales and formerly curate of South Petherton in Somerset, was driven ashore on Antigua and preached a Christian sermon in St John's to a black congregation of a thousand people, most of them slaves.

Dependencies of Antigua

Antigua has two dependencies: Barbuda, a low coral island with an area of sixty-two square miles, lying twenty seven miles to the north, and Redonda, a one thousand foot high rock, thirty miles to the south-west.

Barbuda, like Antigua, had been sighted by Columbus in 1493; originally named Dulcina, it was first settled by Littleton, a planter from St Kitts, in 1628, becoming a dependency of Antigua when that island was settled four years later.

In the seventeenth century Barbuda was used as a stock farm for Nevis and other neighbouring islands, and at the time of a Carib raid there in 1681 there were only twenty white inhabitants. Ten years later Barbuda was leased by William III to Christopher and John Codrington, after whom the island's capital is named, at an annual rent of 'one fat sheep (if demanded)'. The Codringtons leased the island until the year 1870, though they never lived there permanently, using it as a stock farm for their plantations in Antigua and as a shooting estate. A certain amount of subsidiary income was generated thanks to the plight of ships which were wrecked as they attempted to negotiate the dangerous reefs which surround the island. The plantation system was never developed on Barbuda, but the Codringtons imported slaves to tend their crops and their cattle.

On 9th January 1871 Barbuda was leased to Rev W Cowley and George Hopkins for a term of 21 years, but following later leases the Crown resumed possession in 1898. Eventually all land was vested in the Governor and taxes were imposed on the inhabitants. By 1921 the population was 902, most of them descendants of slaves said to have belonged originally to one man.

From 1903 to 1976 a warden on Barbuda regulated the island's affairs and acted as registrar of births, marriages and deaths. Civil registration had been made compulsory in 1868, and Baker's book on the Leeward Islands gives details of birth and death registers (from 1902) and marriage registers (from 1907), then held in the warden's office.

A useful map of Barbuda may be seen on page 124 of *Antigua and Barbuda: Heart of the Caribbean* by Brian Dyde (2nd edition, 1993).

Redonda is an isolated rock, a mile long and a third of a mile broad, lying mid-way between Montserrat and Nevis. To the Caribs this place was 'Ocanamunru', but Columbus named it Santa Maria la Redonda (St Mary the Round). The first known landing there occurred in 1687, but this was an inhospitable place covered with bird guano, which would be of interest eventually to phosphate companies, the first of which began mining operations in the 1860s using hired labourers from Montserrat. By an act of 1872 Redonda was annexed to Antigua and was deemed to lie within the parish of St John's.

By 1898 the population numbered 120 people, all phosphate workers. The mining company relinquished its lease in 1930, and Redonda has been uninhabited ever since.

RECORDS (UK REPOSITORIES)

The National Archives, London
Colonial Office correspondence, sessional papers, gazettes, etc. Classes CO152/16, CO152/21 and CO152/25 include baptisms, marriages and burials for various Antigua parishes. Transcripts of some of these registers appear in *Caribbeana* (see below).

Nominal censuses for Antigua taken in 1677/8 (CO1/42) and in 1753 (CO152/27) are printed in V L Oliver's *History of the Island of Antigua* (1896-9) volume 1, pages lviii-lxi and cix-cxv respectively.

Plantation records among those of the West Indian Incumbered Estates Commission, 1770-1893 (CO 441) include papers from estates on Antigua.

Treasury: T71 includes records generated by the Slave Compensation Commission, 1817-1832, and claims are indexed in T71/923.

The British Library, etc.
The British Newspaper Library holds several Antigua newspapers, the earliest of which dates from 1826.

For details of other record holdings in London repositories relevant to Antigua, including those of the Methodist Missionary Society, the Moravian Union, HM Customs and Excise and the National Maritime Museum, see E C Baker's *A guide to records in the Leeward Islands* (1965) - but take its date of publication into account.

RECORDS (LOCALLY-HELD)

In some ways it is something of a miracle that any significant archives have survived on Antigua itself. St John's was laid flat by a hurricane of 1670, and almost destroyed by fire in 1769 and in 1782. A blaze of 1841 gutted the Customs House, and in 1950 records relating to Antigua and to the Leeward Islands federation which had been stored in the federal building went up in flames. Powerful earthquakes struck in 1690 and in 1843, the latter of which did considerable damage to all but two of the island's churches and destroyed many of the monumental inscriptions ranged around the walls of the church in St John's. A further earthquake destroyed the public library in 1974, and in 1999 the records held in the prison were destroyed by fire. Antigua has been no stranger to hurricanes over the years, and in September 1995 the island was pounded for 36 hours by Hurricane Luis, soon to be followed by floods.

Churches
Compulsory parochial registration of christenings, marriages and burials was introduced in Antigua in 1692, the registering clerks being paid ninepence for each event they recorded. In 1672 it had been decreed that civil marriages solemnized by the Governor, council, or any justice of the peace, should be deemed to be lawful in the absence of any beneficed clergyman.

Five parishes were established on the island in 1681: St John's, St Peter's, St Philip's, St Mary's and St Paul's. In 1725 an area of St Peter's which was inconveniently far from the parish church became the new parish of St George, and both St John's and St Peter's churches later acquired chapels of ease. An idea as to the relative business conducted by the various churches on the eve of the Victorian era can be gleaned from the number of baptisms conducted at each in 1836: St John, 310; St Peter, 116; St Philip, 122; St Mary, 60; St Paul, 74; St George, 74.

E C Baker's *A guide to records in the Leeward Islands* (1965) gives details of Anglican and other church records then held on the island:

At St John's: registers of baptism and burial (1689 onwards) and of marriage (1700 onwards); vestry minutes (1769 onwards).

At St Peter's: registers of baptism and burial (1771 onwards) and of marriage (1835 onwards); church accounts, 1796 onwards; St George's church registers of baptism and burial (1724 onwards) and of marriage (1830 onwards). Registers of St Augustine's and St Matthias's chapels of ease, 1917 and 1918 onwards.

St Mary's: In 1938 A E Gropp had noted the existence of various registers of baptism, burial and marriage from 1839 onwards, vestry minutes from 1684 onwards and censuses for 1821 and 1827. Baker could find none of these in 1965, and heard that they had been destroyed by a later incumbent.

At St Philip's: registers of baptism (1767 onwards) and of marriage (1683-1722, a copy made in 1879); vestry minutes (1798 onwards). Also marriage records relating to St Philip's and St Stephen's (1884 onwards).

Methodist records, including deeds, and registers of baptism, burial and marriage, were then held at the Manse, St John's.

Early documentation relating to the Moravians has since been moved to the church archives in Bethlehem, Pennsylvania, but the Antigua National Archives currently holds Moravian records from the Spring Garden Church (1807-1983), Cedar Hall (1884-1916), Grace Bay (1844-1921) and Grace Field (1834-1959).

The National Archives also holds Roman Catholic baptism, marriage and burial records for the Holy Family Cathedral; these date from 1862, but some are extremely fragile.

Civil registration
Compulsory civil registration of births and deaths on Antigua, organised on a parochial system, dates from 1 August 1856, with marriages from 1868. The Registrar General, Registrar General's Office, High Court, High Street, St John's, holds the appropriate records.

Census

The earliest nineteenth-century census for Antigua dates from 3 June 1844, at which time the population of the island numbered 36,178, to be followed by the first in a decennial series of censuses, taken seven years later in 1851.

Other original records held on the island

As early as 1696 the authorities on Antigua decided that all public records would henceforth be kept in the secretary's office, as a number had already been mislaid or lost. Many records were subsequently lost in a fire which destroyed the Custom House on 2 April 1841.

E C Baker's *A guide to records in the Leeward Islands* (1965) includes a summarized history of the archives of the Leeward Islands and of Antigua (pages viii-x) which makes depressing reading. As early as 1914 the Royal Commission on Public Records was reporting that the archives held in various West Indian islands 'were in a somewhat unsatisfactory state'. V L Oliver, amongst others, visited Antigua just before the First World War; he found records from as early as 1685 in a 'deplorable state of decay' and kept in inadequate storage conditions, and included a report on some of his findings in the third and fourth volumes of *Caribbeana*. Later visitors such as H C Bell, D W Parker and Professor Richard Pares confirmed Oliver's findings, but by the 1940s war-time Britain found itself unable to offer any financial help, and when a fire gutted the federal building in St John's on Antigua on 19th August 1950, those records relating to the Leeward Islands Federation and to Antigua itself which had been stored there were destroyed. Four years later an appreciable quantity of the surviving federal and Antiguan records (including House of Assembly minutes, deeds record books, letter books, probate and court records, Admiralty Court papers, slave registers, 1844 census return enumerators' books and marriage bond books) were shipped to England for safe keeping and were placed in the care of the Public Record Office at Ashridge Park, being Listed in PRO1/1612. These records have since been returned to Antigua and are now in the National Archives.

Meanwhile, Baker's book does its usual thorough job of summarising those surviving records held on Antigua, arranged by repository:

'In the Administration Building: Leeward Islands federal records; Government, estate and trade records from 1725. In Government House: Letter books, copies of despatches, laws of Antigua (mainly 19th and 20th century). In the Court House vaults: Deed record books from 1727; book of wills from 1804, probate registers from 1808, government grants of land from 1668, bankruptcy records from 1890, marriage bonds from 1895, voters' registers from 1859, court record books from 1728, registers of birth, marriage and death by parish from 1856. In the Harbour Master's Office: ships' registers from 1855. Other records were held in the Public Library, the Prison, the Education Office, Antigua Grammar School, the Girls' High School and elsewhere. A number of Antigua newspapers, 1814-1882, were in the Public Library.'

Antiguan archives are now housed in a modern building at Antigua and Barbuda National Archives, Rappaport Centre, Victoria Park, St John's. Research enquiries are accepted by post, but researchers need to be as specific as possible about what information they have and what it is that they are looking for.

The National Archives now holds the following archives featured in Baker's original Listing, and is currently compiling a detailed guide to its holdings:

Records from the Administration Building; estate record books; special reports; programmes; records from Government House; records from the Court House; records from the Harbour Master's Office (from 1921); records from the Education Office; records from the Antigua Girls' High School and the Antigua Grammar School; Misses Branch records; Anglican Church records; Antigua newspapers.

Records held at Her Majesty's Prison were destroyed by fire in 1999.

The Antigua Historical and Archaeological Society is based at the Museum of Antigua and Barbuda, PO Box 103, Long Street, St John's.

SECONDARY SOURCES: PRINTED WORKS, ETC.

Mercifully, genealogical sources for Antigua in print, typescript, manuscript and microform are very plentiful.

The major source for printed transcripts of historical material is *History of the island of Antigua, one of the Leeward Caribees in the West Indies, from the first settlement in 1635 to the present time* by V L Oliver, published by him in a limited edition of 150 copies from 1894 to 1899. An even more limited reprint edition published by Jim Lynch of Toronto in 1999 was sold out almost as soon as it appeared, but the LDS church has a copy of the book on microfilm (film # 1149539).

Oliver lived on Antigua in 1888 and 1889, copying documents and monumental inscriptions to add to what he already knew about his own and other island families. This material was augmented by a significant amount of transcription work carried out for him at the Public Record in London by Mrs Vernona T C Smith, whose own papers are now with the Society of Genealogists in London.

Oliver set himself a defined task: to make available in printed form as much source material for the history of Antigua as he could, uncluttered by narrative or commentary of his own. His *History* begins with transcripts of documents relating to the history and topography of the island, including full versions of name lists compiled in 1678 and 1753. He then launches into a series of alphabetically-arranged pedigrees of the grander settler families, supported by information from deeds, wills, parish registers, family bibles and the like. Oliver had not anticipated the need to produce a third volume, but eventually he did so, including in it transcripts of deeds, warrants, slave compensation claims and parish registers, together with abstracts of wills, extracts from the Close Rolls and from the *Gentleman's Magazine*, Lists of Governors and officials and much else.

Each of the three volumes of the *History* carries its own separate index, featuring hundreds of thousands of names in all, and portraits, topographical views and maps are scattered throughout the work. Rarely can the history and genealogy of a place the size of Antigua have been featured in such detail in one extended publication.

No other published books on Antigua can match the scope and detail of Oliver's *History*, but there is much of interest to the genealogist in a two-volume work published in 1844 under the title *Antigua and the Antiguans: a full account of the colony and its inhabitants from the time of the Caribs to the present day, interspersed with anecdotes and legends, also, an impartial view of slavery and the free labour systems, the statistics of the island, and biographical notices of the principal families*. A reprint appeared in 1991, published by MacMillan Education Ltd in conjunction with the Antigua Map Shop.

This work was published anonymously, but the author is known to have been a Mrs Lanaghan, a lady from Cork in Ireland who married an Antiguan and came to live on the island. Here we have 700 pages of text which mix fact and fiction in a charming manner. Mrs Lanaghan has much humane commentary to make on the question of slavery and loves to recount legends at length, but the genealogical enquirer will be principally interested in her descriptions of churches and churchyards, the details she gives of monumental inscriptions in St John's church (volume 1, pages 222-234) and the collection of genealogies of some of the principal families (Warner, Winthorpe, Byam, Williams, Codrington, Mathew, MacKinnon, Thomas, Carlisle, Lavington, Fitzroy, Willoughby, Martin and Freeman) in volume 2, pages 308-355.

Amongst the oldest monumental inscriptions noted by Mrs Lanaghan in the churchyard of St John's were those for Col Philip Lee (1704); Capt Bastien Baijer (1715); Thomas Oasterman (1724) and Frederic Cope (1739). Several fine monuments relating to the more prominent island families lined the inside walls of the church. One of these commemorates the fate of poor Eliza Musgrave, wife of William, who was thrown out of her carriage when the horse became restive and broke the shafts (*No warning given! Unceremonious fate!/ A sudden rush from life's meridian joys!/ A wrench from all she loved*); the white marble memorial plaque even has an imaginary picture of this tragic accident sculpted upon it in basso-relievo. Mrs Lanaghan was not impressed...

Parish registers
A number of parish register transcripts appear in volume three of V L Oliver's *History of Antigua* (1896-1899) and in his *Caribbeana* (1910-1920).

Extracts by Oliver of military baptisms, marriages and burials for Antigua appear in *Miscellanea Genealogica et Heraldica*, second series, volume 4 (1892), .

The Society of Genealogists in London has a volume of manuscript transcripts of various parish registers for Antigua, presented by V L Oliver.

A simple gravestone for Welsh-born John Edwards, in the graveyard of Lady of the Valley church, Antigua. Photograph by John Titford.

Monumental inscriptions
Monumental inscriptions of the British West Indies by J H Lawrence-Archer (1875) has a few transcriptions of MIs for Antigua (pages 405-414), taken from the book *Antigua and the Antiguans* (1844). V L Oliver's *The monumental inscriptions of the British West Indies* (1927) includes a small collection (pages 1-4) of Antiguan MIs which supplement those arranged parish-by-parish in the Appendix section of volume three of the same author's *History of Antigua* (1896-9). *Caribbeana* has a number of transcriptions of MIs in England with Antigua connections.

The famous genealogist Vere Langford Oliver arranged for a substantial and detailed memorial to his many 'ancestors and kinsfolk' to be placed in St John's Cathedral, Antigua. This plaque is at the base of that memorial. Photograph by John Titford.

St John's Cathedral, Antigua. Photograph by John Titford.

Details of inscriptions in the English Harbour Military Burial Ground are printed in *Notes and Queries*, 10th series, vol 5.

Probate records

V L Oliver's *History of Antigua* (1896-9) has a significant collection of summaries of local and Prerogative Court of Canterbury probate material, from the seventeenth to the nineteenth century, in the Appendix section of volume three. *Caribbeana* contains various calendars and transcripts of wills and administrations relative to Antigua and other West Indian islands, including wills proved and administrations granted in the PCC. A lengthy abstract of the PCC will of James Vaughan of Antigua (1681) is featured in *Miscellanea Genealogica et Heraldica*, second series, vol 4 (1892), p 255.

Deeds and other records

History of Antigua and *Caribbeana* include various transcripts of deeds, pedigrees and so on, relative to Antigua.

FURTHER READING

The Antigua Almanac and Register including Montserrat 1842. Antigua, G Hart, printed at the office of the *Weekly Register*. Offered for sale by K Books of York in April 1999: 'possibly the only known copy?'

Berleant-Schiller, R; Lowes, S; Benjamin, M *Antigua and Barbuda*. World Bibliographical Series, volume 182. 1995.

Clark, W *Ten views in the island of Antigua*. 1823. A copy sold for £21,500 in a Bonham's sale in December 1998.

Dyde, B *Antigua and Barbuda: heart of the Caribbean*. MacMillan Caribbean. 2nd edition, 1993.

Dyde, B *A history of Antigua: the unsuspected isle*. MacMillan Education (Caribbean). 2000.

Galenson, D 'Servants bound for Antigua 1752-56'. *Genealogists' Magazine*, volume 19, no 8, Dec 1978, pages 277-9. Features manuscript indentures, held at Somerset Record Office, relating to the Tudway family estates at Parham Hill Plantation.

Harper, B *A short history of the heads of the government of the island of Antigua*. Antigua. 1962.

Harlow, V T *Christopher Codrington 1669-1710*. 1928.

Jane, C W E *Shirley Heights: the story of the Red Coats in Antigua*. Antigua, 1982.

Johnson, J *Historical and descriptive account of Antigua*. 1830.

Jones, Mrs [the only survivor]. *Account of the loss of the Wesleyan missionaries, Messrs. White, Hillier, Truscott, Oke and Jones, etc. in the Maria mail-boat off the island of Antigua, Feb.28, 1826.* 1826.

Langford, J *A brief account of the sufferings of the servants of the Lord called Quakers, from their first arrival in the island of Antegoa, under the several Governors, from the year 1660 to 1695.* 1706.

'A. Layman'. *The story of the cathedral and parish church of St John, Antigua, 1678-1932.* 1933.

Nicholson, D V *Antigua, Barbuda and Redonda: a historical sketch.* Antigua, 1991.

Scott, Rev R J E *The Church Calendar for the Diocese of Antigua in the province of the West Indies.* 1893.

Titford, J 'Settlers of the Old Empire: The West Indies: Antigua', 2 parts, *Family Tree Magazine,* June 2001 and September 2001

Tooley, R *The printed maps of Antigua 1689-1899.* 1969.

Maps

Some printed maps of Antigua are particularly useful in establishing the names and locating the estates of various planters and settlers. A small map of 1729, published by H Moll in the Strand, London, features the surnames of proprietors according to location, and a large and impressive map drawn by Robert Baker, 1746-9, carries a substantial alphabetical list of subscribers' names, 'with references to the divisions in which they have land'. A reproduction of the Baker map may be obtained from Kauai Fine Arts, PO Box 1079, Lawai, Hawaii 96765, USA. See also *Maps and plans in the Public Record Office, Volume 2: America and the West Indies*, edited by P A Penfold, 1974.

WEBSITES

www.rootsweb.ancestry.com/~atgwgw/
Historic Antigua and Barbuda, provided by avid researcher Christopher M Codrington. Includes details of the Antigua National Archives, the Museum of Antigua and Barbuda, a List of major reference works, a message board, details of search tools, maps, and much else.

www.rootsweb.ancestry.com/~caribgw/cgw_archive/archive.htm and:
www.rootsweb.ancestry.com/~caribgw/cgw_archive/antigua/baptism1.htm
Extracts from Antigua baptism records.

http://boards.rootsweb.com/localities.caribbean.antigua.general/mb.ashx
Rootsweb message board: Antigua.

http://Lists.rootsweb.ancestry.com/index/intl/ATG/ANTIGUA.html
Rootsweb mailing list: Antigua.

www.cousinconnect.com/p/a/13//sa/
CousinConnect.com Antigua and Barbuda genealogy queries.

www.familysearch.org/eng/Library/FHLC/frameset_fhlc.asp
The LDS Family History Library catalog. Search on 'Antigua' for a good collection of material, some of it on microfilm, including: Civil Registration records, Board of Trade correspondence, Court of Common Pleas court records and acts and registers of slaves.

The International Genealogical Index (now within FamilySearch) and related records should also be searched for individuals from Antigua.

English Harbour, Antigua. An engraving published in 1756.

CHAPTER FIVE
Bahamas

LOCATION

West Indies, east of Florida, north of the Caribbean islands. The name Bahamas comes from the Spanish word *bajamar*, meaning 'shallow water'. Of over 2000 islands in the Bahamas, only twenty-two are inhabited, including: Grand Bahama, New Providence (not to be confused with the island called 'Providence' off the coast of Nicaragua), Eleuthera (from a Greek word meaning 'free'), San Salvador (formerly Watling Island), Cat Island, Andros Island, Great Exuma, Great Inagua, Great and Little Abaco, Acklins Island, Long Island, Crooked Island, Mayaguana, Harbour Island, Rum Island, Bimini Islands, Spanish Wells, Berry Islands and Ragged Islands. The capital, founded in 1695 and named in honour of King William III, is Nassau.

HISTORY

Columbus discovered the Bahamas in 1492; although the islands were claimed by Spain, no settlements were made there, and in the seventeenth century control was exercised by a series of individuals granted rights by the English Crown, and - from 1647 to 1649 - by the Company of Eleutherian Adventurers. Eleuthera was settled in 1648 by seventy English

Puritans, and New Providence in 1656. Some colonists from Bermuda moved to settle in the Bahamas at various times from the 1640s onwards. The lords proprietors of Carolina had control over the Bahamas from 1670 to 1718, in which year, having been beset by pirates and all manner of corruption, the islands succeeded in becoming a Crown Colony ruled by a Governor. Later in the same century, American and Spanish interest in the islands was seen off, and Britain confirmed its sovereignty at the time of the Treaty of Madrid in 1783.

George Street, Nassau, Bahamas, with Government House (built in 1801) in the background.

The population of the Bahamas doubled in 1784 with the arrival of Empire Loyalists and their slaves from Georgia and the Carolinas, and a significant amount of growth took place in Nassau during the American Civil War of the 1860s, when the town became the main supply base for blockade-runners from the South.

The Turks and Caicos islands were under the control of the Bahamas from 1799 to 1838, when they were joined with Jamaica. The Bahamas achieved dominion status in 1973, becoming known as the Commonwealth of the Bahamas. Hurricane Floyd inflicted much damage on the islands in 1999.

ECONOMY

Rum, salt and crawfish have steadily become major Bahamian exports, and tourism has long been a mainstay of the islands' economy.

A sponge-sorting yard, Nassau, Bahamas. Is the man in the pith helmet supervising? Buying? By the end of the nineteenth century, sponge-fishing in the Bahamas employed over five hundred vessels and almost six thousand workers.

PEOPLE

- In 1629 the Bahamas were granted by King Charles I of England to Robert Heath, Lord of the Bahamas, along with the Carolinas.

- Captain William Sayle was Governor of Eleuthera (1648-1657); the first Governor of the Bahamas was Hugh Wentworth (1671), followed by John Wentworth (1671-1676); the first Royal Governor was Captain Woodes Rogers, who had been born in Bristol and baptised in Poole, Dorset (1718-1721); the first Governor-General was Sir John Paul (1973).

- From 1706 the pirates Captain Thomas Barrow and Captain Benjamin Hornigold effectively acted as rulers of key areas of the Bahamas.

- Early missionaries: Rev William Guy (at Providence, 1731), followed by Rev Hooper and by Rev William Smith, the first settled missionary officially established there by the Society for the Propagation of the Gospel in Foreign Parts.

- The Methodist Mission in the Bahamas was founded by William Turton, a planter's son from Barbados, in 1800. Other early Methodist missionaries included William Wilson, James Horne and Revs Crofts, Haigh, Whitehouse, Corlett, Cheesbrough and Bleby.

RECORDS (UK REPOSITORIES)

The National Archives, London. Colonial Office: correspondence, etc. (from 1696), censuses (1731,1734), land records (from 1734). Also: High Court and Vice Admiralty Court records (from 1673), War Office papers (from 1660), Board of Treasury Commissioners' records (eighteenth and nineteenth century loyalist claims), Privy Council Office plantation books (from 1676), Home Office denizations and naturalizations (from 1789). Treasury: T71 includes records generated by the Slave Compensation Commission, 1822-1834, and claims are indexed in T71/936.

Guildhall Library, London. Microfilm copies of the following registers for the Bahamas, from the Fulham Papers: baptisms 1721-28, marriages and burials 1723-28.

London Metropolitan Archives. Bahamas baptisms 1813-16 and marriages 1811, are with the 'International memoranda' records.

The Society of Genealogists, London, has a manuscript register of monumental inscriptions at Christ Church, Nassau, by 'H B' (1938).

RECORDS (LOCALLY-HELD)

Churches
Anglican: From 1734 to 1868, the Anglican church was the established church in the Bahamas. Until 1768, Christ Church was the single parish covering the entire colony. In that year Harbour Island became the parish of St John. In 1795, the colony was further divided, and the following parishes created: St Patrick (Eleuthera); St Andrew (Exuma and its Cays); St David (Long Cay, Crooked Island and Acklins); St Salvador (Cat Island); St Paul (Long Island); St George (Turks

Island and Caicos). Various other parishes were formed in the nineteenth century, and in 1861 the Diocese of Nassau was created, the church being disestablished seven years later. In the late nineteenth century, the islands came under considerable Anglo-Catholic influence, with the result that several prominent families became Methodists in protest; as a counterbalance, a considerable number of black people joined the Anglican church at this time, attracted by the increasing ritualism. The Department of Archives holds Anglican Church records for the period 1733 - 1992.

Methodists: The Methodists started work in the Bahamas in the closing years of the eighteenth century, the first chapel being built in 1794. Registers are held centrally at Methodist headquarters in Nassau.

Baptists: The first Baptist church was built 1790-1802, and a Baptist mission followed in 1833. Many other chapels were founded in the nineteenth century, and there are now over 200 Baptist churches on the islands.

Presbyterians: The Presbyterian church in Bahamas was founded in 1798, the first kirk being started in 1810. There is also a Presbyterian church in Freeport.

Roman Catholics: The first Roman Catholic priest to visit the islands arrived as late as 1845. Only in 1858 were the islands attached to the diocese of Charleston, South Carolina, the first church (St Francis Xavier) being built in 1885. Nassau became a Prefecture Apostolic in 1929, a Vicariate Apostolic in 1941 and a Diocese in 1960.

Jews. The first few Jews arrived on the island in the seventeenth century, and a Moses Franks served as attorney general and chief justice in the eighteenth century. There are some very old Jewish graves in Nassau.

Civil registration
Civil registration of births, marriages and deaths began on the islands in 1850. However, the records of the Registrar General's Office, PO Box N532, Nassau, include an index of marriages from 1799, together with records of birth (from 1850), death (from 1853) and marriage (from 1863).

Census
Two sets of enumerators' papers are included in the Colonial Secretary's records. These are the 1891 and 1953 working papers. The latter deposit, which is largest, contains valuable information such as the names, address, age, birth date and place, occupation or profession, religious affiliations, literacy and race of the people.

Probate records

Wills and administrations survive from 1700 in the Department of Archives, Nassau.

Dowers

In Bahamian society a man's wife is entitled to one third of all his estate (Dower Rights). When land or property is sold by the husband, the woman must renounce all claim to the land or property - without this renunciation the land cannot be sold. The Department of Archives holds a number of volumes of Dower Renunciations which were deposited by the Registrar General's Department. These span the years 1791-1910, but do not run continuously. Some Dower records are mixed with deeds and conveyances, which cover the period 1859-1951. The records give the names of parties involved, the type of transaction and the location of the property. The volumes are also on microfilm.

Cemetery records

For many years the Department of Archives has been involved in the transcription of headstones in a number of cemeteries, and publications on Christ Church Cemetery, St. Matthew's Cemetery and Eastern Burial Grounds have been produced. Cemetery Records have been deposited in the Archives from the Ministry of Works for the years 1897-1963.

Bahamas Department of Archives, PO Box SS-6341, Nassau. For a comprehensive account of the department's holdings as at 1973 (and an account of other public and private archive repositories), see Saunders and Carson's *Guide to the records of the Bahamas*.

The following records were microfilmed in 1956: conveyances, land grants, mortgages, bonds, deeds, wills and inventories (with indexes), proceedings of the Courts of Ordinary and Chancery, lists of freed slaves (1740-1834), details of slave trials (1785-89), minutes of the Executive Council (1789-1802) and the Colonial Secretary's book (1733-51). The Department also holds official government papers to 1964, maps, photographs and some parish registers.

The Department of Archives' website has this to say about the Registrar General's Department: 'This office which dates back to 1764 possesses a rich reservoir of records of genealogical importance. Its responsibility for births, marriages, deaths, land grants, deeds, conveyances and slaves resulted in the generation of innumerable documents. Although the department has made a large deposit of original and duplicate manuscripts to the Archives it continues to hold a vast amount of original and microfilmed records. The government's birth, marriage and death records span the years 1851-1979. Church Records from various denominations have also been deposited by the Registrar and these cover the period 1802-1976. The government records have been microfilmed but not those from the Churches. The original documents can only be seen at the discretion of the Research Room Supervisor'.

The Nassau Public Library, established in 1847, has a unique collection of material, especially newspapers from the late eighteenth century onwards (the earliest being a copy of the *Bahamas Gazette* for 1784).

FURTHER READING

Albury, P *The story of the Bahamas*. 1975.

Bethell, A T *The early settlers of the Bahamas and colonists of North America*. Packed full with names and many biographies, including a name-list from the 1671 census. 1937, reprinted 1999.

Cash, P, Gordon, S and Saunders, G *Sources for Bahamian history*. 1991.

Craton, M *A history of the Bahamas*. Second edition, 1968.

Johnson, C K 'Index of Land Grants in the Bahamas Islands' [1778-1850]. *Caribbean Historical and Genealogical Journal* II 1, January 1994.

Johnston, E C and Hollis Hallett, C F E *Early colonists of the Bahamas*. 1996. Thousands of names of individuals.

Kent Family History Society: Monumental inscriptions in St Matthew's Church and Cemetery and the Eastern Burial Ground, Nassau. Microfiche, 1986. The earliest references are to the early nineteenth century

Lester, G *In Sunny Isles*.1897. Methodism in the Bahamas.

Looking Back: A Guide to Genealogical Records in the Department of Archives [Bahamas]. 1996.

Malcolm. Sir H *Historical documents relating to the Bahama islands*. 1910. Gives certain key documents in full.

Mosely, M *The Bahamas handbook*. 1926.

Nassau: a detailed map of 1788, showing streets, etc: in *Caribbean historical & genealogical journal*, October 1997 (vol 5, no 4), page 27.

Oliver, V L *Caribbeana*. 1910-1920. References to the Bahamas, *passim*, including lists of wills proved in the Prerogative Court of Canterbury, 1743-1810, 1813-1816.

Oliver, V L *Monumental inscriptions of the British West Indies*. 1927. Monumental inscriptions from various places in the Bahamas, pages 240-248.

Riley, S *Homeward bound: a history of the Bahama Islands to 1850*. 1983. Plenty of names and name-lists.

Saunders, D G and Carson, E A *Guide to the records of the Bahamas*. 1973. *Supplement* to the same, 1980.

Siebert, W H *Legacy of the American revolution to the British West Indies and Bahamas: a chapter out of the history of the American loyalists.* 1913.

Symonette, M C & Canzoneri, A *Baptists in the Bahamas.* 1977.

Whittleton, E 'Family history in the Bahamas'. *The Genealogists' Magazine* volume 18, December 1975. Essentially a short historical account of the islands.

WEBSITES

www.rootsweb.com/~bhswgw/
Bahamas GenWeb, including access to useful online name lists (1671 census, Supreme Court Wills Index, etc).

http://Lists.rootsweb.com/index/intl/BHS/BAHAMAS.html
Rootsweb Bahamas Mailing List

www.bahamasnationalarchives.bs
Bahamas National Archives.

http://bahamashistoricalsociety.com
The Bahamas Historical Society.

www.cousinconnect.com/p/a/18/
CousinConnect.com Bahamas genealogy queries.

www.familysearch.org/eng/Library/FHLC/frameset_fhlc.asp
The LDS Family History Library catalog. Search on 'Bahamas' for a good collection of material, some of it on microfilm: birth, marriage and death registers, chancery records, indentures, including mortgages, wills, etc, dowers, land and property records, estate appraisals, leases, probate records.

The International Genealogical Index (now within FamilySearch) and related records should also be searched for individuals from the Bahamas.

CHAPTER SIX
Barbados

LOCATION

The island of Barbados is of coral formation, lacking rivers or streams and generally flat, with the exception of the north-eastern area known as the Scotland District. Twenty-one miles long and fourteen miles wide, with a total area of 166 square miles (rather larger than the Isle of Wight) and a present-day population of 258,000, it is one of the most densely-populated parts of the world.

From the earliest times it was considered to be the most strategically important of the Leeward and Windward Islands, occupying, as it does, the most easterly position of the archipelago. In effect, the island was Britain's foremost colonial possession in the Western Hemisphere, and it was in Barbados and in St Kitt's that England founded its first colonies in the southern part of America. The capital is Bridgetown.

HISTORY

There is no final consensus as to where the name Barbados comes from, though the most popular explanation would derive it from the Portuguese name for the bearded fig tree. There is also a certain amount of disagreement as to the date(s) of the original settlement of the island,

though the story would appear to be as follows. The English took possession briefly in 1605, when the crew of a vessel called the *Oliphe Blossome,* fitted out by Sir Oliph Leigh and on its way to Guiana, landed on the leeward coast and erected a cross, inscribing on a tree nearby: 'James K. of E. and of this Island'. Yet the first full English settlement dates from twenty one years later, when the ship *William and John*, with about forty emigrants on board, landed in 1626 on what was then an uninhabited island which had been abandoned by its Carib settlers a hundred years previously. The settlement they founded would become known as St James's Town, later renamed Holetown.

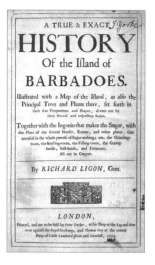

The title-page of Richard Ligon's History of the island of Barbadoes, published in 1673.

As the seventeenth century wore on, a variety of settlers arrived by choice or under compulsion. Some were small-scale farmers or husbandmen, others the younger sons of gentry or nobility. There were young men seeking adventure and wealth, or escaping from religious or political persecution or bad debts. All these would rub shoulders with indentured servants, convicted criminals and kidnapped people of both sexes. The descendants of Scots, Irish and Welsh who served as indentured servants (sold as white servants for seven years) were known as 'red legs' from their sunburnt skin, while the two hundred or so wealthy settler families who dominated the island for centuries are referred to as 'high whites'.

The divisions of the English Civil War were played out with a vengeance on the island, Cavalier against Roundhead. By 1656 the total Christian population was 25,000, comprised very largely of former Cavaliers, some of whom had been captured in battle and transported, while others had taken flight from what they saw as a post-war Cromwellian despotism. Cromwell, not best pleased, despatched a fleet of seven ships to the island under the command of Admiral Sir George Ayscue. After a stubborn defence the Royalists yielded on honourable terms, which were embodied in Articles of Agreement signed on January 11th, 1652. At the Restoration thirteen gentlemen of Barbados were created baronets in consideration of their sufferings and loyalty during the Civil War.

Some years later the population was swelled by the arrival of a hundred or so men whose punishment at the hand of Judge Jeffreys was to be forcibly removed from the homeland following the unsuccessful Monmouth Rebellion of 1685. Some of their descendants still live on the eastern part of the island to this day. Further enforced immigration took place in the wake of the Jacobite rebellions of 1715 and 1745.

Difficult as it is to attack from the sea because it lies upwind from the other Caribbean islands, Barbados remained uninterruptedly in English possession from its founding until it achieved dominion status in 1966, after having been a member of the Windward Islands Group (1833-1885), and the chief component in the West Indies Federation (1958 to 1962).

Richard Ligon's map of Barbados. 1657.

ECONOMY

Tobacco and indigo were the main source of the island's wealth during the seventeenth century, but thanks to Jewish immigrants who brought with them a knowledge of sugar culture they had learned in Brazil, it was on Barbados that the first sugar-cane was planted upon the soil of the British dominions, and proved to be hugely profitable. At the same time, a number of white settlers and their families were leaving the island, some moving to other places in the Caribbean, but many to make a new home in Virginia, Georgia and (especially) the Carolinas. It has been estimated that during the years 1660 to 1667, no fewer than ten thousand people, mainly landless freemen and small farmers, left Barbados, to be followed in 1668 to 1672 by four to five thousand more, mainly of the planter class, and from 1678 to 1682 by a further two thousand. As the plantation system took hold on the island, black slaves from West Africa were brought in to fill the labour gap. With the decay of the sugar trade from 1730 onwards, many Barbados planters moved permanently to South Carolina.

Two major historical survivals on the island are the former plantation houses of St Nicholas Abbey (built by Benjamin Berringer in about the year 1650) and Drax Hall. Together they have been described as 'The finest British colonial dwellings in America'.

The British abolished the slave trade in 1807, and full emancipation came to Barbadian slaves in 1838.

The Sea Island Cotton industry was revived in 1902 with some success, though sugar is still the main crop and tourism has proved to be a great success on the island in recent years.

PEOPLE

• The ship William and John, which arrived in 1627, was owned by a wealthy London merchant called Sir William Courteen.

• In his book *The cavaliers & roundheads of Barbados 1650-1652*, N Darnell Davis provides a fascinating list of a shipload of immigrants who arrived in Barbados in 1626-7:

'If no list of the settlers who arrived in the William and John is accessible, the names of those who left England in the Peter fortunately have been preserved among the State Papers in the Public Record Office, London, where they are to be found in Domestic Charles I, Vol 54, No. 83. Here is the list in all its original ruggedness of spelling: Rg. 23rd Feby 1627 (-7). The names of the men in Capt Powell's ship: A note of the menes their names that are shippte: Mr. Wodwoth, Richard Hobsone, Alexander Anante, Robart Radford, Samle. White, William Watsone, Stewen Wufle, Henry Newmane, George Powell, Henry Slingsleye, John Cadmore, Thomas Cooper, Mr. Broke Surgent, John Parker, John Aurree, John Rodes, Henry Ropere, Abereham Beneeime (sic), William Walker, Danell Cookee, Marke Stokes, Cornelios Jereshman, John Lambarte, John Speake, Thomas Clifete, John Prysen, Sameuell Burbe, Henry Austine, George Witte, John Cadmane, William Gilburt, John Rogers, Makum Scowle, William Browne, Henry Halle, John Hownely, Henry Fortine, Thomas Baxster, Dawe Fowle, William Wodmarse, John Blowar, John Latiner, Isake Fott, Henry Wanley, Archabole Asborne, Henry Henly, Jeme Lee, Thomas Coolee, Edward Perenall, Robarte Cooper, Antepas Medcafe, Willian Broker, William Nedese, John Celcarte, William Lebeter, Robart

Dicksone, Nickles Joyles, Mathew Andersen, Elias Pinder, John Edwardes, Lenard Harwid, Fraces Harber (sic), John Gainer, William Boltman, William Miles, John Grigese, Nickles Isake, Thomas Ringroome, William Tregane, Edward Primrose, Peter Stronge, John Jenkenyes, John Woode, Frances Weste.'

- The first Governor was Captain Henry Powell (1627-1628).

- Codrington College is an Anglican theological college in the parish of St John. It was founded by Christopher Codrington, who died in 1710 leaving portions of his estates - two slave labour plantations on Barbados and areas of Barbuda - to the Society for the Propagation of the Gospel in Foreign Parts to establish a college in Barbados. Construction was started in 1714, and the College was eventually opened on September 9, 1745.

- Early Moravian missionaries in Barbados include Benjamin Brookshaw and John Fozzard.

- Methodism encountered a great deal of initial resistance on Barbados, but by 1793 the Methodists had built a small chapel in Bridgetown, thanks to the strenuous efforts of Benjamin Pearce. Later ministers included Isaac Bradnack, Richard Pattison, John Robinson, James Whitworth, Jeremiah Boothby and others.

- Captain William Bate, son of Nathaniel Bate of Little Chester, Derby, began life as a sugar planter and as an officer in the defence force of Barbados. He became a member of the island's council, was promoted to Colonel, and was buried at Bridgetown in 1680, having never seen his estates in Derbyshire again. (See 'Escape to Barbados' by Frank Bates, *Family Tree Magazine*, June 1990, page 28ff).

RECORDS (UK REPOSITORIES)

The National Archives, London
Colonial Office records relating to Barbados - correspondence (from 1689), sessional papers, gazettes, etc - and to the Windward Islands and to the West Indies (general) are relevant sources. Transcriptions of various other Colonial Office records (parish registers and censuses) appear in books by Hotten and Brandow (see below) and details from a census of 1715 for the parishes of St Michael, St George and Christ Church are printed in the *Journal of the Barbados Museum and Historical Society*, vol IV, page 72.

Treasury: T1/4395 contains details of claims made following a hurricane of 11 August 1831. T71 includes records generated by the Slave Compensation Commission, 1817-1834, and claims are indexed in T71/940.

The British Library
There are copies of many registers and lists of wills for Barbados by Edwin Fitzpatrick in the British Library Manuscripts Section.

Alphabetical list of wills proved in Barbados, 1776-1880. Additional Manuscript 37,067. Marriages in Barbados, 1643-1700. Additional Manuscript 38,825.

A collection of all the monumental inscriptions prior to 1750 in Barbados, also similar inscriptions in Jamaica. J H Lawrence-Archer. 1857-8. Additional Manuscript MS 23,608. Includes many family notes not included in his book (see below).

School of Oriental and African Studies, London. Holds the archive of the Methodist Missionary Society, and has details of Methodist marriages in Barbados, 1830-34 and 1857-86.

RECORDS (LOCALLY-HELD)

An account of archive holdings in Barbados, originally provided by the Barbados Department of Archives, has been made available online at:

www.rootsweb.ancestry.com/~brbwgw/Archives1.htm *and at*:
www.rootsweb.ancestry.com/~atgwgw/resources/bsource.html

In 1959 the Rockefeller foundation provided funding to enable the University of the West Indies to carry out a survey of surviving historical records in Barbados. The resultant survey, which was carried out in 1960-1961, covered most Government Departments, the local (parish) governments, secondary schools, Anglican, Methodist, Moravian and Roman Catholic churches, a few business firms, the Public Library, and the Barbados Museum and Historical Society. The results of the survey, published as *A Guide to Records in Barbados* by M J Chandler (1964), form the core of the account which follows, with supplementary notes and updating (to 2006) added. Chandler's book, though it reflects the situation as it existed in the 1960s, rather than the way things are in the twenty-first century, is scholarly and comprehensive, and can still be used to advantage.

Churches
Barbados is divided into eleven parishes (each with its own church), the boundaries of which have remained unaltered since 1652. In the nineteenth century many additional churches were built, each having responsibility for its own district. The eleven parishes remained as the units of local government, and although the vestries were abolished in 1959, the parish boundaries still remain for some administrative

purposes, and all 'parochial registers' are still arranged under the original parish, although the district churches are now autonomous.

Here are the eleven parishes, giving the starting dates of surviving registers for each:

Christ Church: Bapt 1637 Marr 1643 Bur 1643; St Philip: Bapt 1648 Marr 1672/3 Bur 1673 (all imperfect before 1757); St Michael [Bridgetown]: Bapt 1648/9 Marr 1648/9 Bur 1648/9; St James [Holestown]: Bapt 1693 Marr 1693 Bur 1693; St Joseph: Bapt 1718 Marr 1717/8 Bur 1717/8; St Thomas: Bapt 1728 Marr 1723 Bur 1723; St Lucy: Bapt 1714 Marr 1749 Bur 1748; St Peter [(Speightstown, formerly known as 'Old Bristol']: Bapt 1779 Marr 1779 Bur 1779 (lacking baptisms 1825-1834); St George: Bapt 1801 Marr 1801 Bur 1801; St John: Bapt 1805 Marr 1657 Bur 1657 (baptisms imperfect before 1825); St Andrew: Bapt 1825 Marr 1825 Bur 1825.

The earlier registers of the parishes of St George and St Andrew were destroyed in a hurricane, and occasional gaps in any given series of registers should be expected.

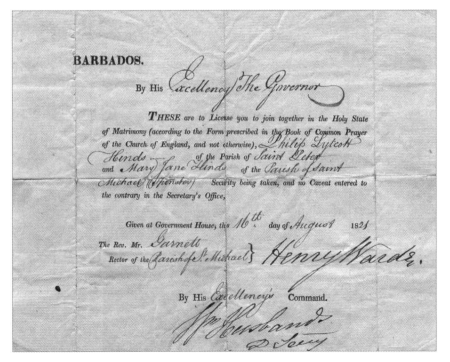

A marriage licence, Barbados, 1821. Philip Lytcott Hinds is to marry Mary Jane Hinds. It was usual at this period for the island's Governor to issue marriage licences - and Governor Henry Warde has duly signed his name here.

Thus, of the thirty-three series involved, only fourteen begin in the seventeenth century, twelve in the eighteenth century and seven in the nineteenth century. Only after 1825 are records fully complete for all parishes, though fortunately two of the most populous parishes, Christ Church and St Michael (the parish of the principal town, Bridgetown), are represented among the earliest registers. Parochial registers up to 1930 and indexes up to 1884 are housed at the Department of Archives. All surviving pre-1800 baptism and marriage registers have been transcribed and published by Joanne McRee Sanders (see below). For a detailed study of the parochial registers, see Geraldine Lane's *Tracing ancestors in Barbados*, pages 22-38.

In 1855 a central registry was established; copies of the existing registers were deposited in the Colonial Secretary's office, where they were indexed, and instructions were given that in future copies of registers from the parishes were to be submitted to the registry each year. There is a fine series of indexes (1637-1848, sixteen volumes, 1849-1884, sixteen volumes, etc) covering all existing 'parochial registers', and these continue up to the present day. Registers of baptisms, marriages and burials were presumably kept from the time each parish was founded, but the surviving records are by no means complete, nor were they when the Central Registry was created.

Until 1885 only Anglican registers were copied, but thereafter all denominations had to submit their own records: *Moravian* (from 1769), *Methodist*, *Roman Catholic*, *Garrison* and *Jewish* (from 1660) registers were also copied in a separate series with its own indices (3 Vols.) up to 1886. See Geraldine Lane's *Tracing ancestors in Barbados*, pages 39-48, for more details of Catholic, Jewish and nonconformist registers, page 101 for a table listing other relevant parochial records, and pages 106-108 for details of vital records relating to St Ann's Garrison. Offices located in some island cemeteries contain registers which can be consulted by arrangement.

Barbados: A collage of old registers for St James parish. Top left, baptism of slaves; top right, baptisms, marriages and burials, 1694; bottom left, burials from 1868 until the closure of the graveyard in 1887; bottom right, baptisms. By an act of 1855, copies were to be made and returned to the secretary's office of all registers kept by the parishes for which no duplicate had previously been returned. Reproduced by kind permission of the Rector of St James parish church.

District registers

Compulsory registration of births came into force in Barbados in 1890, of marriages in 1930 and of deaths in 1925. Registers and indexes are held at the Registration Department, Supreme Court of Barbados, Law Courts, Coleridge Street, Bridgetown. A limited search service is available for overseas enquirers.

Probate records

Wills, 1647-1959 and indexes are at the Department of Archives. Three series of wills exist: original wills (very fragile, imperfect before 1723, and only reasonably complete from about 1800), wills record books (copies of original wills, also fragile) and wills re-copied record books (these being the volumes that are now normally available to researchers). Indexes to recopied wills are available in two series: 1647-1800, by surname, year by year, and 1801-1945. The recopied will books from 1914 to 1945 are held at the Registration Department, though for this period it might be possible to see the original will in the Department of Archives. Wills from 1946 to 1959 have not been copied, so the original can be requested, and all wills from 1960 onwards are held at the Department of Archives. There are also indexes to original wills, 1743-1859 and 1860-1959, but such wills prior to 1914 can only be seen, if not too fragile, if it proves impossible to consult the recopied version. There is an index to wills that were filed but never proved, 1820-1959.

The Department of Archives holds surviving records of letters of administration, 1714-1959, but there are gaps, especially for the period 1714-1764. There is no comprehensive index, but most volumes have an individual index. Such records from 1960 onwards are at the Registration Department.

Inventories of testators' property provide additional information, including, at times, details of servants and slaves. The Department of Archives holds around 1800 of these for Barbados, covering the period 1780-1888, and there are indexes, arranged first by parish, then by surname.

Barbados wills and administrations, 1639-1725, have been abstracted and published by Joanne McRee Sanders (see below).

Deeds, etc
The earliest deeds record book (including land conveyances, leases, marriage settlements, bills of lading, letters of exchange and court decisions) dates from 1647, but only about half of the series to 1718 is still extant, and even for the period 1718 - 1781, the series is still incomplete. Moreover, many of the volumes cannot be used because of their bad state of preservation. Comprehensive indices to grantors date from 1801, but to grantees, only from 1879. Some of the earlier record books have individual indices to grantors, but many have none.

A number of deeds between 1636 and 1840 were entered into re-copied record books (a series of 47 volumes, compared with a possible 194 volumes of the original series in the same period). There is a comprehensive index (4 vols.) to grantors and grantees for the recopied volumes. Because of the limitations and difficulties of using the original series, searches before 1800 are usually only possible in the re-copied series.

The record books of powers of attorney and miscellaneous documents date from 1666, but are not complete prior to 1770. These records may be of particular interest to researchers, as individuals leaving the island would commonly execute and record a power of attorney to a representative in the island. There is no comprehensive index of powers from 1698 onwards.

Method of indexing. Each index in the foregoing series of registers and record books was compiled in a combination alphabetical-chronological order. The alphabetical arrangement is by initial letter of surnames only, the remaining arrangement being chronological, and sometimes by parish also. It is therefore no easy matter to search for a given name unless some date limitations (5-10 years, or even less in the nineteenth century) are given.

For further details, see Geraldine Lane's *Tracing ancestors in Barbados*, pages 81-86.

Inhabitants' lists
No continuous record of inhabitants exists, but the following may be noted:

- 1638. *List of inhabitants possessing over 10 acres* (transcript). A list of 'Barbados landholders in 1638 recently given grants', taken from *Some memoirs of the first settlement of the island of Barbados* by William Duke (1743), is given in the October 1997 issue of *Caribbean historical & genealogical journal* (vol 5, no 4), page 15.

- 1679/80. *Names of landowners* (transcript, indexed). Some parishes are reproduced in Hotten's *Original Lists...* and the remainder in Brandow's *Omitted chapters* and in Kent's *Barbados and America* - see below. For a description of the 1679/80 census, see *Journal of the Barbados Museum and Historical Society*, vol.33, page 57.

- 1715. *Census* (transcript, indexed). Names from certain parishes were published in *Journal of the Barbados Museum and Historical Society*, vols. 4 to 9, and a definitive listing for all the parishes appears in *Barbados and America* by D L Kent (1980).

- c.1740 - c.1835. *Parochial lists of inhabitants.* Thirteen items only.

- Rate books: St Michael (1683/5-1716, 1722-1729, 1749-1765, 1768-1810, 1823-1829, 1841 to date); St Philip (1874 to date); St Lucy (1881-1885, 1921 to date); St George (1891 to date). Other parishes: various dates from 1905 onwards. Many of these documents - even the more recent ones - are in poor condition and incomplete.

- *Voters registers*: 1807-1938; 1952 to date.

- No *census enumerations* between 1715 and 1900 exist. The 1960 and later census enumerations are not available for research.

Immigration and emigration
No early original records of immigration or emigration exist. Some records, not originating in Barbados, have been published - see below.

Shipping

No continuous record of arrivals and departures exists, but slight evidence of shipping movements may be obtained from various sources, mostly relating to cargoes and duties, for the following years: 1708-1723, 1730-1734, 1736, 1766, 1786, 1807-1809, 1817-1819, 1824, circa 1824-1835, 1839, 1842-1843, 1851-1852, and from newspapers. Only the newspapers (see below) report names of some passengers arriving or departing. There are also ships' protests for 1818-1819, 1835 and 1841 to date, but these also deal mainly with goods.

Index to plantations

Some original records relating to plantations are held by the Department of Archives and by the National Library Service. The department has compiled a card index from directories showing owners of plantations under the plantation name, mainly during the nineteenth and twentieth centuries. For further details, see Geraldine Lane's *Tracing ancestors in Barbados*, pages 87-90.

Newspapers

There are newspapers in Barbados for 1783-1784, 1787-1789, and for most years from 1805 onwards. Although the earliest Barbados newspaper is believed to have been published in 1731, only a few single issues are known to exist of an earlier date than those held in the island's library. The collection may be viewed on microfilm at the Barbados National Library Service, Public Services Division, Coleridge Street, Bridgetown 2, where directories and almanacs are also held, and where staff will carry out limited paid research for those from overseas.

Extracts from the newspapers between 1783 and 1870, mostly relating to Barbadian affairs and families, have been published in Volumes 1 to 33 of *The Journal of The Barbados Museum and Historical Society*. Also see *Caribbeana*, below.

In 1964 a Department of Archives was established by the Barbados Government and can now be found at Lazaretto Building, Black Rock, St Michael. The department has been accumulating records which were formerly kept by the agencies originally responsible for their creation. Many, but not all, of the records listed in Chandler's *Guide*, above, have already been transferred to the Archives, and such transfers are continuing. The Department of Archives has kept a watchful eye over those records not yet in its custody, and is always ready to advise on the whereabouts of any material listed in the original *Guide*. The Department does not undertake extended genealogical research for enquirers, but will on request give the names and contacts for any research agent currently active. Researchers at the department have access to the notebooks of the late Mr. H. G. Hutchinson, who specialised in searching genealogies.

Maps

A number of maps of Barbados, which include names of landowners, can be seen in the galleries of the Barbados Museum. The best-known are as follows: Ligon's, c.1650; Ford's, c.1680; Moll's, 1728; Bowen's, 1747; Mayo's, 1756, Barrallier's, 1825.

The Barbados Museum and Historical Society, St Ann's Garrison, St Michael, also has a considerable genealogical collection, including family files, the genealogical notes of Mrs Diana Campbell and the notebooks of the late Mr. E. M. Shilstone (see below).

Many of the Barbados archives have been filmed by the University of the West Indies.

SECONDARY SOURCES: PRINTED WORKS, etc.

As so often, it is Vere Langford Oliver who has made one of the most significant contributions to the publication of books and articles on the genealogy of Barbados. Works by him and by other authors/editors are summarized here.

Monumental inscriptions

The earliest surviving tombstone in Barbados, dating from 1659 and formerly in the parish church of Christ Church, is in the Barbados Museum: *Here lyeth/William Balston/Esq/Dec'd the 26 October/Ano Dom/1659*. Many such memorials which had been situated within churches were lost when a hurricane, destroyed the parish churches of Christ Church, St John, St Joseph, St Lucy, St Peter, St Philip and St Thomas in 1831. A detailed account of the hurricane, which struck Barbados, St Vincent and St Lucia in August 1831, can be found in *Four years' residence in the West Indies* by F W N Bailey (1833).

During a visit to Barbados in 1913/1914, Oliver recorded in full the memorial inscriptions then to be found in the island's Anglican churches and churchyards, resulting in the publication, the following year, of his *Monumental inscriptions in Barbados*, which includes some memorial stones found in plantation burial grounds. This was later complemented by the same author's *Monumental inscriptions of the British West Indies*. 1927, which gives details from Monumental inscriptions in the new portion of the Military Cemetery at Needhams Point (pages 255-260). Many inscriptions in various Barbadian churchyards had previously been published in the *Gentleman's Magazine* (1863). M.I.s at Nedham's Point Naval and Military Cemetery are featured in *Notes and Queries* (1922) as are those for St Paul (1928). Those for St Michael, the Cathedral, are in the *Journal of the Barbados Museum* (1948 and 1964).

A broken gravestone, St Michael's, Barbados. Fleetwood Thomas Hugh Wilson was a Captain in the 8th Hussars and Auditor-general, of Barbados. Photograph by John Titford.

Volunteers have made Oliver's work freely available in full at www.tombstones.bb, have brought it down to the year 1950, have included M.I.s for other denominations, and have added information from some burial registers.

See also:

- Gleadall, M E *Monumental inscriptions in the Barbados Military Cemetery.* 2000.

- Lawrence Archer, J.H. *Monumental inscriptions of the West Indies.* 1875. The great majority of recorded inscriptions are from Jamaica, but pages 345-401 feature details of selected monumental inscriptions from Barbados, some with illustrated armorials and genealogical notes. See Lawrence-Archer's manuscript, now held in the British Library, above.

- Shilstone, E M. *Monumental inscriptions in the Jewish Synagogue at Bridgetown Barbados with historical notes from 1630.* 1988. A fascinating study by a non-Jew who became intrigued by the subject. A number of Sephardim Jews, mainly those of Portuguese origin who had settled in Brazil to escape the Inquisition, made their way to Barbados and were well established within Bridgetown from the earliest years of settlement. Some names appearing in this book, like Montefiore, will be familiar to those who have some contact with Jewish activities in the City of London and elsewhere to this day, while the Jewish name of DaCosta may still be seen prominently displayed on shop signs in Bridgetown.

Vital records, pedigrees, etc

V L Oliver's *Caribbeana* contains: Barbados marriages and deaths 1783-89, and registers 1815-18 (vols. 1-3); a list of surviving wills prior to 1801 (vols 4, 5), and those proved in the PCC 1628-1812 (vols. 2, 3); extracts from Barbadian newspapers 1807-1809 (vol.2); births, marriages, deaths from the *Barbados Mercury and Bridgetown Gazette,* 1805-1818 (vols 1, 2); marriages and deaths from the same, 1783-4 (vol.3); abstracts of deeds, 1635-54 (vols 4,5).

Many pedigrees and notes previously printed in *Caribbeana* , and in the *Journal of the Barbados Museum and Historical Society*, were collected together by James Brandow and reprinted under the title *Genealogies of Barbados Families* (1983).

An outstanding source for students of family history in Barbados is the books compiled by Joanne McRee Sanders, a magnificent series of published transcripts of Barbados baptism, marriage and probate records, taken from original documents now housed in the Barbados Department of Archives: *Barbados records*: *Baptisms, 1637-1800.* 1984; *Marriages, 1643-1800.* Vols. 1-2. 1982; *Wills, 1639-1725.* Vols. 1-3. 1979-1981. All volumes were published by the Genealogical Publishing Company. There are several gaps in these registers, as noted by the author, and a summary table of these can be seen in Geraldine Lane's *Tracing ancestors in Barbados*, page 137. Ancestry.co.uk have now made these books available on-line by way of a searchable database: entitled 'English Settlers in Barbados, 1637-1800': 'Approximately 200,000 individuals are referenced within these pre-eminent works on Barbados genealogical source records'.

The following well-known printed work also contains very significant transcripts relating to Barbados, including inhabitants' lists, parish register extracts, details of tickets granted to persons leaving Barbados, 1679, etc:

Hotten, J.C. *The original lists of persons of quality, emigrants, religious exiles, political rebels, serving men sold for a term of years, apprentices, children stolen, maidens pressed and others who went from Great Britain to the American plantations, 1600-1700, with their ages, the localities where they formerly lived in the mother country, the names of the ships in which they embarked and other interesting particulars.* Various editions from 1874 onwards.

This work is supplemented by *Omitted chapters from Hotten's original lists, etc.* by J C Brandow (1983), and by *Barbados and America* by D L Kent (1980).

The Journal of the Barbados Museum and Historical Society has been published by the Society since its foundation in 1933. Volumes 14-19, for example, give details of 'Servants to foreign plantations from Bristol, England to Barbados, 1654-1686', and volume 27 has details of parochial returns (to the Plantation Office in London) for five parishes, 1715/1716. A typescript name index to a run of volumes of the *Journal* may be consulted at the Museum and also at the Department of Archives.

FURTHER READING

Beckles, H M *A history of Barbados : from Amerindian settlement to Caribbean single market.* 2nd edition, 2006.

Blackman, F *Methodism: two hundred years in Barbados.* 1988.

Cadbury, H J 'Barbados Quakers, 1683 to 1761' and '186 Barbados Quakeresses in 1677' in *Journal of the Barbados Museum and Historical Society*, IX (1941-1942), pages 29-31, 195-197.

Campbell, P F. *Some early Barbadian history.* 1993. Includes an alphabetical transcription of an inhabitants' list of Barbados for 1638 (see website, below).

Campbell, P F. *The church in Barbados in the seventeenth century.* 1982. Includes biographies and chronological lists of ministers by parish.

Davis, N Darnell *The cavaliers & roundheads of Barbados 1650-1652.* 1887. Includes an extensive list of surnames, pages 95-97, and names of early immigrants to Barbados, 1626-7, etc.

Dobson, D *Barbados and Scotland links 1627-1877.* 2005.

Gragg, L *Englishmen transplanted: the English colonization of Barbados 1627-1660.* 2003.

Handler, J S *A guide to source materials for the study of Barbados history, 1627-1834.* 1971. *Supplement* to the same. 1991.

Handler, J S, R Hughes, M Newton, P L V Welch, E M Wiltshire *Freedmen of Barbados: names and notes for genealogical and family history research.* 2nd ed, 2007. The names of nearly 2,000 Barbadians, arranged alphabetically by surname.

Harlow, V T *A history of Barbados. 1625-85.* 1926.

Hartland, M *A concise and illustrated military history of Barbados 1627-2007.* c.2007.

Hill, Barbara (Ed. Henry Fraser). *Historic churches of Barbados.* 1984.

Hoyos, F A. *Barbados. A history from Amerindians to Independence.* 1978.

Lane, G *Tracing ancestors in Barbados: a practical guide.* 2006. A user-friendly and comprehensive guide, tailor-made for the family historian by Geraldine Lane, who passed away a mere two years after its publication, but who has left it behind as a lasting legacy.

Lewis, K *The Moravian missions in Barbados*. 1988.

Murphy, Nathan W. 'To be sent to America: Indentured Servants Registered at Lyme Regis, Dorset, England, 1683-1689'. *Genealogists' Magazine*, Volume 29, no 3 (September 2007). These immigrants are included in the free online Immigrant Servants Database.

Myers, A C *Quaker arrivals at Philadelphia 1682-1750*. 1902. Includes abstracts of a number of Quaker certificates of removal from Barbados to Philadelphia.

Potter, R B and M S Graham *Barbados*, in the World Bibliographical Series, 76. 1987.

Poyer, J *The history of Barbados, from the first discovery of the islands in 1605, till the accession of Lord Seaforth, 1801*. 1808.

Radford, D A and A C White, 'The Irish in Barbados'. *The Irish at Home and Abroad: A Newsletter of Irish Genealogy and Heritage*. Volume 2, no 3 (1994/1995). Despite its title, this focuses on all early Barbados records, not just those pertaining to the Irish.

Schomburgk, R.H. *The history of Barbados*. 1848 (reprinted 1971).

Sinckler, E G *The Barbados Handbook*. 1913.

Stanford, C J. 'Genealogical sources in Barbados' in *The Genealogists' Magazine*, Vol.17, March 1974. pp.489-498.

Titford, J 'Barbados: some of its parishes, churches, and monumental inscriptions'. *Family Tree Magazine,* May 1997 (pages 55-57) and June 1997 (pages 56-58).

Wigfield, W McD *The Monmouth rebels 1685*. 1985. Has a two-page alphabetical list of 'Purchasers of the Monmouth rebels in Barbados', pages xix-xx.

WEBSITES

www.rootsweb.ancestry.com/~atgwgw/resources/bsource.html
RootsWeb: Barbados. Includes a name list of subscribers to William Mayo's Map of Barbados, circa 1717.

www.rootsweb.ancestry.com/~brbwgw/
Chronicle Barbados: Centre for Barbados Studies in History and Genealogy. Essential for the links it features and for the information it has to offer, including transcripts of the following: Association Oath Rolls 1696; Land Holdings 1630-1644; Inhabitants 1679: Christ Church, St. George, St. James, St. Michael; Census 1680: Christ Church, St. George, St. James, St. John, St. Joseph, St. Lucy, St. Michael, St. Peter All Saints, St. Phillip, St. Thomas; Bristol Servants; Regiment of Dragoons 1672; Eminent Planters - 1673

www.rootsweb.ancestry.com/~caribgw/cgw_archive/barbados/baptism1.htm
Barbados: Christ Church baptisms

www.barbmuse.org.bb/
Barbados Museum and Historical Society. Website currently under construction.

www.candoo.com/genresources/1638barbadoslist.txt
List of the names of the inhabitants of Barbados in the Year 1638 who then possessed more than ten Acres of Land. From P.F.Campbell's *Some Early Barbadian History* (1993).

www.candoo.com/projects/newspapers.htm
Jim Lynch: Old Barbados Newspapers.

http://boards.rootsweb.com/localities.caribbean.barbados.general/mb.ashx
RootsWeb message board: Barbados.

http://genforum.genealogy.com/barbados/
Barbados genealogy forum

www.barbados.org/museum2.htm
Barbados Museum.

www.cousinconnect.com/p/a/21/
CousinConnect.com Barbados genealogy queries.

www.barbadosancestors.com/
Tracing Ancestors in Barbados. Barbados-based researcher Geraldine Lane, who died in March 2008, compiled a comprehensive guide to records held on the island. Details of the book can be found here, together with information on research services provided by Barbados-based genealogy researchers. Includes an update feature. 'Once you have taken your research as far as you can you may find you need some help with records held on the island. Feel free to contact the Barbados-based research team at this point, giving an outline of the research needed. After assessment of the work involved, the amount and method of payment will be discussed and agreed before work commences'. There is an email address for enquiries, and a form to fill in if it is found to be helpful.

https://wiki.familysearch.org/en/Barbados
A developing site, worth keeping an eye on over time.

www.familysearch.org/eng/Library/FHLC/frameset_fhlc.asp
The LDS Family History Library catalog. Search on 'Barbados' for a good collection of material, some of it on microfilm: civil registration, probate, censuses, parish registers, military, cemeteries. emigration and immigration, maps.

The International Genealogical Index (now within FamilySearch) and related records should also be searched for individuals from Barbados.

** Ernest Wiltshire has compiled a database containing over 60,000 names from a variety of sources in Barbados, both published and unpublished, and has attempted to reconstruct the complex inter-relationships between various early settler families. It is hoped that this may eventually be made publicly available at the Department of Archives or on the internet.

St Thomas's church, Barbados. Photograph by John Titford.

CHAPTER SEVEN
Bermuda

Alternative names: Somers/Summer Islands

LOCATION

Bermuda, situated in the western north Atlantic, and constituting the most northerly coral islands in the world, is emphatically *not* in the Caribbean, though it is often spoken of in association with the islands of the West Indies, not least by the Colonial Office in London. Lying 800 miles to the north of St Kitts, 580 miles from North Carolina and 677 miles from the City of New York, it is the second most isolated piece of land in the world after St Helena.

Bermuda consists of a group of 300 or so small islands arranged in the shape of a sickle, of which the seven which form the essential core are linked by bridges or causeways; the total area of the whole is nineteen square miles - about the size of Manhattan - and nowhere is it possible to be more than a mile from the sea. The chief islands are: St George's, St David's, Great Bermuda; Somerset, Watford, Boaz, Ireland, Marsha, Long, Hawkins, Nelly, Darrells, Buck, Hinson, Ports, Burt, Nonsuch, Castle, Coney, Paget, Ordnance and Smiths. The original capital (from 1612) was St George (named after Admiral Sir George Somers), but from 1815 it has been Hamilton, on Great Bermuda, the smallest capital town within the old British Empire.

HISTORY

Juan de Bermudez, an early sixteenth-century Spanish traveller, gave Bermuda the name which it has enjoyed for much of its known history. The Spanish made no settlement there, and the first Englishman to set foot on Bermuda was Henry May, who survived a shipwreck in 1593 and whose account of his experiences was later published. In 1609 Admiral Sir George Somers' ship the *Sea Venture* was also wrecked off what is now St Catherine's Beach whilst en route to Virginia with a group of would-be colonists, and for a while the new-found territory acquired his name, being known as the Somers Islands. Shakespeare, hearing of this famous shipwreck, used it as the inspiration for the opening scenes of *The Tempest*, with its reference to the 'still vex'd Bermoothes'. Bermuda is thus almost as old a British possession as Barbados, and even older in terms of settlement.

When Somers set off again for Virginia in two new ships built under the direction of the shipwright Richard Frobisher (a native of Gravesend) the following year, he left behind two men - Robert Waters, a murderer, and Christopher Carter, a deserter, who became the first Bermuda settlers, soon to be joined by Admiral Somers' former servant, a man named Chard.

In 1612 the ship *Plough* arrived bearing Master Richard Moore, a carpenter by trade, who brought with him a party of fifty or so new settlers and a Virginia Company Commission as Governor.

St George, Bermuda, was established in 1612, and the Bermuda Company came into being three years later. In the 1640s various Bermudians of a puritan persuasion made an attempt to settle on the island of Eleuthera in the Bahamas.

Various immigrants arrived in Bermuda over time: some were gentry families living on their own means, others were less salubrious characters forced upon the islands by the Company. A number of Scots Highlanders were held in bondage in Bermuda following the Battle of Worcester in 1651, and several Irish convicts were transported there in the early nineteenth century.

A police station, Bermuda. In the foreground sits the magistrate, with members of his staff behind him.

In 1684 the charter of the Bermuda Company was revoked, and the islands became a Crown Colony the following year. A naval base for Bermuda was established on Ireland Island, built initially by slaves and then (until 1863) by convict labour, helping the islands to become something of a 'Gibraltar of the Western Hemisphere'. Bermuda remains a British Dependent Territory, though ties with the USA have always been strong.

ECONOMY

Eden of the Atlantic
A land of rest and play, of scenic beauty and natural wonders, of tropic yet temperate sunshine, Bermuda is the ideal resort for those who wish to escape the rigours of winter. Here one can spend delightful days golfing (six courses), yachting, bathing, walking, cycling, etc. Beautifully appointed hotels offer home comforts and convenience.

Copies of Tourists Guide Book obtainable free of charge from the Secretary, West India Committee, 14 Trinity Square, London, E.C., or from the Bermuda Trade Development Board (see under)

BERMUDA

This Advertisement is authorised by the
BERMUDA TRADE DEVELOPMENT BOARD
Hamilton, Bermuda
[A Department of the Bermuda Government]
to whom enquiries may also be addressed
London Office :—
37, Chancery Lane, W.C.

Early attempts to establish a viable economy based upon ambergris and tobacco eventually failed. Privateering and wrecking offered a living for some, and Bermudians built ships for whaling and trade, together with speedy light vessels for blockade-running during the American Civil War. Others were employed in gathering salt for export from the Bahamas and the Turks Islands. Tourism and offshore banking steadily grew in importance, and by the late 1970s the citizens of Bermuda had an average income that ranked among the highest in the world.

Bermuda, Eden of the Atlantic.
From a book published in 1927.

PEOPLE

- The first Governor was George Somers (1609-1610), a native of Lyme Regis in Dorset, followed by Matthew Somers (1610-1611). Captain Daniel Tucker, a Virginia planter, was the first Governor to be commissioned following the granting of a charter to the Bermuda Company by King James I in 1615, and the first Governor under the Crown was Col Richard Coney (1683-1687).

- On 26 November 1609 Admiral George Somers' cook, Thomas Powell, was married to Elizabeth Persons, the maid servant of another member of the company. The following year two children were born to members of the settlers' party: John Rose had a daughter, christened on 11 February 1610 and named 'Bermuda', and Edward Eason's son, christened on 25 March following, became 'Bermudas'.

- Less happy events beset the crew of the Sea Venture. Henry Ravens (master's mate) and Thomas Whittingham (Cape Merchant) went missing, presumed lost at sea; Robert Waters, a sailor, killed fellow crewman Edward Samuels and then escaped into the woods; Stephen Hopkins was sentenced to death (but then pardoned) for acting in a seditious manner, while Henry Paine, a gentleman venturer who struck the Captain of the Guard, was shot at sundown on 14 March 1610.

- Thomas Outerbridge, an emigrant from England (Oughtibridge is the name of a parish in Yorkshire), settled in Bermuda in 1619, and individuals bearing his surname can be found in great profusion there to this day.

- An early macabre tale relating to Bermuda concerns a man called Andrew Hilliard, whose fishing companions all died from starvation in an open boat, with the result that he ended up using the corpse of one of them as a source of much-needed food and as a cistern to collect rainwater.

- In 1618 a surveyor named Richard Norwood began to divide the islands into eight tribes or parishes, each named after a prominent British peer or knight: Hamilton, Smith's, Cavendish (later Devonshire), Pembroke, Paget, Southampton, Mansil's (later Warwick) and Sandy's.

- Bermuda was beset by a series of witchcraft trials during the second half of the seventeenth century. Those accused included: Jeanne Gardiner and Anne Bowen (executed, April 1651); John Middleton (accused in 1653 by Margery Tucker, and in turn accused Mrs Christian Stevenson and Goody North); Henry Ward (tried 'for consenting with the devil to bewitch the turkeys of Tommy Atkin'); Alice Moore; Jane Hopkins, 'one of the passengers of the Mayflower' (found guilty of having suckled the Devil, and executed in 1655).

- Eighteenth and early nineteenth century missionaries on Bermuda include: Rev Enoch Matson (Presbyterian); Rev John Stephenson, an Irishman (Methodist); Revs G Coster, M K S Frith, W L Gibbon, J F Lightbourn and others (Society for the Propagation of the Gospel).

Rev William Dowson (died 1846), a Methodist missionary in Bermuda and in the Bahamas.

RECORDS (UK REPOSITORIES)

The National Archives, London. Colonial Office: correspondence (from 1689), entry books (from 1615) etc. Admiralty: Baptisms and burials (from 1826) for the naval base at Ireland Island, and some similar records for Boaz Garrison and Ireland Island dating from the twentieth century. Treasury: T71 includes records generated by the Slave Compensation Commission, 1821-1834, and claims are indexed in T71/935.

RECORDS (LOCALLY-HELD)

Churches
Anglicans: In 1622 a system of nine parishes was established and the Bermuda Company required that annual returns of the numbers of registrations be made from each parish, but this injunction had to be repeated regularly, and clearly the Company did not receive these returns.

Three parishes have registers starting in the seventeenth century: Southampton (1619 from a copy made in 1723), Pembroke (1645) and Devonshire (1668). No registers survive from the other six parishes. St George's had one in 1720 when it was referred to in a court case. It has disappeared, as have any others that had been kept.

The situation only grew worse in the eighteenth century. Christ Church, Warwick, begins in 1789, but apart from this only two fragments (Hamilton 1745-1748, and Smith's 1758-1761) survive as church registers. The loss is only very partially made up by four personal registers kept by Rev. John Moore (1743-1776), Rev. Alexander Richardson (1755-1802), Rev. Alexander Ewing (1791-1820) and Rev. Marischal Keith (1793-1796). These do, however, contain records from many (and in some cases all) parishes, as there were only a few clergymen on the island in the eighteenth century.

The paucity of this survival means that wills are not merely a valuable supplemental source of information for Bermuda, but are absolutely vital. Printed abstracts of all Bermuda wills to 1835 have been printed (see below).

In 1825, ecclesiastical jurisdiction was transferred from the Bishop of London to the Bishop of Nova Scotia. A new archdeacon (Rev Aubrey George Spencer) was appointed and he immediately ordered that new registers be bought and kept, and enforced this edict. From that time onwards, therefore, registration improved considerably.

Methodists. Registration of Methodist baptisms started in 1810 and marriages in 1826, and has been fairly continuous since then. The Methodists did not have their own cemetery until they were permitted to do so in 1880; although a handful of deaths are recorded in the 1820s, no regular register predates 1866, and Bermuda Methodist burials are not as well recorded as are baptisms and marriages. Until 1846, there was only the Central Circuit; in that year St George's Circuit was created. Later Bailey's Bay Circuit and Southampton and Sandys became separate circuits.

Presbyterians: The first nonconformist church on the islands was built by the Presbyterians in Warwick. Its register starts in 1771, but was not regularly kept until 1789. Another church, St Andrew's, was opened in 1846

Roman Catholics: A Roman Catholic chapel in Hamilton opened in 1870, and Hamilton-in-Bermuda was established as a diocese in 1970.

Civil registration. The Registry General, Ministry of Labor and Home Affairs, Administration Building, 30 Parliament Street, Hamilton, has birth and marriage records (from 1866), death records (from 1865). NB: until 1910 the child's name does not appear on a birth certificate [sic]; marriage certificates do not include parents' names; death certificates include parents' names (though not the mother's maiden name).

Bermuda National Archives, Government Administration Building, 30 Parliament Street, Hamilton HM 12. Holdings include: parish registers (the earliest, for Southampton Parish, begins in 1619); various court records (chancery, quarter sessions, assize, Court of King's Bench, etc); land records, grants, deeds; manumissions, bills of sale and freedom certificates of slaves; shipping registers; oaths, naturalisation records; probate records (from 1640).

SECONDARY SOURCES: PRINTED WORKS, etc.

Family historians with an interest in Bermuda have every reason to be thankful for the tireless efforts of the husband-and-wife team Archie C and Clara F E Hollis Hallett, who have transcribed and published (under their own imprint of the Juniperhill Press) an impressive range of relevant archive material:

Hallett, C F E Hollis. *Bermuda Index 1784-1914: an index of births, marriages, deaths, as recorded in Bermuda newspapers*. Two volumes, 1989.
Hallett, A C Hollis. *Early Bermuda records 1619-1826: a guide to the parish and clergy registers with some assessment lists and petitions*. 1991.
Hallett, A C Hollis. *Early Bermuda wills 1629-1835, summarised and indexed*. 1993.

Hallett, C F E. *Forty years of convict labour. Bermuda 1823-1863*. 1999. Convicts working at the Bermuda Naval Dockyard.

Hallett, C F E Hollis. *Nineteenth century Bermuda wills 1835-1913*. 2000.

Hallett, A C Hollis. *Nineteenth century church registers of Bermuda*. 1997.

In effect, while Bermuda is unlucky enough to have lost many of its earlier registers, it is fortunate in that virtually everything that has survived before 1900 is available in print, as are indexes to wills, 1629-1913.

FURTHER READING

Anderson, C L *Lincolnshire convicts to Australia, Bermuda and Gibraltar: a study of two thousand convicts*. 1993.

Bermuda Directory (1881, further editions to 1914)

Chambers, J 'Transported to Bermuda', in *The family and local history handbook*, Seventh edition, pages 28-30.

Chapin, H *Bermuda privateers 1625-1703 and 1739-1748*. 1923, 1925.

Davies, G *Extracts from the Bermuda Gazette*. 1984.

Gandy, W *The Association Oath Rolls of the British Plantations AD 1696*. 1922. Extensive name-lists for Bermuda, pages 48-60.

Green, T H *Monumental inscriptions of the Royal Naval Cemetery, Ireland Island, Bermuda*. Typescript. 1983. A copy may be seen at the Society of Genealogists in London. [NB: in general, monumental inscriptions in Bermuda graveyards are rarely found, many tombs bearing simply a brass plaque with the family name on it].

Hotten, J C *The original lists of persons of quality...who went from Great Britain to the American plantations, 1600-1700*. Various editions from 1874 onwards. Lists of names relating to 'The Sommer Islands', 1673-1679, can be found at pages 301-313.

Kennedy, J de C *Biography of a colonial town: Hamilton, Bermuda 1790-1897*. 1963. Useful lists of rectors, ministers and priests at various Hamilton churches.

Mercer, J.E. *Bermuda Settlers of the Seventeenth Century*. 1982. Abstracts of some of the earliest-known records of Bermuda settlers.

Miscellanea Genealogica et Heraldica. New series, volume 4: Bermuda (St George's) baptisms (1812-1830), marriages (1812-1848), burials (1812-1815). Entries in some cases are fuller than in Hollett's *Early Bermuda records*. New series, volume 3 (the start of a planned series which was soon discontinued): monumental inscriptions in the church of St Peter and St George, Bermuda.

Oliver, V L *Caribbeana*. 1910-1920. Lists of wills of Bermuda residents proved in the Prerogative Court of Canterbury, 1625-1796; 1806-1811; 1813-1816.

Rowe, H *A guide to the records of Bermuda*. Bermuda Archives. 1980.

Strode, H. *The story of Bermuda*. (New York) 1932.

Wistow, H *The Church in Bermuda: a brief sketch*.

WEBSITES

www.rootsweb.com/~bmuwgw/bermuda.htm
Bermuda Genealogical Web Project. Provides access to a wide-ranging collection of online material - wills, ships' passenger lists, details of witchcraft trials (with names), parish surveys, and much else.

http://lists.rootsweb.ancestry.com/index/intl/BMU/BERMUDA.html
Rootsweb Bermuda Mailing List

www.cousinconnect.com/p/a/1142/
CousinConnect.com Bermuda genealogy queries.

www.gov.bm/portal/server.pt
Government of Bermuda. Follow links: Government services A-Z > Archives.

www.bermuda-online.org
Institute of North American & Atlantic Colonial History in Bermuda. Includes several useful links.

www.familysearch.org/eng/Library/FHLC/frameset_fhlc.asp
The LDS Family History Library catalog. Search on 'Bermuda' for a good collection of material, some of it on microfilm: census 1788, Ireland Island church records, Boaz Island garrison baptisms, (from TNA Admiralty records), St Ann Church, Southampton, baptisms and burials 1858-1958, court records, register of freeholders, public records, wills, inventories and administrations.

The International Genealogical Index (now within FamilySearch) and related records should also be searched for individuals from Bermuda.

CHAPTER EIGHT
British Guiana (Guyana)

Alternative names: Demerara/Demerary

LOCATION

British Guiana, now Guyana, the only British colony on the South American mainland, is separated from Surinam(e) in the east by the Corantyne river, and from Brazil in the south by the Akarai mountains. Several rivers make up the western border with Brazil and Venezuela, and the Essequibo river flows through the centre of the country. Behind a cultivated coastal strip, which is low-lying and needs careful draining, lie ranges of densely-wooded mountains.

HISTORY

The Dutch developed sugar plantations in Demerara in the late sixteenth century, but in the 1790s British privateers took over the colonies of Berbice, Demerara and Essequibo from the Dutch West India Company and they were placed under the jurisdiction of the Governor of Barbados. Struggles for supremacy in the area followed, Britain finding itself in contention with both the Dutch and the French. In 1815, following the Napoleonic Wars, the three colonies were ceded to Britain, and in 1831 they became constituent parts of what became known as British Guiana.

Slaves from Africa and from the islands of the West Indies had been extensively used to work the plantations, but once slavery was abolished, immigrants from the East Indies came to live and work in the colony as indentured labourers, and their descendants now make up more than half the total population - a development which has led to a significant amount of inter-racial tension. Boundary disputes with Venezuela and Brazil beset the colony for many years, but self-rule was achieved in 1961, and five years later the name of Guyana was adopted. The Co-operative Republic of Guyana was formally created on 23 February 1970, with a capital at Georgetown.

An Indian home, British Guiana. A solitary white man squats on the ground, his hat on his knees.

ECONOMY

The rich alluvial soil of the coastland region favours the cultivation of sugar (for many years the principal crop), rice, coconuts and coffee.

PEOPLE

- In 1620 Captain Roger North established a colony in Guiana by the name of Oyapoc. It was destined to be short-lived, and North soon returned to London.

- Lieut-Col Robert Kingston was Governor of Berbice and Demerara (1781-1782); Lieut Col Robert Nicholson was Governor of Essequibo (1781-1782); Abraham Van Batenburg was Governor of Berbice and Essequibo (1796-1802); Antony Beaujon was commander of Demerara (1796-1802); Sir Benjamin D'Urban was the first Governor of British Guiana (1831-1833).

- It was in defence of the manager of his father's estate in Vreed-en-Hoop, Demerara, who had been accused of cruelty to his slaves, that William Ewart Gladstone made his maiden speech in House of Commons in 1833.

- Early Missionaries: *Wesleyan Methodist*: Rev J Hawkshaw, followed by Revs T Talboys (1815), Mortier, Bellamy, Ames, Shrewsbury, Cheeswright, Edmondson, Rayner, Vigis, Hornabrook, and Ranyell. *Church Missionary Society*: Leonard Strong, born in 1797, the son of the rector of Brampton Abbots, Herefordshire (arrived in Demerara 1826), who later joined the ranks of the so-called 'Brethren', and Rev J H Bernau, who wrote *Missionary labours in British Guiana*, published in 1847. *The London Missionary Society* was particularly active in British Guiana, and the following chronological list of missionaries who served there appears in an appendix to *The history of the London Missionary Society 1796-1895* by Richard Lovett (1899):

British Guiana: Demerara and Berbice: Wray, John 1808-1837 (several years later, in 1892, *The life and labours of John Wray, pioneer missionary in British Guiana* by Thomas Rain was published in London); Davies, John 1809-1827; Elliott, Richard 1814-1824; Kempton, John 1814-1815; Smith, John 1817-1824 (a native of Rothwell, Northamptonshire, who encountered strong opposition from the Governor; following his death in 1824, the Smith Memorial Church, Georgetown, was named in his honour); Mercer, James 1818-1822; Ketley, Joseph 1828-1838; Lewis, Michael 1830-1832; Scott, James 1831-1867; Howe, James 1833-1837; Mirams, James 1833-1836; Haywood, Samuel 1834-1850; Rattray, Charles 1834-1871; Ross, John 1834-1835; Watt, Charles Davidson 1834-1844; Kenyon, Daniel 1835-1851; Taylor, Robert Barry 1835-1839 (appointed to South Africa in 1841); Forward, Giles 1836-1840; Murkland, Sidney Smith 1836-1846; Parish, William (schoolmaster) 1837-1837; Edwards, John 1838-1839; Henderson, Thomas (schoolmaster, afterwards ordained) 1838-1870; Morris, John (schoolmaster) 1838-1843; Seaborn, Hugh Sanderson 1838-1839; Davies, Ebenezer 1840-1848; Roome, James (schoolmaster, afterwards missionary) 1840-1866; Thompson, Richard (schoolmaster, afterwards missionary) 1840-1842; Waddington, Joseph

1840-1847; Giles, James (schoolmaster) 1841-1842; Pettigrew, George (schoolmaster, afterwards ordained) 1841-1877; Dalgleish, John 1842-1862 and 1867-1884; Parker, James Laurie (schoolmaster) 1842-1843; Wallbridge, Edwin Angel 1842-1874; McKellar, Alexander 1843-1845; Bowrey, James 1844-1854; Foreman, John (schoolmaster, afterwards ordained) 1846-1888; Hughes, John Henry 1848-1853; Kent, William 1848-1850; Ingram, Henry Brown 1853-1857; Ricards, Robert 1859-1866; Rain, Thomas 1861-1863; Warder, William 1862-1872; Carter, Thomas 1863-1864; Johnson, Alfred William 1864-1866; Cooper, Joseph Jeremiah 1865-1866; Munro, James Wright 1865-1871; Green, James Lampard 1889-1894 (stationed in the Society Islands, 1861-1886).

- Quntin Hogg, an enlightened late nineteenth century sugar plantation owner in Demerara, gave financial support to the Moravian Mission Board to pay for chaplains to work on his estates.

- *The Royal Gazette for Demerary and Essequebo*, 26th. January 1819, carries the text of a proclamation dated 22nd January 1819 by Major General John Murray:

'Lieutenant Governor and Commander-in-Chief, in and over the United Colony of Demerary and Essequebo &c.' concerning the illegality and consequent invalidity of certain marriages contracted in the colony. The proclamation declares that 'all marriages, which may have been contracted and celebrated within this Colony, in the manner prescribed in a proclamation of the late Major-General H.L.Carmichael, bearing date the 2d day of June, 1812, be, and they hereby are, confirmed and established as legal and valid.'

Carmichael's earlier proclamation is repealed, and 'no marriages hereafter contracted within the Colony can be legally valid...unless contracted and celebrated in the manner prescribed by the laws and ordinances actually in force within the said United Colony'.

A list of the names of the following forty-three couples affected was provided by Rev.W G Strachan, minister:

'Henry Blackman Adams and Ann Oxley; James Mings and Susannah Archer; Anthony Miller and Johanna Haselemeir; Philip Phillips and Christina France; Peter Clement and Cora Emery; Samuel Bulcock and Marsiella Collette Post; William Oxley and Christina James; John Anthony Neischer and Princess Howard; Fricco Desbras and Maria Paadevoott; Michael Smith and Johanna Rebecca Garbin; Andrew Battalier and Mary Cornelisen; James Thomas Stephens and Ann Walker Cuvilje; John Hall and Elizabeth Arthar; William M Roach and Mary Jane Nurse; Abel Corbin and Elizabeth Bennett; Thomas Lambly and Charlotte Corbin; Evan Hughes Williams and Elizabeth Knight; George Firebrace Perry and Ann Taylor; John Wade and Maria Margarita Wagear; Francis

Carrol and Frances Lucas; Peter Henry Thompson and Sophia Elizabeth Stoll; John Runnells and Elizabeth McDaniel; Samuel Cordew and Sarah Wake; Johannis Cornelis De Ryk and Janette Elizabeth Thompson; Paul Augustus Ouckama and Mary Elizabeth Downer; James Daley and Kitty Staunton; Thomas Laurence and Frances Merrick; John Whitaker Tull and Ann Cuvilje; John Williamson and Harriet Hunter; William Augustus Crozier and Ann Shillingford; Mauritz Johan Jacobus Mottet and Ann Stamper; Joseph Bentham and Margaret Smith; Henry Bollers and Sarah Gibbs; Christian Frederick Cayler and Mary Bollers; Peter Capelhof Pieters and Maria Langevine; John Vial and Elizabeth Hennecey; Peter Heyliger and Mary Carteache; John Peter Peterson and Cuvelje; Lewis Fox and Elizabeth Berrow; Peter Blackman and Louisa Williams; Christian Marcus Tobie and Wilhelmina Watherham; William Kennard Samms and Margret Desullie; Philip Backer and Jane Agard.'

The original *Gazette* may be seen on microfilm at The British Library Newspaper Library, London.

This was not a unique occurrence: in 1854:

'An act to render valid certain marriages of British subjects in Mexico' was passed, whereby 'All marriages solemnized before the first day of January one thousand eight hundred and fifty four in any place of the Republic of Mexico by or in the presence of Percy W Doyle (both or one of the parties thereto being subjects or a subject of this realm) shall be deemed and held to be as valid in the law as if the same had been solemnized within Her Majesty's Dominions with a due observance of all forms required by law'.

RECORDS (UK REPOSITORIES)

The National Archives, London.
Colonial Office: correspondence (from 1781), sessional papers, gazettes, land grants, mortgages, tax and court records, together with a few documents written in Dutch. Treasury: T71 includes records generated by the Slave Compensation Commission, 1817-1832, and claims are indexed in T71/931-933.

The archival sources for Guyana's history before 1796-1803 are mainly in Dutch, many of them held in Dutch repositories, though much relevant material was handed over to Britain in 1818-1819.

London Metropolitan Archives. Baptisms and marriages 1798.

Society of Genealogists, London. Extracts of burials, 1812-1821.

United Society for the Propagation of the Gospel, London. Baptisms 1821-28, marriages 1827.

Bookers McConnel & Co, Bucklesbury House, Cannon Street, London, once owned many of the sugar plantations in colonial British Guiana and may have some relevant records.

RECORDS (LOCALLY-HELD)

The history of what is now the Guyanan National Archives, formerly at Main Street, Georgetown, but now occupying a new building on Homestretch Avenue, D'Urban Park, has at times been a troubled one, involving neglect and losses. In 1945 a fire destroyed a large part of Georgetown, including the library and a number of other principal buildings, and during 2005 lurid newspaper headlines expressed concern about the safety and condition of the nation's archival heritage: 'National Archives building sold; move threatens historical material...'.

At the present time it is difficult to determine exactly which records are held within the archive office, though they reputedly include land records, mortgages, wills, some transcriptions of monumental inscriptions, and much else. The best we can do - and with a certain degree of optimism - is to give a partial listing of what was known to be in evidence in 1941, when Arthur E Gropp of the New Orleans Middle American Research Institute at Tulane University of Louisiana compiled his book *Guide to libraries and archives in Central America and the West Indies, Panama, Bermuda and British Guiana*:

A collection of 30 titles of newspapers, the earliest being the Berbice Gazette, 1818; the Demerara and Essequebo Gazette, 1819; and the Guiana Chronicle, 1819-1841; Administrative papers of Berbice; Military Register, 1766-1796; Blue Book of Berbice, 1830-31; Blue Book of British Guiana, 1844-1856; Blue Book of Demerara & Essequebo, 1821, 1827-28, 1830-31; Land Grants; Petitions, 1813-1830; Dispatches, Berbice 1812-1823; Account Book, Rio Demerary, 1794-1796.

In the Registrar's Office, Georgetown (*almost all records prior to 1803 are in Dutch*): agreements, 1770-; contracts, 1770-; deeds of release of apprenticeship, 1836; leases, 1770-; mortgages, 1870; parish population records; plans of plots (originals); Royal Gazette (1841-) [Official Gazette from 1851-]; suits (law); transports, 1770- (deeds to land in Essequebo and Demerara); property register (a book for each district by names of places and urban districts by ward; also includes encumbrances on property).

In the Registrar General Office: Births, 1869- ; Deaths, 1869-; Marriages 1903-.

Churches

Records of baptism, marriage and burial prior to 1880 are held by individual churches. In her *History of the Anglican Church* (2000), Blanche Emmeline Duke gives the earliest dates recorded in the registers of the various churches: St Georges, Georgetown, Demerara 1796; All Saints, New Amsterdam, Berbice 1818; Holy Trinity, Anna Regina, Essequibo Coast 1821; St Paul's, East Coast Demerara 1824; St John's, Suddie, Essequibo Coast 1825.

New Amsterdam, British Guiana, circa 1905.

The Church of the Immaculate Conception(Roman Catholic) at Brickdam has the following records: baptisms (from 1869); marriages (from 1873); funerals (from 1913): Cathedral Administrator, Cathedral Parish of the Immaculate Conception, 28 Brickdam Street, Stabroek, Georgetown.

St Andrews Presbyterian Church has many records dating back to 1816; their records are kept by event (birth, deaths, marriages) and by year: Rev Oswald A Best, St Andrew's Manse, 81 Croal Street, Georgetown.

St George's Cathedral: archives are held here, but the oldest records are in fragile condition and presently inaccessible until funds to preserve or digitise them become available: Very Rev Terry David, St George's Cathedral, Deanery Office, 79 Carmichael Street, South Cummingsburg, Georgetown.

Civil registration

Records of births, marriages and deaths are with the office of the Registrar-General, GPO Building, Robb Street, Georgetown, which falls under the auspices of the Ministry of Home Affairs, not the Ministry of Culture. The Guyana public can currently view its records there only on Fridays...The office is also a repository for some, although not all, of the shipping records.

Census

Censuses (reputedly taken every ten years from 1861-1931 - are they nominal censuses?) are the responsibility of the Statistical Bureau, Ministry of Economic Development, Georgetown.

Wills and Deeds.

Held by the Registrar of Deeds, Victoria Law Courts, Georgetown.

Newspapers

When British Guiana gained independence in 1966, the British took back to England copies of many colonial newspapers - among them the *Argosy* and the *Colonist*. The births, marriages and death notices printed in such newspapers may be the only source for such information for many colonists. These newspapers now form part of the British Library collection, where a number have been microfilmed (for a useful listing see: www.rootsweb.ancestry.com/~nyggbs/NewspaperListing.htm); they are unindexed, but Inge Veecock has produced transcripts and indexes for various entries from the *Argosy* and *Colonist* papers (see below).

An extensive listing of repositories in Guyana which held relevant records as at 1985 (the Deeds Registry in Georgetown, the Berbice Legal Registry, etc) can be found in *Research guide to Central America and the Caribbean* (Grieb, K J et al), pages 360-363.

SECONDARY SOURCES: PRINTED WORKS, etc.

Newspapers

A book entitled *Compilation of births marriages and deaths 1864-1880. Announcements as reported in the Colonist newspaper, Georgetown, British*

Guiana and, ditto, in *The Argosy newspaper, Georgetown, 1880-1896* (1996) by I R Veecock is a magnificent name-indexed collection of material for the late nineteenth century, compiled from microfilm copies of *The Colonist* and *The Argosy* held at the British Newspaper Library, London. Never published as such, these volumes appear in the catalogue of the LDS Family History Library, and may be seen, for example, in the library of the Society of Genealogists in London. Recently they have been made available on the website of the Guyana / British Guiana Genealogical Society at: www.rootsweb.ancestry.com/~nyggbs/Argosy/ArgosyBMDs.htm.

Entries include births, marriages and deaths which took place in the colony itself - *Marriage, 18 June 1872: At St Peter's Chapel, Essequebo, by the Revd. William Austin, William Smith, Esq., to Margaret Elizabeth, only daughter of the late David Brodie, Esq., engineer of Belfield, Essequebo* - and also events connected to British Guiana which happened elsewhere: *Marriage. 12 December 1894. At St Edmund's Church, Allestree [Derbyshire], by the Rev. Anchtel Anson, rector of Longford, Derbyshire, and Rural Dean, uncle of the bridegroom, and the Rev.Austin West, vicar of Allestree, Edward Roseberry Anson, of the Civil Service, British Guiana, second son of Edward Hamilton Anson, of H.M. Household, and late of the Bengal Civil Service, to Mary Gertrude, eldest daughter of William Gisborne, of Allestree Hall, Derbyshire, and of Lingen, Herefordshire.*

FURTHER READING

A comprehensive overview of the main printed works relating to British Guiana may be found in *General history of the Caribbean*, volume 6 by B W Higman (UNESCO 1999), pages 590-603.

British Guiana Directory. The 1906 edition, for example, carries a useful List of pensioners: *Mrs Stevenson, widow, pension of $469.02 per annum in right of J D Stevenson, Police Inspector.*

Dalton, H G *The history of British Guiana*. 2 vols. 1855. Contains many names of plantation owners, 1839-1848. Volume One, page 540 onwards, has a significant list of names of those who purchased plantations, 1838-1849: *3 March 1847. Den Amstel plantation. Demerary. Sold for $10,150 to William Lyng. Coffee. Since abandoned. Negro village.*

Daly, V T *The making of Guyana*. 1974.

Lawrence-Archer, J H *Monumental inscriptions of the British West Indies*. 1875. A few MIs from the Cathedral, Georgetown (pages 423-425) and some old Dutch epitaphs (page 426).

Oliver, V L *Caribbeana* (five volumes, 1910-1920) contains various references to British Guiana wills proved at the Prerogative Court of Canterbury, 1668-1816, some transcripts of monumental inscriptions, details of bookplates, and extensive name-lists from the Obituary of the Orphan Chamber of Demerara 1812-1821 (but: 'I have omitted all names of coloured persons').

Oliver, V L *Monumental inscriptions of the British West Indies* (1927). Contains a number of inscriptions copied from tombstones in various places in Demerara (pages 223-239 and 252-254).

Rodway, J *History of British Guiana*. 3 volumes 1891,1893,1894.

Rooke, Beryl *Rooke's genealogical notes on Guyana. A guide to records and sources*, typescript, 1993 (held at Society of Genealogists).

Who's Who in British Guiana. Various editions. Text and many illustrations.

Who is who in British Guiana 1935-1937. This was the first attempt at such a work - and is substantial, at 411 pages. The compilers sent out questionnaires for the purpose, but were disappointed at the results, not least because of the evidence they found as to 'the low degree of intelligence existing in the ranks of our peers', as they put it.

Name of Pensioner.	Officer in right of whom the Pension is drawn.		Pension per Annum.
	Brought forward...	...	...$45,308 10
Moore, Mrs.,	widow	...Rev. J. R. Moore	150 08
Moore, Mrs.,	,,	...J. M. Moore, late assistant Colonial Civil Engineer	600 53
Muir, Mrs.,	,,	...Rev. J. Muir ...	351 26
Nelson, Mrs.,	,,	...Prince Nelson, Prison Warder ...	54 60
Odlum, Mrs.,	,,	...R. W. Odlum, Customs Officer ...	152 58
Oudkirk, Mrs.,	,,	...G. Oudkirk, retired Clerk, Audit Office ...	185 96
Ozanne, Mrs.,	,,	...Dr. G. Ozanne, Resident Surgeon, H.M.P.S. ...	951 42
Pairaudeau, Mrs.,	,,	...E. A. Pairaudeau, Government Surveyor..	619 69
Payne, Mrs.,	,,	...C. L. Payne, Magistrate...	507 01
Pentland, Mrs.,	,,	...Dr. Pentland, Medical Officer	653 60
Percival, Mrs.,	,,	...Exley Percival, Principal, Queen's College	1,042 29
Phillips, Mrs.,	,,	...W. V. Phillips, Customs Officer ...	328 44
Pollard, Mrs.,	,,	...W. B. Pollard, Col. Civil Engineer	1,081 04
Potbury, Mrs.,	,,	...J. A. Potbury, Principal, Queen's College ...	1,001 52
Pringle, minor, child	...Rev. A. C. Pringle	...	163 05
Sabeeno, Mrs.,	widow	...J. A. Sabeeno, Mechanician, Post Office	101 74
Salmon, Mrs.,	,,	...Rev. G. Salmon	294 74
Schrack, Mrs.,	,,	...G. Schrack, 2nd Clerk, Administrator General's Office ...	287 19
Schurer, minor children	..G. H. Schurer, Accountant of Court ...	...	131 24
Seifferth, Mrs.,	widow	...Rev. C. B. Seifferth	363 38
Semper, Mrs.,	,,	...His Honour, H. R. Semper, Puisne Judge	849 02
Shannon, Mrs.,	,,	...Dr. M. Shannon ...	842 03
Shanks, Mrs.,	,,	...A. D. Shanks, Prison Officer	186 06
Sheriff, Mrs.,	,,	...W. A. M. Sheriff, Puisne Judge ...	1,246 00
	Carried forward	...	...$57,352 59

LIST OF PENSIONERS.

Part of a list of pensioners from British Guiana Directory 1906.

WEBSITES

www.vc.id.au/tb/index.html
The excellent British Guiana Colonists database, maintained by Tikwis Bebgie. Information on eighteenth and nineteenth century settlers, drawn from a wide range of sources and arranged alphabetically by surname.

www.cousinconnect.com/p/a/74/
CousinConnect.com Guyana genealogy queries.

www.kindredtrails.com/guyana.html
KindredTrails Guyana genealogy.

www.rootsweb.com/~nyggbs/index.htm
The Guyana / British Guiana Genealogical Society. A number of searchable transcriptions have been made freely available, and birth, marriage and death announcements are posted on the site as transcribed from various newspapers: *The Colonist, The Argosy, The Royal Gazette of Demerara & Essequibo,* and the *London Times.*

http://lists.rootsweb.com/index/intl/GUY/GUYANA.html
RootsWeb.com Guyana Mailing List

www.vc.id.au/edg/index.html
Guyana Colonial Newspapers, with transcriptions and indexes.

www.bisa.btinternet.co.uk/mainbody.htm
Brits in South America Database

www.familysearch.org/eng/Library/FHLC/frameset_fhlc.asp
The LDS Family History Library catalog. Search on 'Guyana' to see a list of the few relevant items the library holds.

The International Genealogical Index (now within FamilySearch) and related records should also be searched for individuals from the British Guiana.

JAMES GILMOUR
(Mongolia)

J. K. MACKENZIE
(Tientsin)

JOHN WRAY
(Demerara)

JOHN FOREMAN
(Demerara)

JAMES SMITH
(Demerara)

British Guiana: missionaries at Demerara: James Wray, John Foreman and James Smith. From The History of the London Missionary Society 1795-1895 by Richard Lovett, 1899.

CHAPTER NINE
British Honduras (Belize)

Alternative names: Belize/Balize/Belice, Black River Settlement, Wallis.

LOCATION

Central America, on the east coast of the Yucatan peninsula. The northern half of the country is flat, whilst the south consists of a mixture of plateaux and hill ranges.

HISTORY

British pirates and buccaneers began landing at what was then a Spanish colony in the early seventeenth century. In 1660 the ruler of the Moskito Indians placed himself under British protection, and by 1662 British log-cutters from Jamaica had established the first stable settlement there. In 1749 an unofficial colony, know as the Black River Settlements or British Honduras, was formed, answerable to Jamaica. When the Spanish took over in 1787, the British settlers moved to Belize. The Spanish were finally defeated in 1798 at the Battle of St George's Caye, and when the country as a whole became a separate colony in 1862, it was still subservient to Jamaica, a situation which lasted until 1884, when, as a Crown Colony, it was able to control its own affairs.

It has been estimated that during the 1860s, following the end of the American Civil War, more former confederate soldiers settled in British Honduras than in any other country.

Volunteers returning from parade, Belize, British Honduras, circa 1908.

British Honduras: Government House and part of Belize from Fort George.

The country achieved self-rule on 1 January 1964, and in 1981, when it became a dominion within the British Commonwealth, it took the name of Belize, and the capital was moved from Belize City to Belmopan. The population of Belize in the early years of the twenty-first century numbers barely 250,000.

ECONOMY

British Honduras was long renowned for the quality of its timber, especially mahogany, and for a copious supply of log-wood, used in dyeing. Alternative sources of wood from Africa, together with the invention of synthetic dyes, put an end to the viability of the export trade in these commodities. The country survives now thanks to a small agricultural sector, income from the tourist trade, and aid provided by Great Britain and the United States.

PEOPLE

- William Wallis was a Scottish buccaneer who settled on St George's Caye in 1638.

- The first Superintendent of British Honduras was Robert Hodgson, senior (1749-1758); the first Lieutenant Governor (and also the last Superintendent) was Frederick Seymour (1862-1864), and the last was Sir James Hennessey (1980-1981).

- Rev William Stanford came to British Honduras in 1794 from Jamaica, where he had been a parish priest for 18 years. Clergyman, magistrate, bad-tempered drunkard, fighter of duels, yet as enlightened a slave-owner as could be found at the time, he was once described by the Belize historian Emory King as 'a priest with a bible in one hand, a bottle of rum in the other, and a pistol in his waistband'. He retired (for the last time, but not the first) in 1810.

- The first Wesleyan missionaries in British Honduras were Revs Thomas Wilkinson (1825), Thomas Johnston and James Pilley (1829).

- Captain George Henderson (1809), a visiting sea captain, helped build the colony, as did the Baptist missionary Frederick Crowe (1850) and the entrepreneur A R Gibbs (1883).

- A memorial tablet for John Waldron Wright Esq., formerly a merchant and magistrate of British Honduras who died in London in 1850, may be seen in St Pancras Old Church, London.

- Thomas Potts, who was born in England in 1740 and had children in Belize by Catherine Ferrell and Susannah Burrell, was probably the richest man in the settlement when he died in 1806.

- Admiral Sir William Burnaby came to Belize in February (or early March) 1765 to fight a Spanish army on behalf of the `Baymen' (the term used for British settlers around the Gulf or `Bay' of Honduras), but left in April, having meanwhile codified the laws of the settlement into what was called Burnaby's Code - in effect, the first constitution.

RECORDS (UK REPOSITORIES)

The National Archives, London. Colonial Office correspondence (from 1744), sessional papers, gazettes, etc. War Office: land grants c.1748-1774. Treasury: T71 includes records generated by the Slave Compensation Commission, 1834, and claims are indexed in T71/924.

British Library Manuscripts Department, London. See especially the Sloane collection.

Lambeth Palace Library, Lambeth Palace Road, London SE1 7JU, holds various relevant journals and records of the Society for the Propagation of the Gospel in Foreign Parts (SPG).

Cambridge University Library houses the library of the Royal Commonwealth Society, which holds further SPG records. See also Simpson, D H *The manuscript catalogue of the Library of the Royal Commonwealth Society* (1975), pages 145-149 for manuscripts relating to British Honduras.

RECORDS (LOCALLY-HELD)

The bulk of the records held by the Belize Archives Department, 26/28 Unity Boulevard, Belmopan, consists of the superintendents', lieutenant Governors' and Governors' correspondence and consular despatches 1805 - 1956, but it also houses some birth, marriage and death records, census returns (1826-1991), court records (1817-1978), maps and plans, slave records (1820-1854), etc., as well as copies of some wills and miscellaneous archive material dating from the late eighteenth century. Some church records are also held there, but there are separate record offices (all situated in Belize City) for the Anglican, Methodist, Baptist, Presbyterian and Roman Catholic churches. Jesuit records are held at the Belize Institute for Social Research at St John's College in Belize City.

Civil registration

Vital records of births (from 1885), marriages (from 1881) and deaths (from 1885) are held by the Registrar General, Supreme Court, Belize City.

The Belize National Library in Belize City has information on the epitaphs in St. John's Cathedral, the Honduras Almanac for the early years of the Settlement, and some Colonial Office Records.

Guy Grannum, in *Tracing your West Indian ancestors* (2002, page 132) points out that certain records relating to British Honduras have been lost over the years: principally in 1754, when the Spanish destroyed all buildings during an attack; in 1918 when a fire destroyed the Colonial Secretary's Office and other public buildings, and in 1931 when the colony was struck by a hurricane and tidal wave.

FURTHER READING

Burdon, Sir John A *Archives of British Honduras*. 3 volumes. 1931.

Caiger, S L *British Honduras past and present*. 1951.

Dobson, N *A history of Belize*. 1973.

Fairweather, D N A *A short history of the volunteer forces of British Honduras* (includes several lists of militiamen back to 1824). N.D. (1980?)

King, Emory, Film Commissioner for Belize, is a one-man factory for the production of books on the history of Belize. His many publications include *Belize 1798: the road to glory: the Battle of St George's Caye* (1991) and *The great story of Belize* (2 volumes, 1999).

Oliver, V L There are various references to British Honduras wills proved at the Prerogative Court of Canterbury in this author's five-volume work *Caribbeana* (1910-1920).

Usher, J P *Memorial inscriptions and epitaphs, Belize, British Honduras*. 1907. 62 pages, indexed, covering Belize cemeteries and tablets and tombstones at St George's Caye. A gold mine for family historians. A typical entry, relating to a memorial in the Cathedral, reads:

> *To the memory of/William Thurston/of Surlingham, in the county of Norfolk/who died August 20th 1853/aged 30 years/this tablet was erected/in token of gratitude and esteem/by P E Wodehouse, Esqre/Superintendent of Honduras/in whose family he served faithfully/for many years.*

Woodward, R L *Belize*. World Bibliographical Series, volume 21. 1980.

WEBSITES

www.belizearchives.gov.bz
Belize Archives and Records Service.

www.kindredtrails.com/belize.html
KindredTrails Belize genealogy.

www.cousinconnect.com/p/a/24/
CousinConnect.com Belize genealogy queries.

http://genforum.genealogy.com/belize/
Genealogy.com Belize genealogy forum.

http://archiver.rootsweb.ancestry.com/th/index/BELIZE/
Rootsweb: Belize.

http://lists.rootsweb.ancestry.com/index/intl/BLZ/BELIZE.html
Rootsweb Belize Mailing List

www.worldgenweb.org/index.php/north-america/belize
BelizeGenWeb. With Bulletin Boards and Mailing List.

www.familysearch.org/eng/Library/FHLC/frameset_fhlc.asp
The LDS Family History Library catalog. Search on 'Belize' for a list of relevant material, some of it on microfilm: church, census and civil registration records.

The International Genealogical Index (now within FamilySearch) and related records should also be searched for individuals from British Honduras/ Belize.

CHAPTER TEN
The British Virgin Islands

LOCATION

The British Virgin Islands lie at the point where the Greater and Lesser Antilles meet, sixty miles east of Puerto Rico and north and east of the United States Virgin Islands. Thirty two islands make up the British Virgins, including Tortola, Virgin Gorda (once the principal settlement), Jost Van Dyke, Anegada, Peter Island and Salt Island. Tortola (from the Spanish word for a turtle dove) is the largest island in the group, being twelve miles long and three miles wide at its broadest part; ruggedly hilly, with land rising abruptly from the surrounding sea, it has Road Town as its capital.

HISTORY

Columbus had arrived in the Virgin Islands in 1493; he gave them their name, it is said, in honour of St Ursula and the 11,000 virgins who were murdered by the Huns outside Rome. There was a Dutch presence on Tortola from as early as 1620, but in 1665 an English sea captain by the name of John Wentworth made an attack on the island. English settlers from Anguilla arrived a year later, and in 1672 Colonel William Stapleton took control of the island for Britain, driving out a number of Dutch

freebooters, at which time about eighty English, Irish and Welsh settlers were living there alongside a dozen or so Dutch families.

The early British settlers were fortunate enough to be able to develop strong contacts with merchants and financiers in Liverpool, who supplied them with slaves and necessary goods. The islands were practically abandoned as a result of Spanish attacks in the year 1685, but pirates, buccaneers and freebooters found Tortola very much to their liking, and plied their illicit trade from there and from a number of neighbouring islets which bore names such as Rum Island, Beef Island, Dutchman's Cap, Prickly Pear, Broken Jerusalem - and Dead Man's Chest, immortalised by Robert Louis Stevenson in *Treasure Island*. Even law-abiding settlers often found ways of sharing in the profits of the illicit trade being carried on all around them, and many turned to privateering themselves. In 1709 Governor Parke remarked of the Virgin Islanders that 'they live like wild people without order or Government, and have neither Divine nor Lawyer amongst them, they take each others words in marriage; they think themselves Christians because they are descended from such'.

From the 1730s the British Virgin Islands acquired settlers from a number of neighbouring islands threatened with war, including some who were keen to escape debt or punishment for crimes, and began to enjoy a period of great prosperity based upon successful plantation agriculture, woodcutting, and a significant amount of trade, both legitimate and illegitimate. By 1756 the population of the islands as a whole had risen to 1,184 whites and 6,121 slaves. Tortola was finally granted its charter in 1773 and a much-needed legislature was established.

The British Virgin Islands had prospered during times of war, not least during the American War of Independence; when a degree of international peace came in 1815, it heralded a decline in their fortunes and a number of white planters eventually left to seek better opportunities elsewhere. The islands were united with St Kitts, Nevis and Anguilla from 1816 to 1833, and were later part of the Leeward Islands grouping, eventually becoming a separate colony in 1960 and autonomous in 1967. They are now one of the few 'British Oversees Territories'.

Not all the Virgin Islands are British. The United States of America purchased the rights of Denmark in the West Indies in 1917, acquiring (for the sum of twenty five million dollars) the group which had previously been the Danish Virgin Islands, including St Thomas, St John and St Croix. Ownership of these islands had been a matter of some dispute during the seventeenth and eighteenth centuries; the rival claims of Britain and Denmark over St Thomas and St John were settled in Denmark's favour in 1718, and St Croix, home to a number of English, Dutch and French settlers from 1645, was finally legitimised as a Danish Colony by 1733. In the early years of the nineteenth century all three islands were held sporadically by Britain until a final settlement of 1815.

ECONOMY

Sugar cane was cultivated in the British Virgins as on other Caribbean islands, with slaves from a number of tribes (Angolians, Congolese, Nagois, Mocoes, Ibos, Pawpaws, Senegalese and Mandingos) being brought from Africa to work in the fields. In more recent years the limited agricultural economy has been outshone by the profitability of offshore business industries and of tourism - BVI being a favourite destination for couples wishing to marry in a place with a sunny climate and an intriguing name.

PEOPLE

- In 1807 a 17 year old blacksmith from Cornwall, Robert Jeffery, who had been impressed on board a British man-of-war, was left ashore by Captain Lake on Sombrero, alias 'Spanish Hat', a bare rock lying in the channel dividing the Virgin Islands from the other Leeward Islands, for having taken two quarts of spruce beer. Lake was eventually court martialled and dismissed from service for his inhumane treatment of the hapless castaway.

- In a letter to the Council of Trade and Plantations in London dated 27 September 1697, Christopher Codrington, Governor of the Leeward Islands, reported that one of the last families to live on Tortola had been that of Thomas Biss, an Englishman who had Sir William Stapleton's commission as Governor to settle there, and that the only inhabitants at that time were Jonathan Turner and his wife, 'who live there in the woods, breed stock, plant a little cotton and go fishing'.

- Quakers visited the West Indies as early as the 1670s, but it was in the 1720s that Joshua Fielding, a London merchant, left England with William Piggott on a journey to the Americas, landed in the Virgin islands and helped to establish a viable group of Quaker believers at a time when there were no other places of worship there. The beliefs and rules of conduct of the Friends did not always sit easily with the immorality and lawlessness of the wider population of the islands at this period. In 1745 the first Anglican clergyman there, John Latham, appointed in an attempt to combat the growth of Quakerism, married one of the Friends' leading women, Dorcas Powell; she was promptly disowned by the horrified Women's Monthly Meeting. The active Quaker presence on the British Virgin Islands during the mid eighteenth century lasted a mere forty-five years; the official monthly meetings ceased in 1772, and all five meeting houses were destroyed in a great hurricane in 1780. For all that, the general influence of the Friends during this time and in particular their humane treatment of their slaves would have a long-term salutary effect on the life and morals of the islands.

Various Quaker believers and ministers with origins in England who were known to have been in the Virgin Islands during the eighteenth century include: James Birkett, a young merchant from Lancaster, who had settled in Antigua and arrived in Tortola in 1738; Thomas Chalkley, minister and sea captain, who was born in Southwark in 1675, settled in Philadelphia, but died on Tortola during a visit there in 1741 and was buried in a graveyard on Fat Hog Bay; John Estaugh, a minister, born in England in 1676, who arrived in Tortola in 1742 with John Cadwallader from Pennsylvania, both of them dying there in the same year; Peter Fearon, a much-travelled minister, who was born in England in 1683, arrived in the Virgin Islands in 1746 and died in 1762; Samuel Nottingham (1716-1787), minister and originally a blacksmith, born at Wellingborough, Northants, who married Mary Hunt, widow of Captain Hunt, the former Governor of Tortola, in 1749; Thomas Gawthrop (1709-1780), soldier and traveller, who was born at Skipton, Yorkshire, and later lived in Westmorland; Thomas Lancaster, minister, who was born in England in about 1703 and later settled in Pennsylvania, where he married Phoebe Wardell; Alexander Balneives, Collector of Customs, Member of the Council and a Justice of the Peace on Tortola, who was born in Scotland.

John Pickering, first Lieutenant Governor of Tortola (1741) and a convert to Quakerism, was the son of an Englishman, Abednego Pickering of Anguilla, who had arrived in Tortola in the early 1720s. By the time John Pickering died in 1768, his only surviving child, Isaac, was living in England at Fox Lease, Hampshire.

Two Quakers of particular talent and drive who were born in the Virgin Islands were destined to have an impact on the wider international scene. Dr John Coakley Lettsom, physician and philanthropist, was born on Jost Van Dyke in 1744 and died in London in 1815, being buried in Bunhill Fields. On his father's side he could trace his ancestry back to the village of Letsom in Cheshire, while through his mother he was descended from Sir Caesar Coakley, an Irish Baronet. Lettsom was educated at Penketh in Lancashire under Gilbert Thompson and then apprenticed to Abraham Sutcliffe, an apothecary living at Settle in Yorkshire, before embarking on his illustrious career far from the island of his birth. Dr William Thornton, son of the Englishman William Thornton and his wife Dorcas Downing Zeagers, was born on Jost Van Dyke in 1759; given a 'rudimentary' education at Lancaster in England while staying with his aunts, Jane and Mary Thornton, he became a druggist's clerk in Ulverston before studying Medicine at Edinburgh and eventually achieving fame thanks to his efforts to improve the treatment of slaves and to his architectural career in the newly-established capital of the United States at Washington DC, where he designed the Capitol building itself.

Birthplace of Dr John Coakley Lettsom (1744-1815), physician and philanthropist, on Little Jost Van Dyke, British Virgin Islands. From The Gentleman's Magazine supplement, lxxxv Part 2, page 577.

• Methodism began to take root in the Virgin Islands following the arrival of Thomas Coke and others in the February of 1789. Ministers who would work there over the years would include Messrs Hammett, Turner (who reported in 1798 that there were 2,739 Methodists on the islands, 16 of them white), Isham, Murdock, Brownell, Evans and Hodgson.

RECORDS (UK REPOSITORIES)

The National Archives, London
Colonial Office records relating to the British Virgin Islands - correspondence (from 1711), sessional papers, etc - and to the Leeward Islands as a whole are relevant sources. There are separate entry books of correspondence (ten volumes, CO 244) for the island of St Croix while it was in British hands from 1808 to 1815. CO152/12, no.67 (viii) is a nominal census for Tortola, taken in 1717 and including country of origin of the inhabitants. Treasury: T71 includes records generated by the Slave Compensation Commission, 1818-1834, and claims are indexed in T71/929.

RECORDS (LOCALLY-HELD)

Churches

Registration of christenings, marriages and funerals throughout the islands was introduced by 'An act for regulating a Vestry for declaring the whole of the Virgin Islands one parish' of 1811.

Anglicans: Anglican church records held in the parish church of St George the Martyr, Road Town, Tortola, include baptism registers from 1825, marriages from 1833 and burials from 1819. With these are records relating to St Paul's church and also vestry minutes (1823-1828 and from 1921 onwards) and registers of baptism (from 1903) and of marriage (from 1923) relating to St Mary's church, Virgin Gorda. An attractive photograph of St George's church may be seen in Simon Winchester's book *Outposts* (1987).

Methodists: Methodist church records held on the islands include registers of baptism from 1815, marriages from 1877 and burials from 1845.

Civil registration

Compulsory civil registration on the British Virgin Islands was introduced by an ordinance of 1858, later amended and complemented by further legislation. Registers of birth, marriage and death are deposited with the Office of the Registrar of births, deaths and marriages, Government of the British Virgin Islands, Central Administration Complex, Road Town, Tortola. Registration districts are: Virgin Gorda; Anegada; East End; Road Town, West End and Jost Van Dyke.

Census

The first of a series of decennial censuses for the Virgin Islands was taken in November 1871. By 1891 the population numbered 4,639 persons.

It is likely that at least some early census records have now been lost, but some more recent censuses are held at the Development Planning Unit, Government of the British Virgin Islands, Administration Complex, Road Town, Tortola.

Other original records held on the islands

For full details of archival holdings as they existed on the islands in 1965, together with a list of some records of the Leeward Islands Federation held on Antigua and a history of the archives of these islands, see *A guide to records in the Leeward*

Islands by E C Baker (1965). The situation in 1965 was that various records were held in the Record Room, Tortola Treasury Building (deed record books containing copies of acts, indentures, inventories, judgments, powers of attorney and wills [1801-1831], eighteenth to twentieth centuries, together with correspondence, land and house tax registers, etc.), while others were in the Registrar's Office (twentieth-century deed record books and registers of deeds) and elsewhere.

The Islands' archives, some currently held in the Archives Room and some in the Library at Flemming Street, Road Town, Tortola, are still being developed as part of a millennium project; a new location for them is being sought, and it is hoped to produce a catalogue of holdings eventually. The developing website www.nationalarchives.gov.vg/ (Virgin Islands Archives and Records Management Unit) includes a chronological account of the often-disastrous disregard for the islands' archival heritage - e.g.: '2001-2002 - through poor planning and disregard for protocol, historical documents including deeds and wills from 1779 - 1826 were destroyed'. Since then several stable doors have been closed after a number of archival horses have bolted...

GENEALOGICAL SOURCES HELD ELSEWHERE

A certain amount of information relative to the British Virgin Islands, including records of land ownership, may be found in the Public Library and in the Library of the College of the Virgin Islands in Charlotte Amalia, capital of St Thomas in the United States Virgin Islands.

SECONDARY SOURCES: PRINTED WORKS, etc.

A detailed and widely-researched account of the Quaker presence on Tortola in the eighteenth century is given in *Tortola: a Quaker experiment of long ago in the tropics* by Charles F Jenkins, first published in 1923 and reprinted with a foreword by Harriet F Durham in 1971.

Jenkins's book includes appendices which give a great number of names taken from details of births, marriages and deaths and from lists of adult members featured in the minute books of the Monthly Meetings of Friends on the island during the period 1740 to 1763. The following surnames are featured:

Babston; Bacon; Baher; Balneives; Birkett; Bishop; Block; Blunder; Brabston; Bradley; Britt; Brown; Callwood; Chalwill; Clandaniel; Clark; Conne (?); Crulle; Daniel; Downing; Elliott; Everett; Fleming; George; Graves; Grim; Haddin; Hornbe; Humpheys; Hunt;

Johnson; Lake; Lane; Lawrence; Lettsom; McGumery(?); Martin; Mattis (Maddix); Morris; Mulloon; Nash; Nottingham; Parke; Percival; Pickering; Pow(e); Powell; Rapsot; Rawleigh (Raleigh); Reynolds; Richardson; Ryan; Shute; Smith; Strong; Thomas; Thornton; Timberman; Underhill; Vanterpool; Vascraging; Walker; Williams; Wily (Wyle); Woolrich; Zeagers.

A particularly striking illustration of the Friends' burial ground in Tortola, taken from a contemporary drawing, appears on page 87 of *A history of the British Virgin Islands* by Isaac Dookhan, 1975.

Monumental inscriptions
V L Oliver's *The monumental inscriptions of the British West Indies* (1927) contains no material from the British Virgin Islands, but does include part of the text of a letter concerning military cemeteries there, written to the author by Major H Peebles, Commissioner at Tortola, dated 9th.August 1920:

'The sum of £3 is allocated in this Presidency for the upkeep of historic sites, etc.; this amount is adequate to maintain the existing Military Cemetery in this Presidency. The old Military Cemetery, which was of some considerable size, situated on the North side of Road Town, has now disappeared, owing to the sea encroaching, and is beyond reclaiming.'

Probate records
Caribbeana by V L Oliver has lists of British Virgin Islands testators whose wills were proved in the Prerogative Court of Canterbury, 1762-1798 and 1800-1811.

Deeds and other records
Caribbeana has a certain number of references to Virgin Islands deeds, together with genealogical notes and pedigrees on the families of Hodge, Purcell, Georges, Lettsom and Norton.

FURTHER READING:

De Booy, T and J T Faris *The Virgin Islands - our new possessions and the British Islands*. 1918.
Derriman, J *An account of the sufferings of Jeffery the seaman, marooned, during his abode on the desolate rock of Sombrero*. 1991.
Dookhan, I *A history of the British Virgin Islands* 1672-1970. 1975.
Fishlock, W C *The Virgin Islands, B.W.I.: a handbook of general information*. 1912.
Harrigan, N and Varlack, P *The British Virgin Islands, a chronology*. 1970.
Harrigan, N. and Varlack, P. *The Virgin Islands Story*. 1975.

Harrigan, N. and Varlack, P. *The Virgins: a descriptive and historical profile*. 1977.

Jarvis, J A *The Virgin Islands and their people*. 1944.

Lewisohn, F *Tales of Tortola and the British Virgin Islands*. 1966.

Moll, V P *The Virgin Islands*. World Bibliographical series.

Pickering, V W *Early history of the British Virgin Islands: from Columbus to emancipation*. 1983.

Suckling, G *Historical account of the Virgin Islands in the West Indies*. 1780.

Titford, J 'Settlers of the Old Empire: The West Indies: British Virgin Islands', *Family Tree Magazine,* September 2000

The Virgin Islands Handbook. 1912.

WEBSITES

www.rootsweb.ancestry.com/~bviwgw/
British Virgin Islands GenWeb. Currently includes transcriptions of Wesleyan church records, 1815-1824; Quaker records 1740-1760 and marriages at St George's Episcopal Church, 1862-1866 (also accessible at: **www.rootsweb.ancestry.com/~caribgw/cgw_archive/archive.htm**)

www.candoo.com/genresources/bvi.htm
Features a listing of LDS Church microfilm records for BVI.

www.britishislesgenweb.org/bvi/
British Virgin Islands Genealogy Project: useful links to BVI bulletin boards and mailing lists.

http://lists.rootsweb.ancestry.com/index/intl/VGB/BRITISH-VIRGIN-ISLANDS.html
B.V.I. Rootsweb mailing list.

www.familysearch.org/eng/Library/FHLC/frameset_fhlc.asp
The LDS Family History Library catalog. Search on 'British Virgin Islands' for a collection of material, some of it on microfilm: baptisms, marriages and burials at St George's Episcopal Church, Road Town, Tortola; civil registration records and indexes; records of the Wesleyan Methodist Church (Tortola Circuit); extracts from the records of Tortola Monthly Meeting of Friends 1740-1760 by George Vaux (taken from original records in Philadelphia).

The International Genealogical Index (now within FamilySearch) and related records should also be searched for individuals from the British Virgin Islands.

Beach view, Grand Cayman.

Cat Boat, Cayman Islands.

Cayman Islands map.

CHAPTER ELEVEN
Cayman Islands

LOCATION

The three flat, sandy, dryish coral islands in this group - Grand Cayman (the largest), Little Cayman and Cayman Brac - lie 150 miles south of Havana, Cuba, and 180 miles west-north-west of Jamaica. The chief settlements are George Town, the capital, on the south-west side of Grand Cayman, and Bodden Town, on the south coast. A series of hurricanes did their worst during the nineteenth century, and the arrival of Hurricane Ivan in 2004 caused a great deal of devastation.

HISTORY

Columbus sighted the Caymans in 1503, and named them 'Las Tortugas', there being a large number of turtles in evidence. The present name is a development of 'Las Caymanas', a testimony to the large number of sea crocodiles found there.

In 1670 the islands were ceded to Britain by the treaty of Madrid, but there was no serious attempt to settle them until the eighteenth century and even later, although they proved to be a temporary place of sojourn for pirates, privateers, buccaneers, Cromwellian soldiers, shipwrecked sailors and the like. Until 1900 they were governed locally by Justices of the Peace.

Having been (reluctantly) a dependency of Jamaica from 1863 onwards, the Caymans became a unit territory within the Federation of the West Indies in 1959 and a separate British colony three years later, at which time Jamaica became independent. Unlike any of the other British Overseas Territories in the Caribbean, the Caymans have no political parties.

ECONOMY

The export of sharkskin and turtles once formed the basis of the islands' economy, but in recent years the Caymans have become well-known as a centre for tourism and (since the 1970s) financial services - even, at one time, for money laundering. There is no direct taxation, and as of 2003 more than 60,000 companies were registered in the Cayman Islands. Since they offer financial secrecy and discretion, the Caymans have become what one commentator has called 'a Little Switzerland-on-Sea'. About 90% of the islands' food and consumer goods must be imported, but Caymanians enjoy one of the highest standards of living in the world. The influence of both Britain and America is much in evidence.

PEOPLE

- The first recorded English visitor to the Caymans was Sir Francis Drake, who was there in 1586.

- The first recorded permanent inhabitant in the islands, Isaac Bodden, was born in Grand Cayman in about 1700. It has been said that when Henry Morgan from Jamaica came ashore at Grand Cayman with four of his men and buried his plunder there, a gunner named Bodden/Bawden deserted and could not be found. A wise move: Morgan promptly killed Bodden's three companions.

- In 1734 Daniel Campbell, Mary Campbell and John Middleton took out a patent of land in Jamaica for all the land on the north side of Grand Cayman. The next patents were taken out in 1741 by Mrs Mary Bodden (possibly a variant on the surname 'Bawdon' 'Bawden' or 'Bowdon'), William Foster, Murray Crymble and Sam Spofforth.

- In *Handbook of the Cayman Islands* (1909) G S S Hirst gives the surnames (then still 'well represented in the dependency') and brief biographical details of a number of 'hardy mariners' who were shipwrecked on or near the Cayman Islands: Henning, from Greenock, Scotland, about 1840; Chisholm, from Scotland, 1846; Arch, from Stratford on Avon, 1853; Kirkconnel, from Scotland, about 1840. And also: James Sherar Jackson, who came from Westmorland in about 1807; James

Goodchild Cox, from Ipswich, Suffolk, born in 1769, arrived in 1781 or 1782; William Eden, from Devizes, Wiltshire, came about 1766, buried at Pearl Lagoon, Nicaragua; Stephen Walter, from Scotland, a soldier, arrived about 1750; William Parsons, arrived about 1750, left three sons and so began a dynasty; Wood, from Sligo, Ireland; John Webster, from Yorkshire, married Elizabeth Bodden, died at Bodden Town in 1805, aged 28. Amongst the commonest surnames on the Caymans have been Bodden, Eden, Merren and Ebanks.

• Individuals who held various senior administrative posts in the islands include the following: William Cartwright (Chief Magistrate, circa 1750); Frederick Shedden Sanguinetti (Commissioner 1900-1906); Alan Hilliard Donald (Administrator 1958-1960); Kenneth Crook (Governor 1972-1974).

• The first resident Wesleyan Methodist minister on the islands was Rev Mark Bird (1839), to be followed in quick succession by Rev William Redfern (1840), Rev Edward Lockyer (1841), Rev George Savery (1843), Rev John Green (1845) and others.

The Anglican church left the islands in 1839, and the Methodists in 1845. The Presbyterian church appears to have taken over all the property of the Anglicans in George Town; its first minister was Rev William Elmslie (1846-1853).

RECORDS (UK REPOSITORIES)

The National Archives, London. Colonial Office: sessional papers, gazettes, etc; Grand Cayman census 1802 (naming heads of households). Treasury: T71 includes records generated by the Slave Compensation Commission, 1834.

Further relevant material can be found with TNA records relating to Jamaica (together with those held in Jamaica itself), and in TNA classes 'Admiralty' (captains' and masters' logs) and 'High Court of Admiralty' (oyer and terminer).

RECORDS (LOCALLY-HELD)

Churches
Before the beginning of the nineteenth century there would seem to have been no organised religious effort on the islands. Today the main local denomination is Presbyterian, with Anglican, Baptist and Catholic minorities.

Anglicans: The Church had been established by law by 1835, though the first resident clergyman had only arrived as late as 1831, and the first church consecrated in 1834. However, the Anglicans withdrew in 1838 after two crippling hurricanes.

Methodists: Methodists made every effort to establish a presence on the islands in the late 1830s and early 1840s, but nothing permanent came of their efforts until well into the twentieth century.

Presbyterians: Presbyterians started work on the islands in 1846; they have been there ever since, and now constitute the principal denomination.

Baptists: The Baptists first arrived in the islands about 1885, and concentrated much of their work on the Lesser Caymans, where there had been no churches until they arrived.

Government House, Grand Cayman.

Civil registration. Records of birth, marriage and death from 1886 onwards are with the Registrar, General Registry Department, Tower Building, Grand Cayman.

Original records relating to the Cayman Islands have had a pitiful history. Many were destroyed by hurricanes in 1876 and 1932, others by a fire in the Government Administration Building in 1972, and some were lost whilst in transit to Jamaica in the early twentieth century.

Records which have survived include those regarding judicial matters and property transactions from 1810 onwards. The Cayman Islands National Archive is at Government Administration Building, Grand Cayman, and various newspapers and government publications are held by the Cayman Central Library on Edward Street.

The Cayman Islands National Museum is in the restored Old Courts Building in George Town.

FURTHER READING

Brunt, M A *The Cayman Islands*. 1994.
Hirst, G S S *Notes on the history of the Cayman Islands*. 1910. Reprinted, five parts in three volumes, 1967. Hirst had been the administrator of the islands for four years, and undertook to print all the documents he could find which he considered to be relevant (many of which have since perished). This book is a wonderful

compendium of material, including copies of deeds, wills, legal documents and cases, pedigrees and details of ships and their owners, together with extensive notes on individuals and families (Bodden, Foster, Tatum, Jennett, Ebanks, Hunter, Hyde, Rivers, Clarke, Collins, Hill, Leitch, Webster, Merren, Chisholm, Henning, Yates, McCoy, Glover, Page, Phelan, Eden, Coe, Bush, Drayton, Crighton, McKeith, Arch, Miller, Henderson, McTaggart, Panton, Morton - and Watler, a family said to be descended from Stephen Watler, a deserter from Cromwell's army). There is also a copy of a marriage entry for Isaac Bawden, mariner, and Sarah Lamar, widow, 'both of Caymanas' dated 9 November 1735, lists of Justices of the Peace and of storekeepers on the islands in 1910. An examination of gravestones in the churchyard of St George's in George Town (consecrated in 1834) revealed only one of any real antiquity: that for William Henry Solly of Sandwich in Kent, mate of *HMS Edinburgh*, who died at sea on 4 May 1839.

McCoy, H M *Journey into Partnership: a history of the Presbyterian (United) Church in Grand Cayman*. 1997.

Smith, R C *The maritime heritage of the Cayman Islands*. 1991.

Williams, N *A history of the Cayman Islands*. 1970. A popular history written by Neville Williams, a former Deputy Keeper of the Public Records in Britain. The book gives some names mentioned in the 1802 census on pages 34-35.

WEBSITES

www.museum.ky
Cayman Islands National Museum.

www.britishislesgenweb.org/~cayman
Cayman Islands GenWeb Project.

http://caribbeanancestry.com/forum/modules/xforum/viewforum.
php?forum=11
Caribbean genealogy forum: Cayman Islands.

www.cousinconnect.com/p/a/1144/
CousinConnect.com Cayman Islands genealogy queries.

http://lcweb2.loc.gov/hlas
The annual *Handbook of Latin American Studies*. An important source for details of books and articles concerning the Cayman Islands.

www.familysearch.org/eng/Library/FHLC/frameset_fhlc.asp
The LDS Family History Library catalog gives details of microform copies of Cayman Islands indexes of deaths 1878-1930 and of marriages 1871-1930 from the Registrar General of Jamaica.

The International Genealogical Index (now within FamilySearch) and related records should also be searched for individuals from the Cayman Islands.

CHAPTER TWELVE
Dominica

Alternative name: Sunday Island

LOCATION

In the eastern Caribbean, half-way between the French islands of Guadeloupe and Martinique. The Commonwealth of Dominica, pronounced 'Domineeka', the largest and most northerly of the Windward Islands (twenty nine miles long and sixteen miles broad), should not be confused with the Dominican Republic (formerly Santo Domingo). It is a wild and mountainous volcanic island, ruggedly beautiful, with a great many rivers. The capital is Roseau, on the western coast, and the only other significant settlement is Portsmouth, on Prince Rupert's Bay. Particularly virulent Hurricanes caused great devastation on the island in 1778-9, 1787, 1806, 1813, 1817, 1825, 1834, 1916 and then in 1979-80, when the Dominican economy was almost totally crippled as a result. The town of Roseau was destroyed by fire in 1781.

HISTORY

Columbus came across Dominica on a Sunday (hence its name) in 1493, and the island was first settled by the French in 1635, despite ferocious opposition from the indigenous Caribs (Kalinagos). A strong French

121

cultural, religious and linguistic influence has pervaded the island since that time. In the late eighteenth and early nineteenth centuries Dominica was controlled by Britain and France in turns. At a time when the island was British in the 1760s, the chief surveyor, John Byres, constructed a detailed map of it in preparation for a public auction in which speculators living in Britain, many of whom hardly knew where Dominica was, bought portions of its real estate - and later regretted having done so. In the event, many British settlers on Dominica were young bachelors who took local women as mistresses.

In 1782 Admiral Rodney defeated the French navy in the Caribbean in no uncertain terms, and the strategically-important island of Dominica was ceded to Britain by the terms of the Treaty of Paris the following year. Further French invasions in 1795 and 1805 ended in failure. In 1833 Dominica became a colony under the administration of the Leeward Islands, but was switched to the Windward Islands in 1940. In 1967 it joined the Associated States of the West Indies, and in 1978 achieved independence as a republic, remaining a member of the Commonwealth. The population is predominantly Roman Catholic.

ECONOMY

Owing to the difficulty of its terrain, only about a quarter of the island is cultivated, and estates have always been small. The French successfully established a coffee-growing industry, but timber also proved to be a vital source of wealth. Latterly the economy has been based upon agriculture, especially the cultivation of bananas and the products of the lime tree, and there is an embryonic tourist industry.

PEOPLE

- Early British visitors to the island included Sir John Hawkins, Sir Francis Drake, George Clifford Earl of Cumberland, Sir Richard Grenville and (in 1652) Prince Rupert of the Rhine, after whom Prince Rupert's Bay was named.

- Individuals to hold various senior administrative posts in the island include: William Young (Governor 1768-1771); George Metcalfe (Acting President 1805-1808); Brigadier James Montgomery (Governor 1808-1809); Charles Marsh Schomberg (Lieutenant Governor 1833-1834); J P Lockhart (Acting President 1834-1837); Henry Light (Lieutenant Governor 1837-1838); D S Laidlaw (Acting President 1843-1845); George MacDonald (Governor 1845-1851); Alexander Wilson Moir (President 1872-1873); Philip Arthur Templer (Administrator 1895-1899); Geoffrey Colin Guy (Governor 1967-1968).

- Anthony Richardson, onetime MP for Aylesbury, whose male line ancestors were well established in Byerstead, St Bees, Cumberland, though he was born in Maryland, USA, in 1738, went into business with his relation, Anthony Bacon. Anthony Bacon Richardson, eldest son of Anthony Richardson, lived for many years in Dominica but died a bachelor in London and was buried at St Pancras, Middlesex, in 1819.

- Andrew James Cochrane Johnstone, born in 1767, the sixth son of Thomas Cochrane, eighth Earl of Dundonald, but who took the additional surname of Johnstone, was chosen to be Governor of Dominica in 1797. It has been said of him that: 'His rule was marked by tyranny, extortion and vice. He drove a brisk and profitable trade in negroes and kept a harem'.

- Dr John Imray, a Scotsman who had come to Dominica in 1832 at the age of twenty-one and soon became an expert on yellow fever, was perhaps the island's most effective and best-loved physician. Also well-known as a botanist, he died in 1880. A splendid marble memorial to his memory in St George's Church was shattered by Hurricane David in 1979, along with a large plaque dedicated to Charles Leatham.

- The pioneering Methodist missionary Dr Thomas Coke visited Dominica in 1787, and two years later his colleague Rev William McCornock began a mission there. Later Methodist missionaries on the island included Revs John Cook, Thomas Dumbleton, Joseph Bocock, Robert Shepley, Thomas Richardson, Thomas Pattison, William Gilgrass, George Johnston, John Willis and others. This was a thankless posting: many of these men fell prey to the climate or to yellow fever.

- The first Anglican rector on the island was Henry McLeane, who was at his post in 1764. A large wooden Anglican church was built in Roseau two years later, yet by 1791 Governor Orde was writing: 'The christenings and burials I cannot speak to, there not being a Protestant clergyman in the island...The marriage ceremony is performed by a Justice of the Peace'.

The first English-speaking Roman Catholic priest was Father Henry McCorry, who arrived in 1789.

RECORDS (UK REPOSITORIES)

The National Archives, London. Colonial Office: correspondence (from 1730), sessional papers, gazettes, etc; land records from 1764; quit rents 1790-1803.

Treasury: T71 includes records generated by the Slave Compensation Commission, 1817-1832, and claims are indexed in T71/927.

Further relevant records can be found with those of the Leeward Islands and the Windward Islands.

RECORDS (LOCALLY-HELD)

E C Baker's *A guide to records in the Windward Islands* (1968) provides a useful overview of records relating to the Windward Islands as a whole, and summarises the situation regarding Dominica in particular. This guide includes the usual wide range of official, legal and parochial records and deeds, then held in a range of repositories. *Anglican* church records for the parishes of St George's, Roseau, and St John's, Portsmouth, were then retained by the churches themselves. *Methodist* records were held in the manse in Roseau, and *Roman Catholic* records in the Cathedral Church of the Assumption of Our Lady of God Haven, Roseau. In 1963 Baker undertook to make microfilm copies of fifteen volumes of Dominica Councils' records 1787-1832 and deposited these with the University of the West Indies in Jamaica.

Two streets, Roseau, Dominica.

Although V L Oliver was able to report in volume three of *Caribbeana* (pages 361/362) that he was impressed with the Registrar's office on the island ('a handsome commodious edifice, the records being kept in a small fire-proof room...'), since then records for Dominica have been neglected and stored (if at all) with a lamentable lack of care. At one stage original documents, unsorted and unindexed, were held in a basement archive in Roseau, where they suffered from the effects of insect and rodent attacks and periodic flooding (particularly during the hurricane of 1979). Here were House of Assembly and Board of Legislature minutes (1787 onwards), case papers of the Vice-Court of Admiralty (1792-1872), deed record books (1765 onwards), wills (1790-1938) and runs of the Dominica Blue Book and the Dominica Official Gazette. Further legal records (from 1871) have been held at the court house in Roseau.

The National Documentation Centre is now at Government Headquarters in Roseau, and the Public Library is on Victoria Street.

Civil registration. The registration of births, marriages and deaths on the island began in 1860, and there are separate volumes for each parish. The registry was severely damaged by a fire in 1979, at which time many records were destroyed. The Registrar General's office is on Bay Front, Roseau.

GENEALOGICAL SOURCES HELD ELSEWHERE

Some original records relating to Dominica are held in Antigua, and further relevant material is housed in Roseau (Bishop's House: Moris and Proesman's papers; Allfrey papers) and in Oxford, England (Rhodes House Library, Balfour Library, Pitt Rivers Museum and Tylor Library).

FURTHER READING

Alford Nicholls, Dr H A *Dominica. Illustrated and described.* 1905. A book of photographs of the island taken by Jose Anjo, with explanatory text.
Attwood, T *History of the island of Dominica.* 1791, reprinted 1971. An anecdotal account of the island, written by the then Chief Judge of the island in an attempt to persuade Britain to develop the colony and to attract more immigrants and capital.
Grieve, S *Notes upon the island of Dominica.* 1906.
Honychurch, L *The Dominica story: a history of the island.* 1995.
Oliver V L *Caribbeana* (1910-1920), volumes 2 and 3, has lists of Dominica wills

proved and administrations granted in the Prerogative Court of Canterbury 1768-1812, and there are transcripts of indentures, wills, etc for Dominica in volume 4, pages 125-129.

Oliver, V L *The monumental inscriptions of the British West Indies* (1927) provides the following information on Dominica: 'Parishes were formed in 1764 of which there are today [1927] ten: St George [Roseau], St Mark [Soufrière], St Luke [Pont Michel], St Paul [Mahaut], St Peter [Colihaut], St John [Porstmouth], St Andrew [Vieille Case], St David [La Plaine], St Patrick [Grand Bay] and St Joseph [Layou], but owing to the lack of roads all social and official life is centred in Roseau'. Oliver's book has a significant number of entries for Dominica, featuring inscriptions which he found in the following locations: St George's church and churchyard (many of which the author complements by references to relevant parish register burial entries); the burial ground at the Savannah, Roseau; the Roman Catholic Cathedral, Roseau; the Military Burial Ground, Morne Bruce; Morne Desmoulins. The author adds: 'Dominica being very mountainous, with practically no roads across it, only halter tracks, it is probable that there are private burial grounds in distant estates, but nobody in Roseau seemed to know anything about them.'

Watkins, F H *Handbook of the Leeward Islands*, 1924. Contains a list of estate owners on Dominica (pages 195-197), which includes the well-known British chocolate manufacturers, Rowntree and Company.

WEBSITES

http://caribbeanancestry.com/forum/modules/xforum/viewforum.php?forum=14
Caribbean genealogy forum: Dominica.

www.cousinconnect.com/p/a/53
CousinConnect.com Dominica genealogy queries.

www.britishislesgenweb.org/dominica/
DominicaCaribbeanGenWeb: Dominica Genealogy Project. With Bulletin Boards and Mailing List.

www.familysearch.org/eng/Library/FHLC/frameset_fhlc.asp
The LDS Family History Library catalog. Search on 'Dominica' for a collection of material, some of it on microfilm: parish registers, civil registration and land records. The International Genealogical Index (now within FamilySearch) and related records should also be searched for individuals from Dominica.

CHAPTER THIRTEEN
Grenada

LOCATION

Grenada (pronounced 'Grenayda'), the most southerly of the Windward Islands and formerly the seat of government of the British group, lies ninety miles to the north of Trinidad and one hundred miles south-west of Barbados. A volcanic island with a total land area of 120 square miles, it is very mountainous, with fertile valleys and an abundance of water. The capital, St George's, with its beautiful land-locked harbour, stands on a peninsula at the southern end of the west coast. The original town was twice destroyed by fire in the eighteenth century - in 1771 and again in 1775 - and suffered catastrophic damage when Hurricane Ivan, the tenth most intense Atlantic hurricane ever recorded, struck the island in 2004. Other towns of any size on Grenada are Grenville, Gouyave and Sauters. The more southerly islands in the neighbouring Grenadine group, including Carriacou and Petit Martinique, come under the jurisdiction of Grenada, while the northern Grenadines belonging to St Vincent.

HISTORY

The Caribbean island which was originally known as 'Camerhogne' by the Amerindians and then named 'Concepción' by Columbus in 1498, eventually became 'Grenada'. In 1609 a number of London merchants financed an

expedition to the Island, led by Godfrey, Hall, Lull and Robinson, but their attempt to settle there was repulsed by the Caribs. Grenada was one of the islands granted to the Earl of Carlisle by his cousin King Charles I in 1627, but in 1650 it was the French who moved in as colonists and effectively exterminated the Carib population. Although Grenada would remain a poor relation of the French colonies of Guadeloupe and Martinique, it became home to a significant number of colonists and African slaves. The population in 1700 consisted of 257 whites, 53 free coloured and 525 slaves. A visitor to the island at that time, the Abbé Labat, a priest of the Dominican order, was not too impressed by what he saw: 'The English know better than we how to profit by natural advantages. If Grenada belonged to them, it would long since have changed its aspect, and have become a rich and powerful colony...we behold it still no better than a desert, deficient in population, void of all accommodation, without commerce, poor, and with ill-built and worse furnished hovels to represent dwelling-houses...'.

The French retained Grenada until 1763, when it became part of the British South Caribbean Islands following the Treaty of Paris. The French launched a successful counter-attack in 1779 and gained control of the island once more, only to see it pass to Britain again four years later by the terms of the Treaty of Versailles.

In 1795, in what was known as the Brigands' War, the French republican Victor Hugues made a determined effort to regain possession of the island by encouraging an insurrection by the French inhabitants and the slaves - an explosive mixture of those who felt themselves to be disadvantaged or exploited by the British. It was not until June the following year that the rising was eventually suppressed by Sir Ralph Abercrombie.

Grenada became a separate colony in 1802, eventually being constituted as the capital of the Windward Islands in the 1880s; the Governor of the Windwards was also the ruler of Grenada, but a local administrator was appointed to oversee the island's internal affairs.

Slavery was officially abolished in Grenada in 1834, though former slaves only became fully free in the eyes of the law in 1838. In that year a scheme of indentured immigration began; it would bring over seven thousand immigrants from Malta, the Indian sub-continent, Madeira and Africa before it was discontinued in 1885. Another group of immigrants who arrived in search of employment in the nineteenth century came from Barbados; descendants of English settlers, they formed their own community on a hill named Mount Moritz, just outside the capital. The twentieth century would see many Grenadians leaving their native island to settle in England and elsewhere, though some later returned.

Grenada became a separate colony in 1944, and was created a dominion in February 1974, the smallest 'independent' nation in the Western hemisphere. It was the scene of much diplomatic tension between Britain and America in 1983, when United States forces overran communist elements on the island following a coup. American troops left two years later.

Grenada is currently an independent state within the Commonwealth, with the British monarch as Head of State, represented by a Governor General. Grenada is still a predominantly Catholic country, though the French influence there has died out more than is the case in other islands in the Windward Group. At one time an unusual *patois* - a mixture of European and African dialects - was widely used, though it is less commonly encountered than it used to be.

ECONOMY

Under French rule Grenada developed a healthy economy based upon tobacco and sugar, followed by cotton, cocoa and coffee. The population in 1700 consisted of 257 whites, 53 free coloured and 525 slaves, but once the plantation system was well established, by 1753 the island was home to 1263 whites, 175 free coloured and no fewer than 11991 slaves, with eighty three sugar estates, nearly three million coffee trees, over a hundred and fifty thousand cocoa trees and eight hundred cotton plants.

The market at St George's, Grenada, circa 1913.

The rich soil of Grenada once supported a flourishing sugar industry, which suffered from a series of natural disasters including the activities of the sugar-ant. Exports now include cocoa, bananas and spices - particularly nutmeg (and mace), introduced by the British in the 1780s, which has helped Grenada achieve its status as 'The spice island of the West'. Tourism, as might be expected, also plays a significant role in the local economy.

PEOPLE

- The founding expedition to the Island in 1609 was led by Messrs Godfrey, Hall, Lull and Robinson.

- During the Brigands' War of 1795, fifty-one supporters of the British cause, including the ardent Protestant Lieutenant-Governor, Ninian Home, were taken prisoner by Julien Fédon, a free coloured Grenadian plantation owner. When the British launched a retaliatory attack on his camp at Champ la Mort on April 8th, Fédon, already incensed at the death of his own brother in the fighting, gave orders that forty-eight of his prisoners should be shot, one at a time.

  Appendix Two of *Grenada, Island of Conflict* by George Brizan (1984), page 358, gives the following list of those imprisoned and 'executed' by Fédon in April 1795, taken from Minutes of Legislative Council 1795-98 and from Devas, *History of Grenada*, pages 199-201. Note the preponderance of Scottish surnames:

  Executed: Ninian Home [Lieutenant Governor]; Hon.Alexander Campbell [Member of the Council]; James Farquhar [ADC to Governor Home]; Patrick Fothringham; George Rose; George Walker; Samuel Ought; William Muir; Robert Webster; Michael McCarthy; Patrick Cummings; Anthony Kerr; Thomas Johnson; Phillip Lefelly; John Livingstone; John Jackson; Francis Donald Carruthers; Williams Gilchrist; Christopher McCarthy; Gilbert J Kerr; Richard Davis; Jenkin Rice; Joseph Shea; Duncan McDougall; Mathew Atkinson; William Hawkes; Joseph Barlow; James Cuthbert; John Morris; Peter Thompson; John Thompson; William Bell; John Wise; John Reid; William James; Thomas Brae; Neil Campbell Bannister; James Butler; Edward Johnson; Benjamin Johnston; William Kennard; Hugh McCoull; Joseph Thomas Guy; James R Linton; Joseph Mercer; Edward Mathers; Richard Todd.

  Imprisoned but not executed: Dr John Hay and Rev Francis McMahon [the medical officer and clergyman respectively of Fédon's district] and William Ker.

- Methodists were active on Grenada from the late eighteenth century onwards. Thomas Owens, turning down the lucrative offer of a good living on Grenada as an Anglican clergyman, worked as a Methodist missionary there during the closing decade of the century, and was given moral support by the local rector, Mr Dent, and by a visit from the well-known Wesleyan missionary, Dr Thomas Coke, who later achieved fame as the author of a history of the West Indies. Owens was replaced by Rev Abraham Bishop, a Jerseyman by birth who was unaccustomed to the climate and fell victim to fever after only six months on the island, in 1793 - the year in which a Wesleyan chapel was first erected in St George's. Bishop was succeeded in due course by Revs Richard Pattison, Francis Hallett (formerly parish clerk at St George's Anglican church), Benjamin Pearce, William Sturgeon, Myles Dixon, William Lill, William J Shrewsbury, William Dixon Goy and others.

RECORDS (UK REPOSITORIES)

The National Archives, London
Colonial Office records relating to Grenada - correspondence (from 1747), sessional papers, gazettes, etc - and to the Windward Islands as a whole are relevant sources; there is also a list of landholders for 1772 (CO 101/5, ff.147-151) and a capitation tax roll of people liable to pay tax on slaves, 1763 (CO 101/1, ff.18-31). Treasury: T71 includes records generated by the Slave Compensation Commission, 1817-1834, and claims are indexed in T71/926.

Guy Grannum's book, *Tracing your West Indian ancestors: sources in the Public Record Office* (1995) has two illustrations relating to Grenada in 1892: on page 12 is part of a printed jury list for the island in that year, and a list of Grenadian officials featured in the *Colonial Office List* for 1892 is on page 70. On page 56 of the same author's *Tracing your West Indian ancestors* (2002) is a facsimile of a map of Georgetown, Grenada, in 1765 (CO700/Grenada5) with an extensive manuscript list of associated names. Related details of a sale of town lots in St George's, 1762-1764 can be found in CO101/1, ff.245-246.

RECORDS (LOCALLY-HELD)

Churches
Since the early eighteenth century there have been six parishes on Grenada: Basseterre (St George's - the principal parish); Gouyave (St John's); Grand Pauvre (St Mark's); Sauteurs (St Patrick's); Megrin (St David's); Marquis (St Andrew's), each separated from each other by rivers and streams. The island of Carriacou constituted a separate parish.

The Cathedral, St George's, Grenada. Hurricane Ivan removed the roof in 2004, but left the tower unscathed. Photograph by John Titford.

Anglicans

Grenada was part of the Anglican diocese of Barbados until 1879, when the Windward Islands were formed into a separate diocese, though they had the same Bishop as Barbados until 1927. In 1874 the Church of England was disestablished by law, and a 'Church Council' was introduced to control and manage the affairs of that church on the island.

In the 1830s three Anglican churches (St Patrick's, St Andrew's and St David's) were built on the island, while the Presbyterians established St Andrew's kirk in St George's. By 1848 there were eight Anglican churches and chapels, including one on Carriacou, served by five resident clergymen.

The Church of Scotland had its one church in St George's, the *Methodists* had five places of worship, and there were seven *Roman Catholic churches*, serving over 64% of the population.

During the early period of British rule - especially in the period 1783-1795 - Roman Catholics on Grenada found themselves mercilessly persecuted, especially by some members of the Scottish Protestant party, who were vehemently opposed to all things Catholic, and by others who sought revenge for what they had suffered during several years of French rule. In 1785 it was decreed that baptisms, marriages and burials were null and void unless celebrated in an Anglican church, with a record duly entered in the registers, to be used as legal evidence if required. This law was revised in 1807, but remained substantially intact until 1842. Many French settlers left for Trinidad, taking their slaves with them, while others joined the ill-fated Fédon rebellion in protest at the way they were being treated.

132

Eventually, as some kind of compensation to the beleaguered Catholic community, a grant was made in 1846 towards the erection of Roman Catholic churches in St Patrick's and St John's parishes.

At the time of his survey of archives on the island in 1968, E C Baker found the following parochial records:

Anglican:
At St George's: Registers of baptisms, marriages and burials (1764 onwards); vestry minute books (1807 onwards), etc.
'In the custody of Mr Alister Hughes': St John's, Charlotte Town: Register of burials (1854 onwards).
At St Andrew's, Grenville: Registers of baptisms (1798 onwards), marriages (1816 onwards), burials (1937 onwards), etc.
At St Mark's, Victoria: Registers of baptisms (1860 onwards), marriages (1903 onwards), etc.
At St Patrick's, Sauteurs. Registers of baptisms (1845 onwards); marriages (1845 onwards), burials (1922 onwards), etc.
At the Anglican Church in Carriacou: Registers of baptisms (1877 onwards), marriages (1903 onwards), burials (1950 onwards), etc - also including records of other islands in the Grenadines group.

(As of the early twenty-first century the following holdings can be verified:

• At St George's: Registers of baptisms, etc., from 1816.

• St Patrick's: some of the registers listed by Baker are illegible due to the effects of Hurricane Janet in 1955.

• Carriacou: Burials date from 1960).

Methodist:
At the Manse, St George's: Registers of baptisms (1821 onwards), burials (1826 onwards). Also further registers and records of various Methodist churches on the island. (Note that records of Methodist baptisms in the Windward Islands, 1914-1954, are now held at Methodist Headquarters, Nassau, Bahamas).

Roman Catholic:
At the supreme court registry: Roman Catholic registers of baptism, marriage and burial (in French) for Carriacou (1762-1786); St Jacques, Fort Royale (1765-1785); Grenada and Carriacou (1779-1785); St George's (1782).

At St George's presbytery: Registers of baptisms, marriages and burials (1784 onwards), etc.

At Birchgrove presbytery: Registers of baptisms (1925 onwards) marriages (1957 onwards), burials (1864 onwards), etc.

At St Ervan's presbytery, Grenville: Registers of baptisms, marriages and burials (1840 onwards), etc.

At St David's presbytery: Registers of baptisms, marriages and burials (1851 onwards), etc.

At St John's presbytery, Gouyave: Registers of baptisms (1878 onwards), marriages (1878 onwards); burials (1879 onwards), etc.

At St Mark's presbytery: Registers of baptisms, marriages and burials (1859 onwards), etc.

At St Patrick's presbytery: Registers of baptisms, marriages and burials (1849 onwards), etc.

At the Roman Catholic Church presbytery, Carriacou: Registers of baptisms (1920 onwards), marriages (1903 onwards), burials (1920 onwards), etc. - also including records of other islands in the Grenadines group. Early baptism and burial record were destroyed in a fire in 1920.

(As of the early twenty-first century the following holdings can be verified:

- St George's presbytery: Registers of baptisms from 1900; marriages from 1920; burials from 1940.

- The records from Mount St Ervans have been moved to the Grenville presbytery, St Ervans now being used as a Retreat).

Civil registration

Civil registration was introduced in 1865 by 'An Act for registering Births, Deaths, Baptisms, Marriages and Burials in Grenada' dated 27 December of that year. The Registrar General (Registrar General's Office, Ministry of Health, Church Street, St George's, Grenada) holds records from 1 January 1866 onwards.

Censuses

The first comprehensive census taken on Grenada under British rule dates from 1844. A series of decennial censuses commenced in 1851. The following figures indicate a steady population increase during the nineteenth century, though the significant number of deaths from cholera in 1854 depressed the 1861 figure: 1844: 29,650; 1851: 32,671; 1861: 31,900; 1871: 37,684; 1881: 42,403; 1891: 53,209.

Other original records held on the island

In 1762 and in 1783 the French had been specifically permitted to remove all of the public documents generated under French rule on Grenada to Martinique, and many records relating to British rule disappeared or were destroyed by hostilities at about the same time. Thus it was that when David W Parker visited Grenada in 1924-5, he noted that there were no archives prior to 1764 and a hiatus between 1779 and 1784. He commented on the poor condition of manuscript volumes of Council Minutes, and some of those he did list for the eighteenth century had disappeared, along with other official records, by the time E C Baker visited the island in the 1960s. It also appears that earlier records kept by the Governor had been destroyed in the fire which swept through St George's in 1771.

In 1961 both Monsieur J C Nardin and Michael J Chandler examined what archives they could on the island, only to find that the bindings and early leaves of some books were disintegrating, that the parish registers in St George's presbytery (from 1781 onwards) were perilously brittle, and that various volumes of newspapers had been damaged, lost or sold to the American Antiquarian Society.

E C Baker's *A guide to records in the Windward Islands* (1968) provides (pages 4-29) a useful listing of records then held in various repositories in Grenada, of which a summary follows:

> In the Supreme Court Registry: House of Assembly minutes and other government records from the late eighteenth century onwards; oath books (1781-1812, 1916-1936); deed record books [First Series (conveyances, mortgages, leases, indentures, articles of agreement, assignments, etc., 1763 onwards); Second Series (letters and powers of attorney, manumissions, substitutions, bills of sale, bonds of agreement, assignments, deeds of gift and separation, sales in trust, bills of exchange, etc., 1764 onwards)]; indexes to deed record books, both series (1764 onwards); various other deeds and land records, some indexed; census of French inhabitants (1779, 1783); Lieutenant-Governor's commissions; records of slaves and slave owners; court records (Common Pleas, Chancery, Supreme, Ordinary, Complaints, Escheat, Admiralty, Appeal) lists of jurors, warrants for arrest, wills, probate and letters of administration (1765 onwards); rate books, vaccination records.

In the Government Office: Archives dating mainly from the nineteenth and twentieth centuries: records of the Governor-in-Chief of the Windward Islands; Lieutenant Governor's correspondence; Blue Books; reports, tax rolls, census reports, commercial and financial records; police and prison records, marriage licences, etc.

Various further records were then kept in a number of public and private repositories, including schools, hospitals and prisons.

Civil Registers of births, marriages and deaths were held in the Supreme Court Registry and in the Registrar-General's office.

The Government Building, Hillsborough, on the island of Carriacou, held various registers of births, marriages and deaths, together with other official and legal documents. Baker also provides (pages 28-29) a very extensive list of Grenada newspapers held in various repositories, including the former British Library Newspaper Library. The Grenada *Chronicle*, first published in 1783, was the oldest newspaper published in the Western Hemisphere and the second oldest in the English-speaking world, being of even greater antiquity than *The Times* of London.

An article by Joan E Mount of the Laurentian University in Sudbury, Ontario, published in *Research guide to Central America and the Caribbean* (edited by K J Grieb, University of Wisconsin Press, 1985, pages 381-382), says that most early documents she found in Grenada were then either in the Supreme Court registry on Church Street or in the strong room in Government House in Lucas Street, St George's. She found deeds records back to the 1760s and records of births, marriages and deaths mainly confined to the twentieth century.

Grenadian archives are now housed at the Public Library/National Archives, 2 Carenage, St George's. The Grenada Museum is on Young Street, St George's.

SECONDARY SOURCES: PRINTED WORKS, etc.

A memorial plaque within St George's Cathedral, Grenada. The cathedral roof has been blown off, but plaques like this are still legible. Photograph by John Titford.

Monumental inscriptions

V L Oliver's *The monumental inscriptions of the British West Indies* (1927) includes a collection (pages 199-211 and 250-251) of inscriptions for the island, many embellished with genealogical and historical notes. *Caribbeana* has a number of transcriptions of MIs in England with Grenada connections.

Transcripts of the monumental inscriptions in the church and churchyard of St George are printed in the *Journal of the Barbados Museum* (1949). See also: Burgan, W G L *Some West Indian memorials: being a record of the tablets in St George's, Grenada, with notes.* 1917.

Probate records

Oliver's *Caribbeana* contains various extracts from Grenadian wills, and the names of several settlers on the island appear in calendars of wills proved and administrations granted in the Prerogative Court of Canterbury, 1765-1797 and 1801-1812 (*Caribbeana*, volumes 2 and 3).

Censuses and name lists

A transcript of the census of Grenada taken in 1669 appears in *Caribbean Historical and Genealogical Journal* (Volume 4, no 2, April 1996, pages 7-9). Each head of household is named, all males and all with French names, as would be expected at this period.

GENEALOGICAL SOURCES HELD ELSEWHERE

Deeds and other records

The Archives Nationales in Paris are the principal source for relationships between France and its former colonies in the Caribbean, including Grenada. Some sources for Grenadian history may also be found in Martinique.

FURTHER READING

Anonymous [edited by Jacques Pettijean Roget]. *Histoire de l'isle de Grenade en Amérique, 1649-1659.* 1975.

Brizan, George. *Grenada, Island of Conflict: from Amerindians to People's Revolution.*1984. The first full-length history of the island, compiled by a Grenadian educator and politician. There is a useful map of the island (page xi), showing parish boundaries.

Devas, R P *The history of the island of Grenada.* 1964. Two further books on Grenadian history by the same author, who was a Catholic priest long resident on the island and the father of the study of its local history, were published between 1964 and 1974.

The Grenada Handbook, Directory and Almanac. Published annually since 1896, except in 1919 and 1921. So, for example, the 1916 edition (twenty-first year of issue), compiled by the Colonial Secretary and described as being 'not an official publication', is exceptionally thorough and detailed, with a comprehensive history of the island and many lists of names of officials, clergy, professionals, businesses, licensed dealers etc. and a very detailed folding map.

Kay, F. *This is Grenada.* Revised edition, 1971.

Schoenhals, Kai. *Grenada.* World Bibliographical Series, volume 119. c.1990.

A short history of Grenada. 1974.

Sinclair, Norma *Grenada: Isle of Spice*. Second edition, 1992.

South America, Central America, Mexico, West Indies Directory, 1898. Includes a substantial list of professional and commercial individuals and companies on Grenada. A copy may be seen at the Society of Genealogists in London.

They laboured in the vineyard. Glimpses into Catholicism and Christianity in Grenada. St Paul's, Grenada, Rosary Priory Church. 1997. Includes a chronology of Roman Catholic churches on the island.

Titford, J 'Settlers of the Old Empire. The West Indies: Grenada', 2 parts, *Family Tree Magazine,* December 2001 and March 2002.

[Turnbull, G.] *Narrative of the revolt and insurrection of the French inhabitants in the island of Grenada, by an eye-witness*. 1795. Also similar titles by J Hay, D G Garraway and other authors - see Lewin, E, *Subject catalogue of the Library of the Royal Empire Society*, volume 3 (1932), page 599.

Wells, S *Historical and descriptive sketch of the island of Grenada*. 1890.

WEBSITES

www.britishislesgenweb.org/grenada/
GenWeb genealogy project: Grenada.

http://boards.rootsweb.com/localities.caribbean.grenada/mb.ashx
Rootsweb Message Board: Grenada.

http://grenadiangirl.wordpress.com/
Grenada genealogy.

http://genforum.genealogy.com/grenada/
Grenada genealogy forum.

www.cousinconnect.com/p/a/70/
CousinConnect.com Grenada genealogy queries.

www.familysearch.org/eng/Library/FHLC/frameset_fhlc.asp
The LDS Family History Library catalog. Search on 'Grenada' for a collection of relevant material, some of it on microfilm, including civil registration records and supreme court registers of records (in English, French and Spanish).

The International Genealogical Index (now within FamilySearch) and related records should also be searched for individuals from Grenada.

CHAPTER FOURTEEN
Jamaica

LOCATION

Jamaica, the outcrop of a submerged mountain range, is the largest of the islands in the British West Indies, and was once described as 'one of the brightest jewels in the British Crown', and by King Charles II as his 'darling plantation'. Lying ninety miles to the south of Cuba, it is 144 miles long and 49 miles wide, and with a total area of just over 4,000 square miles, is about twice the size of the English county of Lancashire. It is very mountainous, with many bays and inlets, and the town of Kingston has one of the finest harbours in the West Indies. In 1692 an earthquake devastated the town of Port Royal - at that time the 'finest town in the West Indies - the richest spot in the universe', but also a by-word for unbridled hedonism - when all but two hundred or so of its three thousand houses were destroyed. Three thousand individuals perished, to be followed by a further three thousand who died during a subsequent epidemic. Over the years the island has had to contend with a series of fires (one affecting Port Royal in 1703, and others at Kingston in 1780, 1843, 1862 and 1882), earthquakes (especially at Kingston in 1907) and hurricanes. The capital was Port Royal (until 1692), then Spanish Town (1692-1872) and finally Kingston (from 1872).

At various times the Cayman and the Turks and Caicos islands have been dependencies of Jamaica.

HISTORY

When Columbus first landed in Jamaica in May, 1494, it was occupied by peace-loving Arawak Indians. Initially he called it 'St Jago', after the patron saint of Spain, but before long it reverted to its native name of 'Xaymaca' ('well wooded and watered'). Under Spanish occupation, which began in 1509, the Arawaks were exterminated, and in time African slaves would be brought in to provide the labour force. In 1596 the island was raided by the English under Sir Anthony Shirley, who attacked and plundered Spanish Town, and in 1643 Colonel Jackson, with 520 men from the Windward Islands, landed at Port Royal and exacted a ransom from the defenders. Yet Jamaica remained Spanish for 161 years, and it was not until May 11th, 1655, that it changed hands, yielding to a force under Admiral Penn and General Venables, who had been sent out by Cromwell to take up arms against the neighbouring island of Haiti. They met with little resistance other than that offered by a small group of Spanish settlers and a larger number of former Spanish slaves of African descent who took refuge in the mountains and became known as Maroons - an abbreviation of *cimarron*, derived from the Spanish 'Cima', or mountain top. Thus began the long series of struggles with the Maroons which was finally brought to an end, after the quelling of a rebellion in 1796, by the deportation of a great number of the rebels to Nova Scotia and to Sierra Leone. The Cockpit Country, or 'Look Behind Country,' where the Leeward Maroons hid, and around Nanny Town, where the Windward Maroons took refuge, is still the home of some of their descendants. More than one island in the West Indies had its Maroon population, but none had as high a profile, or was more a thorn in the side of the authorities, than the Maroons of Jamaica.

In 1657-58 an attempt was made to recapture the island for Spain, but most of the colonists were apathetic, and those who were not joined the Maroons. In June 1670 the British occupation of Jamaica was formally recognised by the Treaty of Madrid. Meanwhile, 1659 had seen the establishment of the Island Secretary's Office, and two hundred and twenty years later the Institute of Jamaica would be founded in Kingston to help preserve the island's archival heritage.

Jamaica was never a penal colony as such, but between 1655 and the early eighteenth century a number of persons who had committed crimes (some of them very trivial by modern standards) were transported from Britain to Jamaica or to Barbados. Thus the population of these islands was increased, and Britain rid itself of some of its undesirables. Following the abortive Monmouth Rebellion of 1685, a significant number of former rebels were transported to Jamaica, as well as to Barbados and elsewhere - forced, like the common criminals, into what was in effect a form of white slavery.

Colonisation proceeded apace (the population rising from an estimated 4000 in 1662 to 47000 in 1698), and there was a large influx of soldiers, who did not make good colonists, together with other less-than-desirable refugees, and a number of settlers also came from Barbados, Nevis, Montserrat, Surinam, Bermuda and elsewhere. Between 1678 and 1832 there would be no fewer than twenty-seven distinct slave uprisings on the island, and as late as 1865 a rebellion at Morant Bay would pass into the annals of Jamaican infamy. Not only that, but Jamaica also specialized in the repression of nonconformists of every description, and missionaries, especially Baptists, were persecuted and had their churches burnt down.

The gates of Rose Hall, Jamaica. From Picturesque tour of Jamaica by James Hakewill, 1825.

Harbour Street, Kingston, Jamaica.
An aquatint by James Hakewill, 1824.

When a party of Scotsmen attempted to make a success of their settlement of Darien on the Isthmus of Panama, the English monarch, William III, not best pleased, forbade any trade between Jamaica and the Scots. Darien failed - and a large number of Scots settled in Jamaica as a result, some of them selling themselves as servants to the plantation owners. More Scots settled on the island following the abortive Jacobite rebellions of 1715 and 1745, and also in the 1830s and 1840s. Some Scots were luckier: writing to *Everton's Genealogical Helper*, July-August 1998, Patricia Ann Battey of Anaheim, California, says: 'My second great grandfather, James Lyle, won a lottery in Scotland in 1837. The prize was a plantation in Jamaica. His family emigrated to Jamaica in 1837…'.

From the mid nineteenth century onwards, the ethnic mix of Jamaica was enhanced by the arrival of East Indians, Chinese, Germans, French, Syrians, Lebanese, Cubans, Haitians and others, and Jews had been making their home there over a period of many years. The framework for Jamaica's modern political system was laid in the 1930s with the foundation in 1938 of the People's National Party (PNP) by Norman W Manley, and the Jamaica Labour Party (JLP) by his cousin, Sir Alexander Bustamante in 1944. These two parties have dominated Jamaican politics since universal adult suffrage was introduced in 1944.

In 1958, Jamaica joined the West Indies Federation with nine other British territories but withdrew following a national referendum on the issue in 1961. On 6 August 1962, it became an independent member of the Commonwealth.

ECONOMY

VISIT BEAUTIFUL

JAMAICA
A Tropical Fairyland

Unsurpassed Climate . . . Seaside and Mountain Resorts . . . Bathing, Golf, Tennis, Riding, etc. Best Hotels in West Indies. Ideal Voyage from Avonmouth, Liverpool, New York or Canada.

Write: Tourist Trade Development Board, Kingston, Jamaica, B.W.I., or West India Committee, 14 Trinity Square, London, E.C. 3.

Jamaica: A tropical fairyland. From a book published in 1927.

Port Royal, Jamaica, became the headquarters of the Buccaneers, a daring band of freebooters of all nationalities, who were implacably opposed to Spanish rule. Their headquarters were at Port Royal, which became a town of immense wealth, and eventually Sir Henry Morgan, one of their leaders, became Lieutenant-Governor of Jamaica.

Jamaica's great sugar estates were planted in the early days of English occupation, and were originally worked by immigrants from Surinam(e), but later by African slave labour. Slavery was abolished in 1833 when emancipation was declared, but a system of apprenticeship remained in force until 1838.

The sugar and rum industries reigned supreme until the 1890s, when their dominance was supplanted by the production of fruit. In more recent years, Jamaica has been a major supplier of pimento, coffee and bananas, its cigars are of world quality, and it has benefitted greatly from income generated by the tourist trade, as it tries hard to shake off its reputation as a dangerous place to take a holiday. It also has a flourishing bauxite industry.

PEOPLE

- The first Governors of Jamaica were: Edward D'Oyley (1655-56), William Brayne (1656-57), Edward D'Oyley (again, 1657-62) and Thomas Hickman Windsor (1662-63).

- In 1702 Admiral Benbow - the hero of more than one English folk song - was fatally wounded by chain shot during a sea battle against the French off Jamaica in 1702. He was laid to rest in Kingston Church, where a gravestone bears the simple inscription: 'Here lyeth interred the body of John Benbow, Esq., Admiral of the White, a true pattern of English courage, who lost his life in defence of his Queen and country, November ye 4th, 1702, in ye 52nd year of his age, by a wound in his legge received in an engagement with Mons Du Casse. Much lamented'. A gallant sea-dog…

- Sir Henry Morgan, son of Robert Morgan, a well-to-do yeoman, was born at Llanrhymmy in Monmouthshire in 1635. In time he found his way to Jamaica, where his uncle, Colonel Edward Morgan, had once been Lieutenant Governor and where Morgan himself would eventually hold the same post. He and others helped transform the town of Port Royal into a pirate capital, and it flourished until being destroyed by an earthquake in 1692. By then Morgan, who had been stripped of office in Jamaica in 1683, was already dead: he died in Port Royal and was buried at St Catherine's Church on 26 August 1688.

- The poet and writer Elizabeth Barrett Browning [née Moulton Barrett] (1806–1861), had extensive Jamaican ancestry on both sides of her family. Her paternal grandparents, Charles and Elizabeth Moulton, had married in Jamaica on 28 August 1781, and her father was born there. Robert Browning's paternal ancestry, meanwhile, led back to St Kitts, where his grandfather had held large estates. See: *The Barretts of Jamaica : the family of Elizabeth Barrett Browning* by R A Barrett, 1999.

- The poet Robert Burns (1759–1796) *almost* settled in Jamaica - but not quite. In September 1786 it was only the birth of his twins and the possibility that a second edition of his collection of poems might be published that persuaded him not to use his ticket to Jamaica after all.

- The father of William Ewart Gladstone (1809-1898), who served as Queen Victoria's prime minister no fewer than four times, owned mines in Wales, factories in Lancashire and sugar plantations in Jamaica and elsewhere.

- According to *The history of the London Missionary Society 1796-1895* by Richard Lovett (1899), the following men served that society in Jamaica:

Alloway, William (1834-1877); Barrett, William Garland (1834-1848); Hodge, Matthew (1834-1837); Slatyer, William (1834-1850); Vine, John (1834-1844); Wooldridge, John (1834-1840); Brainsford, Charles (1836-1836); Brown, Hugh (schoolmaster) (1836-1837); Howell, James (schoolmaster) (1836-1840); Russell, Henry (schoolmaster) (1836-1839); Franklin, Benjamin (1838-1847); Gibson, John (schoolmaster, afterwards ordained) (1838-1849); Hillyer, William (schoolmaster, afterwards missionary) (1838-1844; 1853-1866); Jones, Robert (1838-1849); Okell, William (schoolmaster) (1838-1840); Milne, William (schoolmaster, afterwards ordained) (1839-1849); Clark, Thomas Henry (1840-1883); Dickson, Robert (1840-1883); Hodges, Samuel (schoolmaster) (1840-1843); Holland, Edward (1840-1852); Milne, James (schoolmaster, afterwards ordained) (1840-1873); Shelden, David (schoolmaster) (1840-1841); Wilkinson, George (1840-1848); Wheeler, Frederick Walter (1841-1852); Lillie, Peter Jeffrey (schoolmaster, afterwards ordained) (1842-1845; 1849-1853); Andrews, Josiah (1848-1854); Gardner, William James (1850-1874); Hall, George (1851-1853); Beardslee, J O (1853-1855); Fletcher, Duncan (1856-1862); Joyce, Alfred (1862-1875); Dalgleish, John (1863-1867); Williamson, Henry C (1863-1865); Bailey, George (1870-1875); Lea, George Henry (1889-1893).

- Early Methodist missionaries to Jamaica include: William Hammett (1789), William Fish (1792), William Gilgrass (1806).

- The first Moravian missionaries to serve Jamaica were: George Caries, David Taylor, Samuel Church, Samuel Russell, Thomas Shallcross, John Brown, Joseph Powell, John Metcalf, Joseph Jackson, John Fred John, Edward Roberts, Sam Fred Church and Christian Lister.

Sir Henry Blake, Governor of Jamaica, having just unveiled a statue of Queen Victoria in Victoria Park, Kingston, Jamaica, addresses the eager crowds.

RECORDS (UK REPOSITORIES)

The National Archives, London

Colonial Office correspondence, sessional papers, gazettes, etc. CO137/162: various slave marriages, 1821-1825; CO 138/1, pages 61-82: survey of Jamaica, 1670; CO 1/45, folios 96-109: Inhabitants of Port Royal and St John's, 1680; CO 137/28, pages 191-196: St Andrews' parish: landholders, etc, 1754; CO 142/31: landholders, etc, 1754; CO 140/121, pages 353-378: return of maroons from various places, 1831; CO 137/28, pages 197-203, 225-249: return of land grants, 1735-1754; CO 137/162: return of land grants 1805-1824.

Also a number of miscellaneous records, including slave returns, lists of convicts, workhouse returns, etc. On page seven of Guy Grannum's *Tracing your West Indian ancestors: sources in the Public Record Office* (1995) is an illustration of a page from CO 137/162: Return of payments to paupers in Jamaica, 1823-24. The individuals concerned are described variously as white, black and mulatto.

Treasury: T71 includes records generated by the Slave Compensation Commission, 1817-1832, and claims are indexed in T71/915-922.

British Library

A collection of all the monumental inscriptions prior to 1750 in Barbados, also similar inscriptions in Jamaica. J H Lawrence-Archer. 1857-8. Additional Manuscript 23,608. Includes several family notes not included in his book (see below). Further manuscript collections made by Lawrence-Archer can be found in Additional Manuscripts 27,971, 27,969 and 27,975.

Mrs V T C Smith: 312 abstracts of wills of English colonists or landholders with Jamaican connexions, proved in the Prerogative Court of Canterbury 1625-1792. Additional Manuscript 34,184. There is a microfilm copy of this at the Society of Genealogists.

Lists, 1661-1750, compiled by the Jamaican historian C E Long. Additional Manuscript 21,931.

Genealogical collection of Charles Edward Long relating to families connected with Jamaica; including rough pedigrees, together with original letters, chiefly addressed to C E Long, 18th and 19th century. Additional Manuscript 27,968. One volume, folio. Includes extracts from parish registers, etc, made in the 1830s. Some of the family surnames featured are listed in *Caribbeana*, vol 2, page 286. A list of landholders in Jamaica, 1750, featured in *Caribbeana* volume 4, is taken from Additional Manuscript 12,436, presented to the library by C E Long in 1842.

Guildhall Library, London (printed books section).
A typescript index of births 1814-48 and marriages and deaths 1779-1848, appearing in Jamaican newspapers.

Friends House, London
Friends House has a series of minutes and correspondence relating to Jamaica, 1677-1795, which bears witness to a small but active Quaker presence on the island, which seems to have died out during the nineteenth century.

RECORDS (LOCALLY-HELD)

Churches
Anglican. At first the island was divided into the seven original parishes of St Catherine, St John, Port Royal, Clarendon, St David, St Andrew and St Thomas, but by 1661 these had been increased to fifteen, and further sub-divisions happened from time to time thereafter. In the early days not all parishes had churches, and their function was as much administrative as ecclesiastical - which makes their vestry books an important source of historical information. From 1655 to 1824 the established churches in Jamaica came under the jurisdiction of the Bishop of London, after which time a diocese of Jamaica was created.

The history of Jamaica in terms of its parishes, its precincts and its counties is complex, and readers are referred to Stephen Porter's *Jamaican records: a research manual* (1999) for more details. The number of parishes on the island steadily grew in number: by 1705 there were seventeen, and by 1841, twenty-two. In 1867, eight parishes were abolished, and they now number fourteen.

The records for the various parishes on Jamaica were filmed by the Church of Jesus Christ of Latter-Day Saints, and it is these microfilms which are available for consultation at the Registrar General's Department at Twickenham Park, Spanish Town, St Catherine and at the Jamaica Archives and Records Department at King Street, Spanish Town. There is no all-island index, but each parish has an index film. Facsimile pages of Jamaica parish registers, 1664-1880, are now available online (see WEBSITES, below). The keeping of records became more complex after the new diocese was created in 1824, and for the period 1826 to 1869, indexes and records should be approached with care. Many registers were copied and re-copied at various times, so there may be no guarantee that you are consulting an original register. In any event, following the creation of the Diocese of Jamaica, stipendiary curates or curates sent returns to the rector of the parish in the capital town, who then submitted them on a regular basis to the Registry Office in Spanish Town - so all registers are in effect 'Bishops' transcripts'. Following the abolition of slavery - from 1834 onwards - the registers contain large numbers of entries relating to slaves or former slaves, and throughout the registration period, a range of racial terms is commonly found in registers. Many white men acknowledged their mulatto, quadroon or mustee offspring and gave them their surname.

Nonconformist. Various faiths were active on the island as follows: Jews (1500s); Roman Catholics (1494-1655; 1792-); Quakers (1679-1749); Moravians (1754); Baptists (1814 - the date of their first mission, though they had been active on the island from the late eighteenth century); Methodists (1816); Presbyterians (1824); Church of Christ (1858); Salvation Army (1887); African Methodist Episcopal Church (1912); Seventh-Day Adventists (1894). During the nineteenth century, details of marriages which had been solemnized in a nonconformist chapel had to be submitted to the Anglican Bishop. These records (mainly for Baptists, Methodists and Presbyterians) may be found in the Registrar General's Department. Registers of the Wesleyan Methodists are held by the Jamaica Archives.

Jews. Duplicate copies of the Sephardim and Ashkenazim Jewish registers are held by the archives, but the originals are kept by the Jewish community at the Kingston synagogue. For a listing of these, and a bibliography, see *Jamaican records: a research manual* by Stephen Porter. The synagogue at Port Royal burned down in 1815, and there have been various other disasters.

Roman Catholics. Holy Trinity Cathedral, North Street, Kingston, hold all records and registers pertaining to their congregation. Many of these are brittle, and sterling efforts are being made to render those from the period 1800 to 1907 more readily available to researchers. None of them have yet been microfilmed or otherwise copied, and an appointment will need to be made to view the originals at the Roman Catholic Chancery, 21 Hopefield Avenue, Kingston 6. Some of the registers have indexes, either separately or as part of the main volume, but some are not indexed at all. Thanks to the influence of the Haitian refugees, much of the early material is recorded in French. Generally, the registers cover Spanish Town with country districts, and the Kingston Diocese of Holy Trinity. More recent registers are still with the relevant Churches.

Civil registration
Civil registration began in Jamaica in 1878 (births and deaths) and in 1880 (marriages). Records of individual registrars are sent to Spanish Town, and are now kept by the Registrar General's Department, Twickenham Park, Spanish Town, St

Catherine, which incorporates two of the island's record keeping arms - the Island Record Office and the General Record Office. Only the staff are allowed to consult the original documents, which are arranged by parish, and pressure of work in the department can make the obtaining of certificates a long, slow process. The original records have been filmed by the LDS Church, 1880 to 1930, with some indexes.

Probate

A list of Jamaica wills (but not admons) in the Prerogative Court of Canterbury 1655-1816 appears in *Caribbeana*, volumes 2, 4, 5, and another list of wills surviving in Jamaica, 1731-50, is in volume 2.

The earliest will book kept by the Island Record Office in Jamaica dates from 1662, and an index of wills now held by that office (in the Registrar General's Department), 1662-1750, and of wills proved in the Prerogative Court of Canterbury, 1655-1816, is available online (see below).

Copies of proved wills for the past one hundred years or so are kept at the Supreme Court, but these are primarily for the use of the legal profession.

District Courts operated from 1867 until March 1888, when they were replaced by the Resident Magistrates' Courts. There is a Resident Magistrate's Court for each parish. The Supreme Court was established by a law of 1879. Wills are proved in a Resident Magistrate's Court or in the Supreme Court, depending on the value of the estate.

There is a will index at the Registrar General's office, but the approximate year of death and the parish of the testator's residence must be known to use this index effectively. The index gives the liber and folio numbers of the will record. Some of the will books have been recopied and the folio number in the index may no longer be valid unless it states 'old folio' or 'new folio'.

The Registrar General's office holds an index volume listing the instances in which an inventory relating to a will can be found, and also hold records relating to the granting of Letters of Administration.

Maps

Major maps for the island include:

Craskell and Simpson. 1763. Showing owners and occupiers.
Robertson's. 1804. Maps for four counties were made, showing names of proprietors, plantation names, etc.

Land, deeds

After 1660, immigrants would patent land from the Crown, in whose ownership it lay, and thereafter would pay an annual quit rent upon it. After land had been patented, it could be passed down a family, or sold by deed; most of the Crown land had been patented by 1828. The Registrar General's office holds forty-three volumes of patents, 1661-1828, including two index volumes, and over a thousand volumes of deeds of various kinds (sale and purchase of land and slaves, leases, mortgages, bonds, conveyances, trusts, etc) from 1664, including sixty-one index volumes.

Censuses

Censuses have been taken in Jamaica at various time since the year 1844, but it is uncertain whether nominal data from these still exists - or ever existed.

Court records

The Registrar General's Office holds the following:

* Court of Chancery records, c1672 to 1879. Typescript index, 1787-May1827, and see: Butterfield, A M 'Notes on the record of the Supreme Court, the Chancery and Vice-Admiralty Courts of Jamaica' in *Bulletin of the Institute of Historical Research*, volume XVI, no 47, November 1938, pages 88-99.

* Supreme Court, 1680-1894, with indexes, 1750-1857.

* Grant Court or Court of Error, 1709-1752, 1784-1838.

* Court of the Ordinary, 1760-1879.

SECONDARY SOURCES: PRINTED WORKS, etc.

Vital records

Details from a marriage register for St Catherine, 1666-79, now held in the British Library, is printed in V L Oliver's *Caribbeana*, volume 1. Marriages and deaths 1796-1800 are in volume 4 of the same periodical.

Monumental inscriptions

Because Jamaican graveyards can be inhospitable places, where the climate has often not been kind to vulnerable gravestones, we can be grateful that there is a good collection of books which have recorded monumental inscriptions for posterity.

- Lawrence Archer, J H *Monumental inscriptions of the West Indies*. 1875. James Henry Lawrence-Archer was a captain in the 60th rifles, and took a particular interest in those inscriptions which related to his ancestors in Jamaica, There's plenty to go at here: pages 1-342 feature Jamaican monumental inscriptions from churches (inside and outside), plantation burial grounds, etc. See also his manuscript in the British Library, above. 'Annotations' to Lawrence-Archer's work as it relates to Jamaica, provided by Frank Cundall and Noel B Livingston, appear in *Caribbeana*, volume one.

- Roby, J *Church notes and monumental inscriptions of Jamaica in 1824.* Part 1: Monuments of the cathedral church and parish of St. Catherine. 1831. John Roby worked as a Collector of Customs and as Postmaster in Montego Bay.

- Wright, P *Monumental inscriptions of Jamaica.* 1966. Philip Wright's book was published by the Society of Genealogists. It features (mainly Anglican) inscriptions up to 1878, including several estate burial grounds, and has made use of the material already published by Lawrence-Archer and by Roby. By the time this book was published, over half the inscriptions recorded by Lawrence-Archer had disappeared; these lost gravestones are not reproduced here. A supplement of the inscriptions at St Thomas, Golden Grove Cemetery, appears in the *Genealogists Magazine,* 1980.

- Barnett, R D and P Wright *The Jews of Jamaica: tombstone inscriptions 1663-1880.* 1997. Based upon Lawrence-Archer's original work, together with photographs taken by Philip Wright, this book features over 1400 inscriptions. Published in Jerusalem.

- Lewis, Lesley 'English commemorative sculpture in Jamaica'. *Commemorative Art.* November, 1965 - February 1967. This is written from an architect's viewpoint, and has some fine illustrations.

- An early copy of some memorial inscriptions appears in the *Gentleman's Magazine* (1864) and there are others in *Caribbeana*, volumes I and 4. The Society of Genealogists has an undated typescript of yet more inscriptions.

Censuses

Calendar of State Papers, Colonial, America and West Indies, 1669-1674, pages 99-104, has a survey of Jamaica in 1670 (CO 138/1, pp 61-82), arranged alphabetically by surname, parish by parish. This also appears (as Part VIII) in Noel Livingston's *Sketch Pedigrees of some of the Early Settlers in Jamaica* (1909) - a satisfyingly long list, though of males only, compiled by parish, to which is added a list of the trained bands in the same year.

An appendix to *The Jamaica Almanac* for 1838 consists of a *List of proprietors and properties with the number of apprentices where the number exceeds 20. As given to the parochial vestries on 28 March 1837.* As the title suggests, this names properties as well as proprietors.

The National Library of Jamaica is at 12, East Street, Kingston. Frank Cundall, the former secretary/librarian of the Jamaica Institute who died in 1937, did much to build up the library's collections, which feature an excellent collection of newspapers, and much else. The library's holdings include the extensive biographical and historical papers of Sir Noel B Livingston (chiefly covering the period 1790-1825), a catalogue of men born in Jamaica who matriculated at Oxford University, 1689-1885, by William Cowper, and the original fifty-eight volumes of biographical information collected by Walter Augustus Feurtado, which became the basis for the publication of a book entitled *Official and other personages of Jamaica, from 1655 to 1790, to which is added a chapter on the peerage &c in Jamaica*, which appeared in 1896.

Newspapers
Marriages and deaths from the *Columbian Magazine or Monthly Miscellany*, Kingston, Jamaica, 1796-1800, are extracted in *Caribbeana*, volume 4.

FURTHER READING

Andrade, A P M *A record of the Jews in Jamaica from the English conquest to the present time*. 1941. Includes epitaphs from several Jewish cemeteries, etc.
Black, C V *History of Jamaica*. Second edition, 1983.
Bridges, G W *The annals of Jamaica*. Two volumes, 1827-8, reprinted 1968. The author, Rev G W Bridges, was pro-planter and a rabid anti-abolitionist.
Buchner, J H *The Moravians in Jamaica*. 1854.
Campbell, M *The Maroons of Jamaica, 1655-1796: a history of resistance, collaboration & betrayal*. 1988.
Catalogue of the West India reference library. Six volumes, 1980. Holdings of the collection in the National Library of Jamaica.
Chapman, E *Pleasure Island: the book of Jamaica*. 1951.
Clarke, C G *Jamaica in maps*. 1974.
Cornish, H M *The Times commercial directory of Jamaica 1910*.
Coulthard, G R 'The inscriptions on Jewish gravestones in Jamaica'. *Jamaica Journal*, volume 2, no 1, pages 8-9.

Cundall, F *Bibliographica Jamaicensis : a list of Jamaica books & pamphlets, magazine articles, newspapers & maps, most of which are in the library of the Institute of Jamaica*. 1902. A *Supplement* appeared in 1908.

Cundall, F *Chronological outlines of Jamaica history, 1492-1926*. 1927.

Cundall, F *Historic Jamaica*. 1915, reprinted 1971.

Delany, F X *A history of the Catholic church in Jamaica*. 1930.

Delatre, R *A guide to Jamaican reference materials in the West Indies Reference Library*. 1965.

DeSouza, M *Jamaica commercial memorandum book and pocket journal with almanac for 1891*.

Gardner, W J *A history of Jamaica from its discovery by Christopher Columbus to the year 1872; including an account of its trade and agriculture, sketches of the manners, habits and customs of all classes of its inhabitants, and a narrative of the progress of religion and education in the island*. 1909, reprinted 1971.

Handbook of Jamaica. From 1881, yearly to 1939, sporadic thereafter until 1969. Include several name-lists.

Hewson, E *Moravian graveyards in India & Jamaica 1755-1971*. c2007.

Higman, B W *Jamaica surveyed: plantation maps and plans of the 18th and 19th centuries*. 1988.

Ingram, K E *Jamaica*. World bibliographical series, vol.45. 1984.

Ingram, K E *Sources of Jamaican history 1655-1838*. Two volumes, 1976. The author was Chief Librarian for the University of the West Indies at Mona, Jamaica. An exceptionally detailed work, truly the researcher's best friend.

Jamaica almanac. From 1672, and regularly from 1776 until 1879. For a full list, including a location where each may be found, see Ingram, *Sources of Jamaican history 1655-1838*. Some are available on microfilm at the National Library of Jamaica.

Jamaica directory 1878. The first (and only?) edition. 376 pages, much of it consisting of name lists.

'Jamaican rebellion: list of properties burned, reports done in 1834'. In *Caribbean historical & genealogical journal*, October 1997, volume 5, no 4, pages 16-20. Alphabetical name-lists, by parish.

Jenkinson, Sir H *A report on the archives of Jamaica*. 1957. An influential report, covering public, semi-public, private and ecclesiastical archives, complete with recommendations. Laid the foundations for modern archive administration in Jamaica.

Karras, A L *Sojourners in the sun: Scottish migrants in Jamaica and the Chesapeake 1740-1800*. 1992.

Long, E *The history of Jamaica: or, general survey of the ancient and modern state of that island; with reflections on its situations, settlements, inhabitants, climate, products, commerce, laws and government*. 1774, reprinted 1970. Edward Long was a plantation owner of Lucky Valley in Clarendon, though he was born and died in England.

MacDonald, J M *Two centuries in the history of the Presbyterian Church, Jamaica.* 1862.

Mitchell, M E *Jamaican ancestry: how to find out more.* 1998. Written by an enthusiast who knows her way around the subject and is happy to share her passion and her knowledge with the reader.

Osborne, F J *History of the Catholic Church in Jamaica.* 1988.

Pawson, M and D Buisseret *Port Royal, Jamaica.* 2000.

Phillippo, J M *Jamaica: its past and present state.* 1843, reprinted 1969, with a ten-page introduction by Philip Wright. The author was a Baptist missionary.

Porter, S *Jamaican records: a research manual.* 1999. The author is an enthusiastic Jamaican-born family historian with a thorough and detailed knowledge of the subject.

Registrar-General's Department: *Civil status records , 1664-1800, in the Registrar-General's Office, Spanish Town.* 1974.

Roberts, W A *Sir Henry Morgan: buccaneer and Governor.* 1952.

Roby, J *Members of the Assembly of Jamaica, from the institution of that branch of the legislature to the present time, arranged in parochial lists.* 1831

Samuel, Rev P *The Wesleyan Methodist missions in Jamaica and Honduras delineated.* 1850.

Sibley, I K *Dictionary of place-names in Jamaica.* Inez Knibb Sibley was the great-granddaughter of William Knibb, a well-know Baptist missionary.

Sibley, I K *The Baptists of Jamaica, 1793-1965.* 1965.

Who's who in Jamaica. Various editions from 1916 to 1976. Alphabetical listings.

Wigfield, W McD *The Monmouth rebels 1685.* 1985. A significant number of the rebels listed were transported to Jamaica.

Wright, P 'Materials for family history in Jamaica' in *The Genealogists' Magazine*, volume 15, September 1966.

Don Lindo's Genealogy of Jamaica. A CD publication, containing about 75,000 names, over 24,000 marriages and 1136 photos, plus numerous text files. The result of many years of research, it includes several extensive family trees, information extracted from Jamaican newspapers, articles and many other sources. There is a source reference for every entry. The third edition includes burial records at St. Andrew parish church, 1657-2000 (over 7000). Also on the CD are two files listing names of several thousand slaves who were freed before the official abolition of slavery. In many cases the reputed fathers are also listed. Designed for use with 'Brother's Keeper'.

WEBSITES

www.rootsweb.ancestry.com/~jamwgw/early.htm
Madeleine E Mitchell's consolidated alphabetical index to early wills of Jamaica, consisting of PCC Wills, 1655-1816, and wills in the Registrar General's Office, Spanish Town, 1662-1750 (based upon a list of wills formerly on record in the Island Secretaries Office, taken from the papers of Edward Long, Additional Manuscript 21,931 in the British Library).

http://jamaicanfamilysearch.com/
A virtual genealogy library for those researching family history in Jamaica, provided by Patricia Jackson. Includes a huge amount of relevant source material (the 1878 Directory of Jamaica, and much else), some available free, some by subscription only. A gold-mine.

www.rootsweb.ancestry.com/~atgwgw/resources/jsourceindex.html
Resources for Jamaican research.

www.rgd.gov.jm/
Jamaica Registrar General's Department.

www.rootsweb.ancestry.com/~jamwgw/index.htm
Genealogy of Jamaica. The coordinator of this World GenWeb Page is Madeleine Mitchell.

http://users.pullman.com/mitchelm/jamaica.htm
Madeleine Mitchell's Hobby HomePage: Jamaica.

www.rootsweb.ancestry.com/~jamwgw/genjamlk.htm
'Links to other Jamaican Genealogy Pages on the Web' - Madeleine Mitchell.

www.instituteofjamaica.org.jm/
Institute of Jamaica. Publishes the *Jamaica Journal*.

http://jard.gov.jm/home/
Jamaica Archives and Records Department.

www.nlj.gov.jm/
National Library of Jamaica.

http://jamaicanhistorical.tripod.com/
Jamaican Historical Society, Richmond Park Great House, 58 Half Way Tree Road, Kingston. The Society publishes a *Bulletin* twice-yearly, and the *Jamaican Historical Review* irregularly. A family history group was formed in 1997.

www.apex.net.au/~tmj/jam-prob.htm
Wills and probate in Jamaica.

www.rootsweb.ancestry.com/~caribgw/cgw_archive/jamaica/wills.htm
A handful of Jamaican wills not filmed by the LDS.

www.cousinconnect.com/p/a/85/
CousinConnect.com Jamaica genealogy queries.

www.sephardim.org/jamgen/
Jamaican Jewish Genealogy.

www.familysearch.org/eng/Library/FHLC/frameset_fhlc.asp
The LDS Family History Library catalog. Search on 'Jamaica' for an impressive collection of material, some of it on microfilm: almanacs; cemeteries; church history, records and bibliography; civil registration (with indexes); directories; gazetteers; Jewish history and records; maps; military history and records; naturalization and citizenship records; probate records (with indexes); slavery and bondage; vital records indexes. *Follow the links provided to access parish register facsimiles, 1664-1880.*

The International Genealogical Index (now within FamilySearch) and related records should also be searched for individuals from Jamaica.

As of 2001/2, researches in various repositories in Jamaica were being undertaken by: Nadine Atkinson (ncarci@yahoo.com) and by: Nadine Wilkins, Research, Inc, 9 Hopeglade Mews, PO Box 91, Kingston 6 (the same lady…?). Such researchers are like gold dust…

I owe a great debt to books by Madeleine Mitchell and Stephen Porter, and to Tony Martin-Jones' website, for much of the information contained in this chapter on Jamaica.

Kingston Harbour, Jamaica in 1870.

CHAPTER FIFTEEN

Montserrat

LOCATION

Montserrat, very rugged and mountainous, is a pear-shaped volcanic island with an area of 32 square miles which lies 27 miles south-west of Antigua and forms part of the Leeward Islands group. Plymouth, on the south-west coast, has been the capital since the second half of the seventeenth century, and the southern part of the island in general is dominated by the Soufrière Hills, which rise to over 3,000 feet and contain volcanoes which have been far from dormant over the years. Inhabitants of the island are referred to as 'Montserratians'.

HISTORY

Columbus sighted the island during his second voyage of 1493 and named it after a mountain abbey near Barcelona, though to the Carib Indians in whose territory it lay, it was 'Alliouagana' - the land of the prickly bush.

The fact that Montserrat is known as 'The Emerald Isle' bears testimony to a genuine Irish element in its history. In the early seventeenth century there were Irish and English Roman Catholics living in the Protestant colony of St Kitts who were only too keen to make a life elsewhere; they wanted to leave, and the Protestants, regarding them as a threat, were glad to see them go. So

it was that a group of those who sought freedom of religion set off for pastures new; landing on a mountainous neighbouring island which reminded the Irish of home, they landed at a place which became known as Kinsale Strand and set about turning Montserrat into a refuge for those who wished to escape religious persecution.

It is tempting to think of Montserrat as a kind of Irish colony in the Caribbean. Its first Governor, Anthony Brisket, though his ancestry was Italian, was an Irishman with family property in County Cork; he set about recruiting new settlers from his native land, and they were joined by Irish freedmen from Barbados and St Kitts and others who sought sanctuary away from the Protestant ascendancy in Virginia. By 1648 there were a thousand Irish families on the island, soon to be joined by a group of enforced emigrants who had been banished by Cromwell following his victory at Drogheda in 1649.

In the event, the true state of affairs on Montserrat was more complex. English dominance grew to the point where Oliver Cromwell, the scourge of the Irish, was entertained by the Governor of Montserrat in 1655, and it was not until 1668 that the first Roman Catholic priest, Father John Stritch from St Kitts, was allowed to minister openly to his community after several years during which he had posed as a timber merchant and acted as a priest in secret.

In effect there was an Anglo-Irish class of planters, far below whom in terms of social class were those whites, mainly Irish, who ran the subsistence economy or were employed as craftsmen, servants or indentured labourers. Further below them, at the base of the social pyramid, was a significant population of black slaves, supplied by the Guinea Company and later by the Royal African Company, the first of whom were brought to the island by an Irishman named John Burke in 1651. It would be gratifying to be able to report that Irish slave-owners, coming, as they did, from a country which had suffered so much oppression over the years, would have treated their slaves in an especially humane fashion. Most of the available evidence, alas, suggests that they did no such thing.

Many of the Irish lived in the area known as St Patrick's, and not a few felt themselves to be persecuted both in terms of religion and government, to the point where they offered active and passive support to the French during that nation's successful invasion of Montserrat in 1667, a victory which was reversed later the same year as the English regained control as part of the terms of the Treaty of Breda. Further French invasions from 1689 onwards also relied upon the support of Irish Montserratians, and the island suffered a devastating attack in the July of 1712 from which its economy never truly recovered. Roman Catholics were denied basic civil liberties until the last quarter of the eighteenth century, though a certain number, as we have said, were essentially part of the ruling plantocracy.

In 1671 the number of men on Montserrat able to bear arms was stated to be 1175, and there were 523 slaves; at the time of the first official census instituted by William Stapleton, Governor of the Leeward Islands, in 1678-9, there were 761 English people, 1869 Irish, 52 Scots and 992 black slaves. There were significantly fewer women than men in each category, a fact which did little to help civilise this rather wild frontier society. A year later a law was passed prohibiting settlers from leaving the island, but meanwhile the tensions between different groups had grown to such a point that Governor Stapleton was forced to resort to enacting legislation which outlawed the use of opprobrious terms such as 'English Dog', 'Scots Dog', 'Tory', 'Irish Dog', 'Cavalier' and 'Roundhead'.

A slave insurrection on the island was suppressed on St Patrick's Day, 1768, and eventually trouble with the French erupted again during the American War of Independence; in 1782 De Grasse compelled the island to surrender and Montserrat remained in French hands until two years later, when it was returned to England following the Treaty of Versailles.

By 1788 there were only 290 white inhabitants on the island, most of them Roman Catholics, and the 1820s saw such a paucity of whites that a near-crisis in government was the result.

Montserrat became the first Crown Colony of the Leewards in 1866, and is currently numbered among the small group of 'British Overseas Territories'.

Government House, Montserrat, 1924. From a photograph by CEE Browne.

The island and its inhabitants have been the victim of even more severe and more frequent hurricanes than many of its neighbours, from the first recorded instance in 1667 to Hurricane Hugo of October 1989. Volcanic eruptions in the Soufrière Hills began to give trouble in 1995, and in August of 1997 the capital, Plymouth, was burned down and became a ghost town. Over 5000 persons had already left Montserrat to settle in the United Kingdom in the period 1946-1964 as the cotton industry fell into decline, but in the wake of this fresh disaster and the forced emigration it caused, the population was down to 2850 by mid 1998.

ECONOMY

The island's economy, originally based upon the cultivation of tobacco, eventually became reliant upon the sugar industry - as was so often the case throughout the West Indies. The first sugar venture on Montserrat had been established in 1649 by a London merchant called Samuel Atkins.

By the early nineteenth century sugar production was in decline, though it would continue for another hundred years or so, and cotton cultivation and lime growing were proving themselves as viable alternatives. Slavery was finally abolished in 1834, and the post-emancipation period saw the arrival of the Quaker philanthropist Joseph Sturge, whose enlightened commercialism would give rise to the economic activities of what became known as the Montserrat Company, initially concerning itself with the burgeoning lime industry.

Tourism used to make a significant contribution to the island's economy, but following the devastation caused by the volcanic eruptions of 1995-97, Montserrat is now dependent upon aid from the United Kingdom.

PEOPLE

- Here is an extract from a complete list of the inhabitants of Antigua, St Kitts, Nevis and Montserrat compiled for Sir William Stapleton, the Governor of the Leeward Islands, in 1678, and now in The National Archives. These are the men listed in just one 'division' on Montserrat (Lieutenant Colonel Cormack's), from pages 316 and 317 of *Caribbeana*, volume 2, by V L Oliver. Further divisions (Major Gallway's, Captain Richard Basse's, Captain Nicholas Mead's, Captain Peter Cove's, Captain Andrew [or Anthony] Booth's, followed by Cove & Palmetto Point, St Peter's Parish, Northward, Captain John Deveraux's) are featured on pages 317-320 and 342-347 of the same work.

The names of men are given singly or in pairs, and columns against each entry give the associated number of white men, white women and white children. The total population for the Island was 1149 white men, 691 white women, 943 white children and 992 negro men. The Irish outnumbered the English by about two to one, with a handful of Scots.

A List of all the men, woemen, & children whites & blacks, which are conteyned in the severall divisions in the Island of Mounserratt. [1677/8].

Lt.Coll. Cormack & Lt. William Knowles; Ens. Daniell Sullavane; Sergant William Cavanan (?); Sergant James Adams; Sergant Dominick Mead; Sergant Daniell Dowdy; Daniell Robryan; Martin Blake; Richard Burke; Daniel Dunavand; Redmond Gerrald; John Hudshell; John Kelly; Dermond Sullavane; Edmond Royle; Teige Crowly & Teige Quigly; Nicholas Dunavain; John Darcy; John Molly & Edmond Cahosy; James Fitzmorris & James Coldmain; Owen Macloughlan; Daniel Killmury & Teige Rean; Wm Rean & Curnellius Keene; Dennis Murphy & Kirgane; Mathew Woodmas Sen. & Jun.; Dan. Cormody & John Dowdy sen.; Dermond Dowdy & John Dowdy jun.; Henry McDonough; Daniel Murphy & Dan. Croveen; John Hide & Teige Dorane; John Mally & Wm Mahone; Redmond Burk & Nichoas poor [sic]; Curnelius Dundo & Dermond Rerfiggs; Ullick Welch & Teige Donavane; John Horane & Flourence Carty; Garrett Missett & Edm. Rened; Farrell Dowdy & Richard Loy; Dermond Mally & Daniell Dolly; John Sullavane & Teige Corrue; Patrick Darcy & Mathew Darcy; Thomas Bonny & Owen Donahul; Thomas Elliott & John Gillroy; James Gillroy & Owen Dowdy; Peirce Erroll & Roger McGuyer; Mosett Ganan & Thomas Ganan; John Sherdan & Wm More; Daniell Conner & David Borke; John Harby & Tho. Daniell; Thomas Rison & Dermond Lorry; Morgan Regan & John Egan; Henry Lewis & Torrence Baines; Daniell Cunegan & Patrick Carrelam; John Thoill & Patrick Sheia; John Donough & Garrett Sey; Wm Rean & Patrick White; Roger Carroll & John Grynen; Michaell Keagh & John Muphy; James Gerrald & Curnelius Kyon; John Finny & Peter Make; Nicholas Rock & John Dume; Tho. Mullrean & Peter Bryan; Luke Cantelly & Curnelius Meword; Eng. Ric. Sawyers & Ino Sharpe senr; John Sawyer & John Sharpe junr.; John Andrews & Roger Ringe; John Renny & John Maning; Tho. Elway & Thomas Elway junior; Wm Milson, Clement Hokins; Clement Hokins junr & Roger Willicks senr; Roger Willicks junr & John Smith; William Bradley & Wm Heak; John Wyke & Peter Harris; Ric Selliott, Ino Westopher & Tho Westopher; John Harper & Richard Hodges; Francis Bynn & George Hill; James Dunt & John Batten.

- The names of some of the Anglo-Irish plantocracy can be gleaned from a 'remonstrance' of 1668, signed by Anthony Brisket, Thomas Roach, John Deveraux, George Wyke, Roger Bentley, David Galloway and Garret Misset. Added to these were men such as Nicholas Tuite, the Ryans of Cove and Palmetto Point and John and Henry Blake, who arrived in the 1670s and established a family dynasty in the process. John and Henry were sons of John Blake, Mayor of Galway, himself a descendant of Richard Craddle, alias Blake, who had been Sheriff of Connaught in 1306. The Blakes' fellow Galway-man, a Protestant named David Galway, came in the 1660s and became one of the most influential sugar-planters on the island.

- During the late seventeenth and eighteenth centuries a number of planters returned home with their fortunes and became absentee landlords. One such was Captain Carroll, a man of considerable wealth, who left for England in 1678 with 25 members of his household. By the 1720s a resident planter such as Nathaniel Webb from Somerset was the exception rather than the rule. For all that, several place names on the island are derived from the surnames of estate owners, such as Hodges Hill (Anthony Hodges), Trant's Bay (Dominick Trant), Bransby Point (Ensign Bransby) and others.

- The Quaker philanthropist Joseph Sturge (1793–1859) visited the West Indies between November 1836 and April 1837, gathering evidence to demonstrate the flaws of the apprenticeship system. On his return he published a book entitled *The West Indies* in 1837; he proved to be a tireless campaigner, and the following year the apprenticeship system was terminated. Towards the end of his life he bought an estate on Montserrat to prove the economic viability of free labour if efficiently and humanely managed.

RECORDS (UK REPOSITORIES)

The National Archives, London
Colonial Office records relating to Montserrat - correspondence (from 1702), sessional papers, gazettes, etc - and to the Leeward Islands Federation as a whole are relevant sources.

Class CO152/18 has a number of original eighteenth century baptism, burial and marriage records for St Anthony's, St George's and St Peter's, and marriage records for St Patrick's. Class CO152/25 has baptism and burial records for various parishes. For transcripts of these, see *Caribbeana*, below.

Census records for Montserrat, 1677/8 and 1729, may be found in classes CO1/42 and EXT 1/258 (extracted from CO152/18). The 1677/8 census indicates whether each person is English, Irish, Scottish, French or Dutch. Transcripts of these are in *Caribbeana* (see below).

Class CO 152/16, folios 148-151, has an account of losses sustained in an attack by the French on Montserrat in 1712.

Treasury: T71 includes records generated by the Slave Compensation Commission, 1817-1831, and claims are indexed in T71/934.

John Rylands Library, University of Manchester
The library has personal and semi-official papers of Sir William Stapleton, first Governor of the Leeward Islands (1672-1686), including details of accounts, etc., for Montserrat, 1672-1680.

GENEALOGICAL SOURCES HELD ON MONTSERRAT

Churches
The Montserrat Assembly of 1663 divided the island into four parishes or administrative districts: St Peter's (northward), St Anthony's (central), St Patrick's (southward) and St George's (eastern). St Anthony's and St Patrick's were later united to form a single parish.

In 1838 St Mary's Chapel, also called the Town Chapel and the Church of the Emancipation, was built by Anglicans for freed slaves on a site in Plymouth that is said to have been a Catholic cemetery. It later became St Mary's Anglican School.

The date of the first *Roman Catholic* church is unknown, but one could have existed from as early as 1678. By 1700 there were Roman Catholic cemeteries at Streatham, White River and at the site of the former St Mary's School. The year 1826 saw the official recognition of Catholics, and in that year a Roman Catholic clergyman was granted £100 'to furnish a convenient place of worship for his flock'. St Patrick's Roman Catholic Church of Plymouth was built in the period 1842 to 1848 by Father Henry McNiece.

Methodists on the island are first mentioned in 1793, but it wasn't until 1820 that they established a formal mission, and in any case they had a hard struggle to make an impact on what was preponderantly a Roman Catholic island. The first Methodist missionary to be stationed there was John Maddock; after he died from fever after a mere fifteen months in post, he was replaced by Charles Janion, to be followed by Thomas Kennington Hyde, William Clough and Benjamin Gartside. In 1855 the congregation replaced its wooden church and schoolroom at Cavalla Hill with a stone church, and the imposing Bethel Church was built in 1893 to commemorate a hundred years of Methodist activity on the island.

At the time of his survey of archives on the island in 1965, E C Baker found the following parochial records:

At St Anthony's with St Patrick's: registers of baptism, marriage and burial from 1828. 'Baptismal register beginning 1823, noted after 1924, was not to be found.' Also twentieth century vestry minutes and church accounts.

At St Peter's (with the chapels of St John and St James): registers of baptisms from 1889, marriages from 1958 and burials from 1926.

St George's: no registers were found.

Roman Catholic church records, then with Bishop Antoine Demets (but said by L H Gipson in 1970 to be in the archive room of Government House): registers of baptisms, marriages and burials from 1771.

Civil registration

Civil registration of births, deaths and marriages was introduced in the island by an Act of 1861. Duplicate copies of the District Registrars' entries are forwarded at the end of each quarter to the Registrar General, whose extant series of records dates from 12 February 1862 and is held at the Registrar General's Office, Registry Supreme Court, Government Headquarters, PO Box 22, Brades, Montserrat. Where possible an enquiry should state in which of the three districts an event is believed to have occurred.

Census

Decennial censuses for Montserrat were taken from 1871 onwards. In 1891 the population numbered 11762.

Other original records held on the island

Writing in 1914, V L Oliver said that 'The records [of Montserrat] have suffered more destruction ... than in any other island...Huge gaps occur...' E C Baker took up the theme again in 1965: 'Inquiry in the islands about records usually drew an initial response that they had been destroyed in hurricanes, but Montserrat was the only island where I saw clear evidence of such disasters, and of damage by accompanying floods, in the state of the records which survived'.

The French destroyed many documents in 1667, and again in 1712, despite the fact that a number of public records were sent to Monk's Hill Fort in Antigua for safe keeping during the hostilities of that year. Colonel John Hart, appointed Governor of the Leeward Islands in 1721, reported that all the Montserrat records had been burnt by the French in 1712; in 1784 a further war with the same enemy caused significant damage, as did the hurricane of 1899 and the earthquakes of 1928, 1933-35 and 1995-97. A fire of 1972 destroyed most records held in the new courthouse.

Herbert C Bell and David W Parker, visiting Montserrat in 1926, were disturbed to find that various classes of records were scattered about on the floor of the government office in Plymouth, being rained on through open windows and thoroughly damp as a consequence. Things were much better by the time E C Baker visited in 1965, though a disastrous fire in the courthouse seven years later was to destroy many 19th and 20th century records.

Baker's *A guide to records in the Leeward Islands* (1965), provides (pages 29-40) a useful listing of records then held in various repositories in Montserrat, of which a brief summary follows:

In the Archive Room, Government House: deed record books (copies of agreements, appraisements, bills of sale, covenants, deeds of gift, manumissions, leases and releases, powers of attorney, sales of slaves, wills) from 1728; legal court records; register of slaves 1831; government papers; Blue Books from 1842; customs books.

In the Court House, Plymouth: Mainly twentieth century records, including books of wills from 1928, but also registers of birth, marriage and death by parish from 1862.

Various other records were held in the Administration Building, the Prison and the Treasury Building, and there were a number of privately-held company archives.

An article by Joan E Mount of the Laurentian University in Sudbury, Ontario, published in *Research guide to Central America and the Caribbean* (edited by K J Grieb, University of Wisconsin Press, 1985, pages 378-379), reports upon a visit she paid to various Montserrat archive offices. The records then held in Government House were verified against Baker's guide, 'with no major discrepancies found', and she also found a number of archives of various dates in the Courthouse, the Law Library, the Administration Building on Church Street and the Public Library.

The archives of Montserrat are still held in a variety of repositories, and are in need of being organised and stored in appropriate conditions. Meanwhile, the Public Library, Government Headquarters, Plymouth, is responsible for these archives in an informal way, and its own record holdings of more than 2000 items (some bound volumes, some files and some very fragile documents, complete with a very basic card index) include papers taken from the basement of Government House.

SECONDARY SOURCES: PRINTED WORKS, etc.

Parish registers

The following parish register transcripts appear in volume one of *Caribbeana* by V L Oliver (1910). Overall covering years are given, but gaps appear in some series:

St Anthony's. Baptisms 1722-1728, marriages and burials 1723-1729; baptisms and burials, 1739-1745.

St George's. Baptisms and marriages, 1721-1729, burials 1721-1728; baptisms and burials, 1739-1745.

St Peter's. Baptisms 1721-1729, marriages 1722-1729, burials 1721-1728; baptisms and burials, 1739-1745.

St Patrick's. Baptisms 1727-1729, marriages 1723-1729, burials 1721-1723 and 1728.

Monumental inscriptions

V L Oliver's *The monumental inscriptions of the British West Indies* (1927) includes a substantial collection (pages 39-63) of inscriptions for the island, many embellished with genealogical and historical notes. *Caribbeana* has a number of transcriptions of MIs in England with Montserrat connections.

Probate records

Caribbeana contains various calendars and transcripts of wills and administrations relative to Montserrat and other West Indian islands, including wills proved and administrations granted in the Prerogative Court of Canterbury.

Censuses and name lists

Caribbeana has transcripts of the 1677/8 and 1729 censuses for Montserrat in volumes 2 and 4 respectively.

Deeds and other records

Caribbeana includes various transcripts of deeds, pedigrees and other material relative to Montserrat. It is well worth the trouble simply to look through every volume in order to find references which interest you, or at least to make use of the index and contents pages.

FURTHER READING

Akenson, D H *If the Irish ran the world: Montserrat 1630-1730.* 1997.

The Antigua Almanac & Register including Montserrat. 1842. Antigua, Weekly Register Office. 1842.

Berleant-Schiller, R *Montserrat.* The World Bibliographical Series.

'Black Irish and Montserrat, 17th century'. In *Tiara,* volume 13, no 2, Spring 1996.

Britnor, L E *Montserrat.* 1965.

Demets, A *The Catholic Church in Montserrat, West Indies, 1756-1980.* 1980.

English, T.S. *Ireland's only colony: Records of Montserrat, 1632 to the end of the nineteenth century.* Unpublished typescript of 250 pages; includes references to a number of local records which are now too damaged to be of any use. West India

Committee Library, London, 1930. A copy at Montserrat Public Library.

Fergus, H A 'Montserrat colony of Ireland: the myth and the reality'. In *Studies: An Irish Quarterly Review*, University of Dublin, Winter 1981.

Fergus, H A *Montserrat: Emerald Isle of the Caribbean*. Second edition, 1989.

Fergus, H A *Montserrat: history of a Caribbean Colony*. 1994.

Fergus, H A *History of Alliouagana: short history of Montserrat*. Montserrat, 1975. Later described by the author as 'a very slim, rough-hewn volume based mainly on a limited number of secondary sources'.

Gwynn, Rev A 'Documents relating to the Irish in the West Indies'. In *Analecta Hibernica*, 1932.

'How Irish is Montserrat?'. In *Irish Roots*, no 1, 1994.

Kirnon, H *Montserrat and the Montserratians*. New York, 1925.

Messenger, J 'The Black Irish of Montserrat', in *Eire-Ireland*, vol 2, no 1, Minnesota, 1966.

Messenger, J 'The influence of the Irish in Montserrat' in *Caribbean Quarterly*, Volume 13, no 2, June 1967.

'Montserrat island history' in *Saint Domingue Special Interest Group Newsletter*, Volume 5, no 3, July 1993.

Peters, F E *A brief history of Montserrat and her recent hurricanes*. Unpublished, 1929.

Peters, F E *St Anthony's Church, Montserrat, West Indies*. Barbados. 1931. Includes a list of ministers, 1761-1896.

Pulsipher, L M and C M Goodwin *Galways Plantation, Montserrat, West Indies*. 1982.

Somerville, D *The early years of Montserrat: a chronicle of the people who settled this island*. Original typescript in Montserrat Public Library, 1976.

Titford, J 'Settlers of the Old Empire: The West Indies: Montserrat', 2 parts, *Family Tree Magazine,* December 2000 and March 2001.

Watkins, F H *Handbook of the Leeward Islands*, 1924. Contains a list of estate owners on Montserrat (pages 197-198)

Wheeler, M M *Montserrat, West Indies: a chronological history*. Montserrat, 1988.

WEBSITES

www.britishislesgenweb.org/data/list php?148
British Isles GenWeb: General Montserrat queries.

www.rootsweb.ancestry.com/~msrwgw/
Montserrat GenWeb

www.cousinconnect.com/p/a/1150/
CousinConnect.com Montserrat genealogy queries.

www.montserratnationaltrust ms/
The Montserrat National Trust, PO Box 393, Olveston, Montserrat, which has some documents and photographs relating to the history of the island.

www.familysearch.org/eng/Library/FHLC/frameset_fhlc.asp
The LDS Family History Library catalog. A search on 'Montserrat' will bring up very little of real relevance. Alas.

The International Genealogical Index (now within FamilySearch) and related records should also be searched for individuals from Montserrat.

CHAPTER SIXTEEN
Nevis

LOCATION

Nevis lies two miles to the south-east of St Kitts, an island neighbour with which it has not always enjoyed the most harmonious of relationships over the years. A volcanic mountain rising to over 3,000 feet occupies the centre of the island, and in colonial days plantations sloped down to the coast all around it. This single peak, nearly always covered in cloud and with the appearance of being snow-clad, was sighted by Columbus in 1493, and he named the island 'Nuestro Señora de la Nieves' (Our Lady of the snows); this later became 'Nievis' or 'Mevis', and finally 'Nevis', pronounced 'Neevis'. The inhabitants are referred to as 'Nevisians'.

The first town was Jamestown, named after the monarch and situated on the leeward side of the island; following damage sustained there by an earthquake in 1660, Charlestown was built on the shore of a wide bay in the north west, and became the principal settlement.

HISTORY

The exact date of the settlement of Nevis by the English is uncertain. Thomas Warner had arrived there in 1623 and was given a Royal Commission for St Christopher, Nevis, Barbados and Montserrat two years later. In July 1627 Nevis, together with other Caribee islands, was leased by King Charles I to James, Earl of Carlisle, the whole being referred to as 'Carlisle Province' or 'Carliola'. The first settlers on Nevis came from Warner's party of colonists at St Kitts, and when Thomas Littleton of London, merchant, sent out three ships in 1628, his factor found Captain Anthony Hilton as Governor there under Carlisle's patent.

The first English settlers on Nevis were keen to acquire cheap land; mainly from the lower or middle classes, they were craftsmen such as blacksmiths, masons, carpenters and tailors or small-scale farmers. The island also had its complement of bonded and indentured servants, those who signed an agreement to work for five years in return for a free passage. V L Oliver points out that evidence from wills would suggest that most of the early settlers on Nevis came from Bristol, which had strong tobacco trade links with Virginia and the Caribbees.

The population in 1650 was reckoned to be 5,000 persons; five years later there was so much overcrowding that 1,400 men, women and children, together with their servants, left Nevis and the neighbouring islands and made for Jamaica under the leadership of Governor Luke Stokes. Others emigrated to America. In 1664 Nevis came under the protection of the English Crown, a status which it enjoyed throughout colonial times except during the period of two French invasions. After the destruction of the English colony in St Kitts in 1666, Nevis became the most important and prosperous of the Leeward Islands, its Lieutenant Governor taking over the administration of these islands in the absence of the Governor.

Slaves were treated well or badly according to the plantation on which they found themselves, but Nevis had an evil reputation at one time for being one of the chief West Indian markets for the sale of 'black ivory', especially during the period 1660 to 1698 when the Royal African Company had the monopoly for providing slaves. Early parish registers on Nevis refer to 'slaves', a practice which continued until emancipation was granted in the 1830s, after which time a trade would be attached to a person's name. The emancipation of Nevis's 7,225 slaves caused a severe collapse of credit, followed by drought and pestilence, and for many years the island was a ruined spot of British territory; the injection of fresh capital in 1865 had a salutary effect, though it was only following the Second World War that life on the island was significantly improved for the majority of its inhabitants.

In 1724 the Governor, John Hart, had recommended the union of Nevis with St Kitts, but only in 1816 was a colony of St Kitts, Nevis, Anguilla and the Virgin Islands established. Nevis became part of the Leeward Islands again in 1833, and in 1882 St Kitts, Nevis and Anguilla were united to form a single colony. Anguilla broke away from this grouping in 1980, and St Kitts-Nevis became a dominion on 19th September 1983, thus ending three hundred and sixty years of colonial rule.

Nevis has suffered a series of natural disasters over the years: hurricanes wreaked havoc on the island in 1772, 1899, 1924 and 1989; Charlestown was severely damaged by an earthquake in 1843; fevers had carried off half the population in 1689, and smallpox and dire epidemics of cholera occurred in 1853 and 1854. For all that, the island has enjoyed a less troubled history than some of its neighbours.

Government House, Nevis.

ECONOMY

The original tobacco industry on Nevis declined in importance in the face of competition from Virginia, and Nevis eventually turned to the cultivation of sugar as an alternative. Slave labour was imported for this purpose, and those poorer white settlers who remained either found some other work on the plantations or set themselves up as shopkeepers or tradesmen. Cotton would become another major crop, and sea island cotton and coconuts are still cultivated on smallholdings, but tourism now makes a significant contribution to the country's exchequer.

PEOPLE

• Several notable English families settled on Nevis, such as the Russells and the Herberts, and these were less inclined to be absentee landlords than those on neighbouring islands.

- The island gave America one of her greatest statesmen, Alexander Hamilton, who was born there on 11th January, 1757.

- The registers of St John the Baptist Figtree include an entry for the marriage of Lord Nelson: '1787, March 11th., Horatio Nelson, Esquire, Captain of His Majesty's ship the *Boreas*, to Frances Herbert Nisbet, widow', a facsimile of which appears on page 93 of *Escape to the West Indies* by Bradley Smith (3rd edition, New York, 1961, page 93). The Duke of Clarence, afterwards King William IV, attended Nelson as best man, and there is a memorial in the church dedicated to Fanny Nisbet's parents, the Woolwards. In the event Nelson and his bride were not married in the church itself, but at Montpelier House, where a plaque commemorating the event may still be seen on the old gatepost.

RECORDS (UK REPOSITORIES)

The National Archives, London
Colonial Office records relating to Nevis - correspondence (from 1689), sessional papers, gazettes, etc - and to the Leeward Islands Federation as a whole are relevant sources.

Class CO152/16,21 and 25 contains baptism and burial records for the parishes of St Paul's (1726-1727), St John's, St Thomas's and St George's (1733-1734) and St James's (1740-1745). Transcripts of various of these TNA parish records appear in *Caribbeana* (see below).

Name lists of residents of Nevis can be found in CO 1/42,ff.201-217 (for 1677/8) and in CO 152/7,f.47 (for 1707), both of which have been transcribed in *Caribbeana*, volume 3.

Treasury: T71 includes records generated by the Slave Compensation Commission, 1817-1834, and claims are indexed in T71/928.

British Library, etc.
The British Library has copies of the following Nevis newspapers: *The Nevis Guardian* 1871-1873; *The Liberal* 1873; *The Nevis Weekly Recorder* 1959.

RECORDS (LOCALLY-HELD)

In 1706 many public records were destroyed or damaged by the French. Given the history of the island, various records relating to Nevis will be found with those for the Leeward Islands as a whole, and Herbert C Bell and David W Parker in *Guide to West Indian Archive materials in London and in the Islands for the history of the United States*, published in 1926, state that 'Such legislative papers of Nevis as survive have been brought to Basseterre [St Kitts] and are stored with those of St Kitts'. For all that, E C Baker in *A guide to records in the Leeward Islands* (1965), provides (pages 41-45) a substantial listing of records then held in various repositories in Nevis, summarised details of which are incorporated in the sections which follow.

Churches

The five *Anglican* churches of St Paul's, St Thomas's, St James's, St George's and St John's were built in the seventeenth century, being originally of wooden construction. St Paul's is the parish church of Charlestown, and was rebuilt in the 1890s; St Thomas's, on the leeward side of the island, dates from 1643, St George Gingerland from 1670 and St James Windward from 1679. The present St John Fig Tree church was completed in 1838.

There are also *Methodist* and *Catholic* places of worship on the island, together with those of other Christian sects. A cemetery is all that remains of the *Jewish* community which arrived in Nevis in the mid seventeenth century, having been expelled from Brazil by the Portuguese.

Various Acts of Parliament passed in England from 1681 onwards attempted to ensure that records of Anglican baptisms and burials were kept on Nevis, just as on St Kitts. Here are details from Baker's list of Anglican church records then held (1965) at the relevant churches on Nevis:

> *At St Paul's*: registers from 1824 (and V L Oliver noted a register beginning in 1812, of which 'the leaves are rotten, broken and loose').
> *At St Thomas Lowland*: registers from 1827 (Oliver noted a fragmented volume for 1740-1827), parish books; also records relating to St Paul's (registers from 1833), St James Windward (registers from 1849, earlier books from 1787 having probably been burnt in a fire of 1837), St Paul's and St Thomas's (vestry minutes, 1914-1935), St Paul's (services register 1836-1952) and St Christopher-Nevis Clerical Society, minute book of meetings, 1925-1956.
> *At St George the Martyr Gingerland*: registers from 1828, register of services, 1930-1957, and vestry minutes for St John's and St George's, 1894-1938 (St George's only after 1923).
> *At St John the Baptist Figtree*: registers from 1728.

Miscellaneous records

Baker lists miscellaneous records then held in various repositories on the island: in the Court House, Charlestown: common deed record books (accounts, agreements, bills of exchange, of sale and of loading, commissions, deeds of discharge and of gifts, leases and releases, indentures, lists of negroes, manumissions, notes of hand, powers of attorney, writs of enquiry, of partition, of possession and of seizing); books of wills from 1783 (and Oliver noted a volume for 1764-1786); various law court records; bankruptcy records; Charlestown and Bath Cemetery registers; St Paul's parish registers from 1861. Other island records, manuscript and printed, were then held at the Alexandra Hospital, the Public Library, Charlestown, and the Treasury Building.

Writing early in the twentieth century, V L Oliver had this to say about the Registrar's Office in Nevis:

The Registrar's Office here is also in a room at the end of the old Court House in Charlestown. Everything is in good order, and proper cupboards have been provided, but the room is not fire-proof.

Censuses
The first of a series of decennial censuses was taken on Nevis in 1891, in which year the population numbered 13,087. Some census records for Nevis are held by the Nevis Historical and Conservation Society.

Civil registration
Compulsory civil registration of births and deaths on Nevis began in accordance with an act of 1860: 'Whereas it is expedient and necessary to provide the means for a complete Registry of Births and Deaths in this Island, whereby evidence of title to property and statistical information, for purposes of public interest and utility, may be more easily obtained'.

Some Civil Registration records are held by the Nevis Historical and Conservation Society. Information on births and deaths on Nevis from 1861 and for marriages from 1907 is held by The Registrar General's Office, Basseterre Health Centre, Connell Street, Basseterre, St Kitts.

At the present time some Nevis archives are held in the Court House vault in Charlestown, others in the Nelson Museum, Belle Vue, Charlestown, under the management of the Nevis Historical and Conservation Society, PO Box 563, Charlestown. Matters seem promising enough: 'The NHCS archivists consider the support of genealogical research one of the strongest aspects of the archives'. Negotiations are being conducted with the island's government in an attempt to centralise all holdings in one location.

GENEALOGICAL SOURCES HELD ELSEWHERE

Some records for St Kitts and Nevis are in the French National Archives in Paris.

SECONDARY SOURCES: PRINTED WORKS, etc.

Parish registers

Various parish register transcripts for Nevis appear in *Caribbeana* by V L Oliver (6 volumes, 1910-1920).

A transcript of the registers of St George Gingerland, 1716-1724 (from the Fulham Papers of the Bishop of London) may be found in *The early English colonists* by Sadler Phillips (1908) pages 143-158. This is reproduced in full in articles by John Titford in *Family Tree Magazine*, January 2000 and March 2000. A microfilm copy of the same register may also be consulted in the Printed Books Section at Guildhall Library, London.

Oliver's *The monumental inscriptions of the British West Indies* (1927) includes a few miscellaneous transcripts from the parish registers of St Thomas's in the eighteenth and nineteenth centuries (pages 103-104).

Monumental inscriptions

Transcripts of monumental inscriptions for the following parishes appear in *Caribbeana*: St George's (vol.2); St John Fig Tree (vol.1); St Paul's (vol.2); St Thomas Lowland (vol.2).

V L Oliver's *The monumental inscriptions of the British West Indies* (1927) includes a very extensive annotated collection of Nevis inscriptions (pages 64 to 121).

The American Jewish Historical Quarterly, volume 61, no 1 (1971) has an article entitled 'Nevis Island Jewish burial ground'.

Probate records

Caribbeana contains various calendars and transcripts of wills and administrations relative to Nevis and other West Indian islands, including wills proved and administrations granted in the Prerogative Court of Canterbury.

A close perusal of printed calendars of PCC wills and administrations should allow the researcher to unearth references to Nevis. This may be a long haul, but may result in the occasional success:

Bourne, John, of Dagenham, Essex, gent., March 18, 1629-30, but deceased abroad. Described in codicil, Sept.10, 1630, as 'late of Grinstead, Essex, and now of Dulcina alias Neves in the Province of Carliola in the West Indies'. Will [56 St John] proved May 12 1631 by relict Margaret. Probate reserved to John Young. (Abstract of probate acts in the Prerogative Court of Canterbury, 1630-4. J and G F Matthews. 1902. page 68).

Alternatively, of course, it is now possible to carry out a PCC will search on The National Archives website and to enter 'Nevis' in the 'place' box.

Censuses and name lists
A 'List of all the men, women & children whites & blacks, which are contained in the several divisions in the island of Nevis', 1677/8, appears in *Caribbeana*, volume 3, beginning on page 27.

A 'List of the inhabitants of Nevis, with the number of their slaves, 13 March 1707/8', appears in *Caribbeana*, volume 3.

Deeds and other records
Caribbeana includes various transcripts of deeds, pedigrees and other records relative to Nevis.

Nevis Families
Two books by E Byron, *Some Nevis families* (no date: 1970s) and *More families of Nevis* (Basseterre, St Kitts, 1981) contain a variety of anecdotal accounts of a certain number of black and white families on the island, with some genealogical detail. Copies of both books are held by the Nevis Historical and Conservation Society. The first volume begins with an account of the Maynard family:

Prominent among the estate owners of Nevis are the Maynards. William Maynard came from England to Nevis in 1703, and unlike some other English migrants to this island, his descendants remained here to this day, and the Maynard family tree (a most interesting one) can now be seen at Clay Ghaut Estate (the present home of Mr. and Mrs. Norman Maynard) in Nevis.

Other settler families featured in these two volumes include those of Liburd (descended from a nineteenth-century immigrant from England who married a 'dark-skinned Nevisian' named Tabitha Williams), Huggins, Wilkins, Hanley, Evelyn, Nisbett and Archibald.

Further reading

Burdon, K J, Lady. *Handbook to St Kitts-Nevis, a presidency of the Leeward Islands Colony, containing information for residents & visitors concerning the island.* 1920.

Gordon, J *Nevis: Queen of the Caribees.* MacMillan Caribbean. 3rd edition, 1993.

'Jews of Nevis, British West Indies' in *American Jewish Archives,* volume 10, no 2 (1958).

'Nevis, Eastern Caribbean island, historical-genealogical sources' in *Afro-American Historical and Genealogical Society Journal,* volume 9, no 1 (1988).

Stern, M *A list of the tombstones in the Jew's Burial Ground, Nevis.* 1971.

Titford, J 'Settlers of the Old Empire. The West Indies: Nevis', 2 parts, *Family Tree Magazine,* September 1999 and November 1999.

WEBSITES

www.tc.umn.edu/~terre011/genhome.html#index

St Kitts-Nevis Genealogy page. A clearing house for those conducting genealogical research on the families of St Kitts and Nevis. Includes various links (eg to a parish map of Nevis and to Michelle Terrell and Elise Morris's offer to do look-ups in Oliver's *Monumental inscriptions of the British West Indies*) and a surname connector listing genealogists who are researching specific St Kitts-Nevis surnames.

www.candoo.com/genresources/stknevang.htm

Includes a listing of LDS Church microfilm records of St Kitts, Nevis and Anguilla civil registration and parochial records.

www.nevis-nhcs.org/

The Nevis Historical and Conservation Society.

www.cousinconnect.com/p/a/145/

Saint Kitts and Nevis Genealogy Queries

www.familysearch.org/eng/Library/FHLC/frameset_fhlc.asp

The LDS Family History Library catalog. Search on 'Nevis ' for a collection of material, some of it on microfilm: civil registration records for St Kitts, Nevis and Anguilla; land records for St Kitts and Nevis. Also a microfilm copy of original records held at the American Jewish Archives, Cincinnati, Ohio, under the following title: *Photographs and some translations of old tombstones in the cemetery of Nevis, various western hemisphere Jewry, epitaphs 1684-1730.* The text is in English and Hebrew.

The International Genealogical Index (now within FamilySearch) and related records should also be searched for individuals from Nevis.

CHAPTER SEVENTEEN
St Kitts

LOCATION

St Christopher, a volcanic island lying two hundred miles to the south-east of Puerto Rico, is universally referred to as 'St Kitts'. Shaped like an Indian club, a paddle (or even a tadpole), St Kitts is 23 miles long, with an area of 68 square miles. Basseterre, a small town on the south-east coast, is the capital, and the residents refer to themselves as 'Kittians'.

HISTORY

St Kitts is known as 'The mother colony of the West Indies'; it was the first to be established in the area, and it was from here that many of the other neighbouring island colonies were settled. Few colonies have had such vicissitudes of ownership as St Kitts. Columbus came across the island in 1493; originally a Spanish possession, it passed to British rule in the January of 1623/4, when Thomas Warner first settled there; he eventually became the island's first Governor. Various tussles over ownership with the French, who had once occupied parts of the island by an amicable arrangement, followed; St Kitts was ceded to Britain under the terms of the Treaty of Utrecht in 1713, but it was only following the Treaty of Versailles

in 1783 that Britain acquired control of the entire island. Over time various permutations of island groups were established within the British West Indies, and in 1882 St Kitts, Nevis and Anguilla were united to form a single colony; Anguilla broke away from this grouping in 1980, and St Kitts-Nevis became a dominion on 19th September 1983.

St Kitts has had more than its fair share of natural and man-made disasters over the years, apart from the usual devastation caused by hurricanes. In 1674 the Governor of the island reported that all archives had been destroyed or lost during the recent war against the French. A great earthquake rocked the island in 1843; an outbreak of cholera devastated the population eleven years later, and a massive fire in Basseterre rendered five thousand people homeless in 1867, to be followed by a flood in 1880 which resulted in the deaths of over three hundred people.

ECONOMY

Tobacco had been the dominant crop on St Kitts in the early days, but it was soon replaced by sugar (and very little else), and several thousand slaves from the Guinea Coast in West Africa were imported to labour in the cane fields. By the third decade of the eighteenth century there were 10,000 slaves out of a population of 13,000; fifty years later there would be fewer than 2,000 whites and over 20,000 blacks, as the ownership of land became concentrated into fewer and fewer hands. The St Kitts government closed down the increasingly unprofitable sugar industry in 2005, and the island is now heavily dependent upon tourism.

PEOPLE

• Thomas Warner from Suffolk, a captain in James I's bodyguard, settled on St Kitts in 1623/4 at the suggestion of Captain Thomas Painton, a seaman 'as enthusiastic as he was experienced', and with the financial backing of a rich London-based merchant, Ralph Merriefield. Warner returned to England for a spell, and when he finally arrived back at St Kitts in 1626 with three ships carrying a hundred new colonists, he did so with a Royal Patent and as the island's first Governor, with John Jeafferson as his deputy. Warner eventually received a knighthood for his pains; his white marble tomb may still be seen on a rise in the grounds of St Thomas's church, complete with elaborate epitaph.

• In 1628 a St Kitts planter named Littleton obtained a grant from Lord Carlisle of the island of Barbuda, which he named Dulcina, but his settlement there proved to be still-born. Later in the century the Codrington family made more of a success of such a venture.

- In 1689 a commission was granted to Christopher Codrington, making him 'Governor-in-chief in and over our islands of Nevis, St Christopher's, Montserrat, Antegoa, Barbouda, Anguilla and all other our islands... commonly known by the name of our Charibbee Islands...'.

- Famous seafarers such as Nelson, Hood and Rodney all had some form of association with St Kitts in their time.

- The founder of the Methodist mission in St Kitts was William Hammet; he was succeeded by Thomas Owens, John Brownell, Philip Debell (who was struck down by yellow fever within eighteen months of arrival), John Taylor (1801-1803), Messrs Gilgrass, Turner, White and Woolley, Abraham Whitehouse, John Willis, James Whitworth, John Raby, Charles Janion, William Clough and Robert Hawkins.

- James Birkby worked as a missionary for the Moravians in St Kitts and in St Croix.

RECORDS (UK REPOSITORIES)

The National Archives, London
Colonial Office records relating to St Kitts - correspondence (from 1689), sessional papers, gazettes, etc - and to the Leeward Islands Federation as a whole are relevant sources. Classes CO152/18 and CO152/25 include baptisms, marriages and burials for various St Kitts parishes. Transcripts of some of these registers appear in *Caribbeana* (see below).

Census records for St Kitts for 1677/8, 1707, 1707/8 and 1711 may be found in classes CO1/42, CO152/7, CO152/6 and CO152/9 respectively. See also transcripts in *Caribbeana*, below.

CO152/11 contains details of land grants in the former French part of St Kitts (1712-1716), CO152/13 has a list of possessors of the French land in two divisions of the island in 1721 (an illustration taken from this list appears on page 43 of *Tracing your West Indian ancestors in the Public Record Office* by Guy Grannum, PRO Readers' Guide no 11, 1995), and T1/275 has a list of contracts made by the Commissioners for Sale of Land in the island that formerly belonged to the French (1729). In the wake of a French invasion of St Kitts and Nevis in 1711, powers of attorney were granted for compensation. Copies of such powers, 1712-1720, together with some wills, are in CO243/4-5.

Treasury: T71 includes records generated by the Slave Compensation Commission, 1817-1834, and claims are indexed in T71/925.

The British Library, etc.

The British Library Department of Manuscripts has a number of records relating to St Kitts, including parochial baptisms, marriages and burials (Additional Manuscripts 34,181, 41,178, 43,743, 43,866 and 41,295 [Ripon Papers]), and transcriptions of population and tax records for the French part of the island, 1776-1770. The BL also holds several St Kitts newspapers from 1771 onwards.

For details of other record holdings in London repositories relevant to St Kitts, including those of the Methodist Missionary Society and the Moravian Union, see the book by Baker, below; additionally, some records for St Kitts and Nevis are in the French National Archives in Paris.

RECORDS (LOCALLY-HELD)

St George's Church, St Kitts. Photograph by John Titford.

Churches

St Kitts was originally divided into quarters or divisions, but later six parishes were formed: Trinity Palmeto Point; St Thomas Middle Island; St Anne Sandy Point; St John Capesterre; Christ Church Nicola Town and St Mary Cayon. Three further parishes were established in 1727 out of former French districts, namely: St Paul Capesterre, St Peter Basseterre and St George Basseterre. A map of St Kitts showing these nine parishes may be seen at: www.tc.umn.edu/~terre011/skbparish.html

Various Acts of Parliament passed in the Mother Country attempted to ensure that parish registers were kept in colonies such as St Kitts. An 'Act for Ministers' Dues, etc.' of 1681 stipulated that 'the inhabitants of each parish in the Island shall pay...Two Thousand Pounds of Sugar [per year] to each clerk, who is to keep a Register of all Christenings and Burials in each Parish'. In 1705 'An Act for regulating Vestries' provided that a register for christenings, marriages and funerals be maintained by the minister of each parish, while in 1711 a further similar act stipulated that 'in every Parish Church shall be kept two large Paper Books, for the publick Service of the said Parish; one whereof shall be kept for the Parish

Accounts, by the Church-wardens, the other as a Register for Christnings, Marriages and Funerals, to be kept by the Minister only'. And so it continued throughout the eighteenth and nineteenth centuries, similar acts being passed, amended or repealed.

Roman Catholic Church, Basseterre, St Kitts. Photograph by John Titford.

Several churches on the island hold original registers of baptism, marriage and burial, together with vestry minute books and other records. Extant parish registers for St George's (with St Peter's) date from 1747; those for St Mary Cayon from 1825; those for Christ Church, Nicola Town, from 1794; those for St Thomas (with Holy Trinity) Middle Island from 1730; those for St Anne Sandy Point from 1762 and those for St John's and St Mary's church from 1826.

Civil registration

Compulsory civil registration of births and deaths on St Kitts dates from 1st January 1859, as the result of an act which hoped to ensure that 'evidence of title to property may be more easily obtained and statistical information afforded for purposes of public interest and utility, and whereby also crime may be more readily discovered and more efficiently suppressed'. Civil registration of marriages dates from 1885. Filled registers containing the original entries of births, deaths and marriages are kept by the registrars of the parishes, while duplicate copies are held by the Registrar General's Office, PO Box 236, Basseterre. These records may be viewed on-site for a fee. Additionally, death registers from 1880, marriage bonds and registers from 1771 and various deeds, etc are held by The National Archives, Government Headquarters, Church Street (PO Box 186), Basseterre.

Census

An ordinance of 1891 '...to facilitate the taking of a census from time to time in the Presidency of Saint Christopher-Nevis' gave rise to the first of a series of decennial censuses on the island; the population in 1891 was 30,876. Census records left on St Kitts have traditionally been destroyed, though some enumeration sheets from as early as 1844 have survived.

Other original records held on the island

Writing earlier this century, V L Oliver had this to say about the Registrar's Office in the Old Court House in Basseterre:

It is located in a large airy room on the ground floor of the old Court House in the square at Basseterre. The volumes are carefully arranged on shelves, and the only reflection that one can make is that the room is not fire-proof. In the past there has been a great destruction of papers. Chancery suits have rotted away. No marriage licences nor passenger licences exist .. The Registrar reported in 1907 on the bad state of the records to the Chief Justice, their legal custodian, but no action was taken. Some of the parish registers of this island are also in a shocking state of dilapidation... (*Caribbeana*, volume 3, page 360).

In retrospect, Oliver's comment about the lack of fire-proofing was prophetic. In 1982 a fire at the Court House resulted in the destruction of many irreplaceable records relating both to St Kitts and to Nevis. Those wills and probates (from 1841) and land title registers (from 1881) which survived the conflagration are now divided between the National Archives and the New Court House.

The National Archives, Government Headquarters, Church Street, PO Box 186, Basseterre, St Kitts, also holds various original records relating to the government, administration and legal system of the island. It has Official Gazettes, Blue Books, a sizeable collection of newspapers from 1877, wills and probate books (from 1753), collections of bonds, including marriage bonds (from 1771) and testamentary bonds (from 1772), death registers from 1880, cemetery records, registers of slaves, debtors and jurors, shipping lists, census and electoral register documentation, details of divorce and matrimonial causes, estate account books and a large collection of deeds and records relating to land holding.

A number of marriage certificates relating to the Methodist and Moravian Churches on the island (from 1844), originally in the Old Court House, are now held by The National Archives, while records of Methodist and Moravian baptism, marriage and burial are with the respective churches. Certain of the older Moravian records have been transferred to an archive in the Bethlehem, Pennsylvania, United States of America.

The St Christopher Heritage Society, PO Box 888, Basseterre, has over 2000 books, documents, maps, reports, and collections of photos and videos featuring the island's history, environment, culture, economy etc, and is in the process of assembling family trees and recording the family histories of present day Kittians through the transcription of obituaries, eulogies, and newspaper articles.

For full details of the archives which were held on the island back in the palmy days of 1965, together with a list of some records of the Leeward Islands Federation held on Antigua and a history of the archives of these islands, see *A guide to records in the Leeward Islands* by E C Baker (1965). The National Archives in Basseterre are currently using Baker's work as a basis for producing an updated guide to their present holdings.

The *Newsletter* of the Saint-Domingue Special Interest Group, volume 4, number 2 (April 1992) refers to the fact that a certain amount of information on the history of the French involvement in St Kitts was then held by Mr Larry Armony, c/o The Brimstone Hill National Park Society, Taylors Range, Basseterre, St Kitts.

SECONDARY SOURCES: PRINTED WORKS, etc.

Genealogical sources for St Kitts in print, typescript, manuscript and microform are fairly plentiful; the present-day researcher has been well-served by the tireless efforts of genealogists from earlier generations.

Parish registers
Many parish register transcripts for St Kitts appear in *Caribbeana* by V L Oliver (6 volumes, 1910-1920), together with details of births, marriages and deaths featured in the *St Christopher Gazette & Caribbean Courier* and the *St Christopher Advertiser & Weekly Intelligencer*.

The Society of Genealogists in London has a number of typescript transcripts of parish registers for St Kitts which complement the pioneering work done by V L Oliver, though details given on the title pages of various volumes of transcripts do not always accurately reflect the contents.

Gravestone, St Kitts General Cemetery. Wigley is very much a Derbyshire surname, and although Sir Wilfred Wigley came from a family based in St Kitts, he was educated at Derby School. Photograph by John Titford.

Monumental inscriptions
Monumental inscriptions of the British West Indies by J H Lawrence-Archer (1875) has a few transcriptions of MIs for St Kitts (pages 418-420), while V L Oliver's *The monumental inscriptions of the British West Indies* (1927) includes a splendid wide-ranging collection (pages 122-198) of inscriptions for the island, many embellished with genealogical and historical notes. *Caribbeana* has a number of transcriptions of MIs in England with St Kitts connections, and details of inscriptions from St Thomas Middle Island and Trinity Palmetto Point are featured in volume 2.

Probate records
Caribbeana contains various calendars and transcripts of wills and administrations relative to St Kitts and other West Indian islands, including wills proved and administrations granted in the Prerogative Court of Canterbury.

Assiduous use of printed calendars of English wills and administrations - or just plain serendipity - should allow you to unearth references to St Kitts and other early British colonies such as:

> *Gulliford, Daniel. Deceased abroad in the Island of St Christopher. Administration granted to relict, Bridget Gulliford, before Richard Knight, Clerk. 8 June 1630. (Prerogative Court of Canterbury Letters of Administration 1620-1630*. J H Morrison, 1935, page 47).

Alternatively, of course, it is now possible to carry out a PCC will search on The National Archives website and to enter 'St Kitts' or 'St Christopher' in the 'place' box.

Censuses and name lists
Caribbeana has transcripts of inhabitants' lists for St Kitts for 1678 (volume 2) and 1707-8 (volume 3).

Recensement de l'île de Saint-Christophe, anné 1671: liste des personnes figurant dans le terrier by B Rossignol (1987) features a 1671 census listing for St Kitts.

Deeds and other records
Caribbeana includes various transcripts of deeds, pedigrees and the like relative to St Kitts. It is well worth the trouble simply to look through every volume in order to find material of interest, or at least to make use of the index and contents pages.

FURTHER READING

Burdon, K J, Lady *Handbook to St Kitts-Nevis, a presidency of the Leeward Islands Colony, containing information for residents & visitors concerning the island*. 1920.
Dyde, B *St Kitts: cradle of the Caribbean*. MacMillan Caribbean. 2nd edition, 1993.
Moll, V P *St Kitts-Nevis*. World Bibliographical series, vol.174, c1995.
'St Kitts history'. *Caribbean Historical & Genealogical Journal*. Volume 1, no 2. April 1993.
'St Kitts: selective addresses for genealogy'. *Saint Domingue Special Interest Group Newsletter*. Volume 4, no 2. April 1992.
Somerby, H G 'Emigrants for St Christophers, &c.'. *The New England Historical & Genealogical Register*, 25:1 (October 1860), pages 347-359.

Titford, J 'Settlers of the Old Empire: The West Indies: St Kitts', 2 parts, *Family Tree Magazine,* May 1999 and July 1999.

WEBSITES

www.tc.umn.edu/~terre011/genhome.html#index
St Kitts-Nevis Genealogy page. A clearing house for those conducting genealogical research on the families of St Kitts and Nevis. Includes very useful material on St Kitts (including maps, details of St Kitts archive holdings, details of purchase records for the French Lands of St Kitts, c. 1726, etc), together with various links (eg to those who will do look-ups in an index of St Kitts wills to 1800 and in Oliver's *Monumental inscriptions of the British West Indies*) and a surname connector listing genealogists who are researching specific St Kitts-Nevis surnames.

http://boards.ancestry.co.uk/localities.caribbean.stkittsnevis.stkitts/mb.ashx
St Kitts Family History & Genealogy Message Board.

www.cousinconnect.com/p/a/145/
CousinConnect St Kitts and Nevis Genealogy Queries

www.candoo.com/genresources/stknevang.htm
Includes a listing of LDS Church microfilm records of St Kitts, Nevis and Anguilla civil registration and parochial records.

www.familysearch.org/eng/Library/FHLC/frameset_fhlc.asp
The LDS Family History Library catalog. Search on 'St Christopher' for a collection of St Kitts records, some of it on microfilm: French censuses, French parish registers, civil registration, land records.

The International Genealogical Index (now within FamilySearch) and related records should also be searched for individuals from St Kitts.

National Museum, St Kitts. Photograph by John Titford.

CHAPTER EIGHTEEN
St Lucia

Alternative names: Iouanalao, Hewanorra, St Alouisie/ St Alouziel.

LOCATION

St Lucia lies twenty miles to the south of Martinique and thirty miles to the north-east of its Windward Islands neighbour, St Vincent. Essentially oblong in shape, it is much broader in the south than in the north and has a total area of 238 square miles, making it rather larger than the Isle of Man.

St Lucia has been described as 'a wild picturesque island with broken shores...as dainty and beautiful an island as the heart could wish...extremely and fantastically mountainous...', the most famous of its mountains being the Gros Piton and Petit Piton, two rocky peaks rising sheer out of the sea to a height of over 2000 feet, behind which lies the Soufrière, a volcanic crater which still spits forth jets of steam from sulphur springs beneath. Two large plains are more friendly to human habitation than the island's mountains and dense forests, these being Vieux Fort in the south-east, and Gros Islet in the north-west The island's capital, Castries, is situated at the head of a bay of the same name on the leeward western coast; to the north of it lies the bay of Gros Islet and the fortified

outpost known as Pigeon Island, once a favourite haunt of pirates. Soufrière, the second largest of the island's towns (and the oldest, having been established in 1746) may be found further south on the same coast, while the south coast itself is home to the little town of Vieux Fort.

HISTORY

St Lucia, known to the Arawak Indians as Iouanalao, and later as Hewanorra, St Alouisie or St Alouziel, was traditionally said to have derived its present name (pronounced 'Saint Loosha') from the fact that Columbus arrived there on St Lucy's Day (13th December) in the year 1502 - a theory discredited in more recent times. It seems more likely that it was the French who named the island after St Lucy of Syracuse.

The island was for long a battle-ground between the French and the British. The Dutch had paid a visit there in the early years of the seventeenth century and built a fortified base at Vieux Fort, but in the year 1605 St Lucia would become, in effect, the earliest English colony in the West Indies. In that year sixty seven passengers and men bound for Guiana aboard the ship *Olive Branch* (alias the *Oliph Blossome*, named after its owner, Sir Olive Leigh) landed there but were driven off or killed by the Indians after little more than a month. Eleven would-be settlers survived, and four returned to England.

The English may have been the first to settle St Lucia, if only briefly, but the Kings of France also claimed it for themselves from at least as early as 1635, leasing it at various times to the French West India Company and to a number of private individuals. The English would not be brushed aside, however, and would fight both the native inhabitants and the French for possession if they had to. From 1640 onwards various settlers arrived from St Kitts, Bermuda and Barbados, and in 1722 the island was granted by King George I to the Duke of Montague, who sent out his own colonisers who were met with an irresistible French force from Martinique.

The reality of the Anglo-French animosities slowly became apparent: neither nation could maintain power for long, and in 1748 the treaty of Aix-la-Chapelle declared that St Lucia should be neutral territory. Not for long: further armed squabbles were to follow, both before and during the time of the Napoleonic Wars.

The convoluted story of conquest and re-conquest approached its end as the nineteenth century dawned. St Lucia was restored to France at the Peace of Amiens in 1802, but was finally ceded to Britain in 1814, having changed hands no fewer than fourteen times since the early seventeenth century. Hence its nickname, 'Helen of the West Indies' - fought over passionately, as Helen of Troy was, by rival suitors.

In the nineteenth century it was the turn of Scots and others to boost a flagging population. Following the emancipation of the slaves in 1838, a number of indentured labourers were imported from India; by 1917 a total of 4,000 had arrived, and their present-day descendants contribute to the cultural and ethnic mix in evidence on the island. Most present-day inhabitants of St Lucia are of African descent, and many speak a French-English patois; French influence is further in evidence in some aspects of the island's legal system, its architecture, its place-names and its cooking, and a large proportion of the population is Roman Catholic.

In 1838 the island was included in the Windward Islands government, with a Governor resident first in Barbados and then in Grenada. In 1967 it achieved self-government, followed by full independence within the Commonwealth in 1979.

St Lucia has been subject to many natural disasters over the years. During the period 1756 to 1831 it was visited by no fewer than six hurricanes; an earthquake of 1839 did a great amount of damage, and Castries was devastated by four enormous fires between 1796 and 1948, during the last of which irreparable damage was done to public and private files, records and archives. In particular an important collection of historic documents built up by Mr. Tom Ferguson was destroyed.

Coaling, Port Castries, St Lucia. Labour was cheap...

ECONOMY

In 1765 two Frenchmen started the sugar industry at Vieux Fort, and in time slaves from West Africa were imported to work in a series of small sugar plantations. In general terms the African population of St Lucia descends from two tribes - the Dahomey, mainly imported by the French, and the Ashanti, brought in by the British. Sugar, general agriculture, and the export of bananas in particular, has long been a mainstay of the economy of the island, though tourism is now a major foreign exchange earner.

PEOPLE

- John Nicholl, one of the survivors of the abortive *Olive Branch* landing in 1605, published an account of his experiences two years later under the title *An Houre Glasse of Indian Newes*, and the names of various members of the party featured in his book are helpfully abstracted in *Caribbean Historical and Genealogical Journal*, January 1998:

    Captain Nicholas Sen-Johns (in charge of the expedition); Alexander Sen-Johns (his brother); William Turner, John Nicholl, Captain Catlin (the ship's captain); Captain Arthur Chambers (the ship's master); Miles Pet; Philip Glascock; John Rogers; Francis Brace; James Garret; Richard Garrat [sic]; Evans; Tench; Looking; Browne (gold-finer); George Browne (his son), three sailors named John Fleming, Thomas Butler and Owen (a Welshman); John and Christopher (no surnames recorded); Budge; Robert Shaw; William Kettleby; Stokely (later a merchant in Bucklersbury) and Harry, his man.

- On 23 June 1763 the future Empress Josephine of France was born at Paix Bouche in the north of the island, and the ruins of the estate house where the event took place can still be seen.

- The first President of St Lucia was Alexander Moir (1882-1883); a series of Commissioners and Administrators followed, until Frederick Phillips became the first Governor (1967-1971).

- St Lucia has been the home of two distinguished Nobel laureates: the economist Sir Arthur Lewis and the poet and playwright Derek Walcott.

RECORDS (UK REPOSITORIES)

The National Archives, London.
Colonial Office records relating to St Lucia - correspondence (from 1709), sessional papers, gazettes, etc - and to the Windward Islands as a whole are relevant sources. CO 253/7 is a nominal census (in French) for St Lucia taken in 1811, and various other Colonial Office records of a miscellaneous nature contain names of individuals. Treasury: T71 includes records generated by the Slave Compensation Commission, 1815-1834, and claims are indexed in T71/884.
Records before 1814 are held in French archives.

British Library, London
The British Library has a number of St Lucia newspapers not found on the island itself, of which a list appears in E C Baker's *A guide to records in the Windward Islands* (1968), pages 62-63.

RECORDS (LOCALLY-HELD)

Churches
By 1780 there were eleven *quartiers* (districts or quasi-ecclesiastical parishes) on St Lucia, overseen by the Dominicans and the Capuchins. Each was canonically established, but also recognised by the French Civil Law.

Roman Catholic priests in France had long had a responsibility to maintain records of baptism, marriage and burial for civil as well as ecclesiastical purposes, a privilege which was withdrawn from them at the time of the revolution in France, but reinstated in St Lucia once the British took over in 1803. Not all burial records are complete: a number of poorer families on the island would bury their dead without benefit of clergy and without any written record being made.

Protestantism became the dominant religion in St Lucia in 1814, and five years later the first Protestant clergyman was appointed to the island. The Protestant church in Castries opened for worship in 1832, an adjoining graveyard being established two years later.

E C Baker's *A guide to records in the Windward Islands* (1968) includes a list of Roman Catholic, Anglican, Baptist, Methodist, Presbyterian and other denominational church records then held in the Chief Registrar's room. These include registers of baptism, marriage and burial for Castries and for other districts and churches. The earliest records listed are those for the Roman Catholic church in Castries, dating from 1805.

Some records were also held in Holy Trinity Church, Castries: baptisms and marriages from 1825, with burials (including members of the garrison) from 1827; Dennery Church records from 1927; registers of Christchurch, Soufrière (baptisms and burials from 1833, marriages from 1844).

In 1968 Bishop Charles Gachet was forming a Roman Catholic archive collection and was calling in all records more than a hundred years old from the island's churches. Baker lists various such records, including registers of baptism, marriage and burial (from 1770) and a number of vestry minute books. Baker also provides a list of various Roman Catholic parish registers (dating from 1763) which were deposited in the Charteres des Colonies in 1793.

Holy Trinity Church, Castries, St Lucia.
Photograph by John Titford.

Methodist missionaries had first arrived in St Lucia in 1855, but did not establish a permanent presence there until 1910. The fire which swept through Castries in 1948 destroyed the Methodist manse and the records which were kept there; subsequent registers of baptism, marriage and burial were then housed in the new manse. Records of Methodist baptisms in the Windward Islands, 1914 to 1954, are held at Methodist Headquarters in Nassau, Bahamas.

Civil registration
Compulsory registration of births and deaths was introduced in the island by an ordnance of 1868, and records date from 1st January 1869. The registration of marriages is governed by the Civil Code of St Lucia, 1879. Records are held by the Registrar of Civil Status, Peynier Street, Castries.

Census
Decennial censuses on St Lucia began in 1851; the population numbered 26,674 in 1861 and had risen to 51,505 by 1921.

Other original records held on the island
E C Baker's *A guide to records in the Windward Islands* (1968) provides a useful overview of records relating to the Windward Islands as a whole, and summarises the situation regarding St Lucia in particular. David Parker, visiting the island in the 1920s, stumbled across a cache of nearly two tons of manuscripts in a loft above

the treasury, only to find that dust, bats, spiders and other insects had got there first. Parker found no administrative records earlier than 1817, and it would appear that practically all the papers, registers and archives then kept in the Registry of St Lucia were burnt in a fire at Castries in 1796 when the British were attacking the French. Further fires at Castries in 1927 and 1948 did their worst, though most of the registrar's records appear to have been rescued.

Baker's list of records held on the island in 1968 is exceptionally useful, as ever. Here is a brief summary:

> In the Chief Registrar's record room: various court, bankruptcy, inquest, jury and execution records; deeds and land title record books (in French, from 1829); index of wills, 1807-1879; marriage contracts 1847-1879; registers of medical practitioners and Friendly Societies. In the Administrative Building: various legal and administrative records, mainly twentieth century in date. A range of other archive material was then held in the Chief Minister's Office, The Chief Secretary's Office, Government House and elsewhere, including the offices and homes of various private companies and individuals. An important collection of material, some of it early in date, was held by the St Lucia Archaeological and Historical Society, including some deeds and wills, 1808-1850.

Joan E Mount further reported on St Lucia archives in the 1980s (*Research guide to Central America and the Caribbean*, edited by K J Grieb, 1985, pages 378-379). At that time most documentary resources were in the care of the St Lucia Archaeological and Historical Society, who were planning to establish an archive centre which would house, amongst other records, those of the Roman Catholic Church on the island from 1750. The chief registrar's room then held not only records of births and deaths from 1869, but also a sizeable collection of deeds.

Records currently held at the National Archives, PO Box 3060, Clarke Street, Vigie, Castries, include: court, bankruptcy, inquest, jury and execution records; deeds and land title record books; index of wills, 1807-1879; marriage contracts 1847-1879; registers of medical practitioners and Friendly Societies.

The St Lucia Archaeological and Historical Society holds an important collection of early material, including some deeds and wills, 1808-1850.

SECONDARY SOURCES: PRINTED WORKS, etc.

A gravestone, Holy Trinity, Castries, St Lucia. A soldier from Wakefield, Yorkshire, finds his last resting place in St Lucia. Photograph by John Titford.

Monumental inscriptions

V L Oliver's *The monumental inscriptions of the British West Indies* (1927) features four entries taken from inside the church of Holy Trinity, Castries, St Lucia (page 211). These are for: William Pattison (a native of Glasgow, died 12 February 1843, aged 50), Rev Charles Sims (Protestant pastor, died 1842), Mary Jane Reid (daughter of Robert Reid, died 31 August 1852, aged 8) and Sir Charles Bruce (Governor of the Windward Islands, stone laid on 25 November 1894).

Of the naval and military burial grounds on St Lucia mentioned by Oliver - at La Toc, Pigeon Island and Morne Fortuné - the latter in particular still bears eloquent testimony to the French and English soldiers, many of them very young, who lie buried there.

Oliver's *Caribbeana*, volume 4, includes references to two monumental inscriptions of St.Lucia inhabitants to be found in England: one in Cheltenham, Gloucestershire (Charles Knowles Davernet, died 1815) and one in Hove, Sussex, (Lieutenant Henry Sandeman, died 1852).

Probate records

Lists of wills proved and administrations granted in the Prerogative Court of Canterbury featured in Oliver's *Caribbeana* include a number of individuals from St Lucia.

Deeds and other records

Caribbeana is of surprisingly little help to the researcher so far as St Lucia is concerned, though volume two features details of an indenture of 1822 relating to the Union Estate on the island.

FURTHER READING

Breen, H H *St Lucia: historical, statistical and descriptive*. 1844, reprinted 1970. The most substantial book on St Lucia's history. Contains two lists of 'Returns of vacant or intestate successions in the Colony of St Lucia'. The first (pages 384-386), covering 1808 to 1831, includes surnames only, with occasional Christian names, year by year; the second (pages 387-388), covering 1831 to 1844, gives the surname and full Christian name or initials of the person to whom the 'vacant succession' applies, followed by the name of the administrator and a date. In each case the surnames are a mixture of French and British.

Ellis, G *Saint Lucia: Helen of the West Indies*. 3rd.ed.1994.

Garraway, E G *The St Lucia Handbook, Directory and Almanac*. 1899. Includes a Post Office directory of residents, officials, etc. Also later editions.

Jesse, C *Outlines of St Lucia's history*. St Lucia Archaeological and Historical Society. 3rd edition,1970; revised edition 1994.

Jesse, C *Saint Lucia Miscellany*. Vol.1: *St Lucia: the romance of its place-names* (1966); Volume 2: *Early days, 1493-1763* (1969). St Lucia Archaeological and Historical Society.

Molloy, L *Saint Lucia past: a pictorial history*. 1996.

Pilgrim, J H *Snippets of St Lucia's history* (c1960).

South America, Central America, Mexico, West Indies Directory, 1898. Includes a substantial list of professional and commercial individuals and companies on St Lucia. A copy may be seen at the Society of Genealogists in London.

Titford, J 'Settlers of the Old Empire: The West Indies: St Lucia', *Family Tree Magazine*, June 2002.

Waite, L *St Lucia the brave*. 1997. A general history.

WEBSITES

www.britishislesgenweb.org/stlucia/
St Lucia CaribbeanGenWeb: St Lucia Genealogy Project. Links to bulletin boards and a mailing list.

http://boards.ancestry.co.uk/localities.caribbean.stlucia/mb.ashx
Ancestry.co.uk St Lucia message board.

www.cousinconnect.com/p/a/146/
CousinConnect.com St Lucia genealogy enquiries.

www.membres.lycos.fr/schmittg/carte_a.html
Maps of St Lucia, Castries, etc.

www.familysearch.org/eng/Library/FHLC/frameset_fhlc.asp
The LDS Family History Library catalog. Search on 'Saint Lucia' for a limited collection of material, some of it on microfilm, including a French census and French parish registers.

The International Genealogical Index (now within FamilySearch) and related records should also be searched for individuals from St Lucia. |

CHAPTER NINETEEN
St Vincent

Alternative name: Hairoun

LOCATION

St Vincent, lying 97 miles west of Barbados, is an oval-shape volcanic island, eighteen miles long, with a backbone of densely-wooded mountains running from north to south, at the northern end of which lies the Soufrière, an active volcano. The Grenadines constitute a chain of about 600 islands, stretched out over an area of 40 miles. Those in the north are dependencies of St Vincent, while those in the south are dependencies of Grenada. The northern Grenadines include the islands of Bequia (the largest), Mustique, Union Island, Petit St Vincent, Canouan and Palm Island. There are five parishes on St Vincent: Charlotte, St Andrew, St David, St Patrick and St George (home of the capital, Kingstown).

HISTORY

Columbus 'discovered' St Vincent on 22 January (St Vincent's Day), 1498. Although the island was granted by English Kings to various proprietors during the seventeenth and early eighteenth centuries, Carib Indian hostility prevented its being formally settled until 1763, when it was declared to be a British possession by the terms of the Treaty of Paris.

199

Following a series of armed struggles, the so-called Black Caribs (descendants of runaway slaves and others who had taken Carib wives) were granted a reservation in the north of the island in 1773. St Vincent became a British Crown Colony three years later, a status that was confirmed by the Treaty of Versailles in 1783. The Caribs who revolted in 1795 under the leadership of the French radical Victor Hugues were eventually deported to the island of Roatan in the Bay of Honduras, and following the abolition of slavery in 1834, Portuguese (1840s) and East Indian (1860s) workers were imported to make up a labour shortfall. From 1763 to 1776, and from 1833 to 1956, St Vincent was a member of the Windward Islands; in 1969 it became a member of the Associated States of the West Indies, and ten years later it was the last of the Windward Islands to gain independence, becoming a Dominion known as St Vincent and the Grenadines.

ECONOMY

Eighteenth century settlers cultivated coffee, tobacco, indigo, cotton and sugar on plantations worked by African slaves. In more recent times the growing of bananas, Sea Island cotton and arrowroot starch, together with tourism, have been the main source of revenue. Natural disasters have conspired to disrupt the economy over the years, the worst of which have been various eruptions of the Soufrière volcano (in 1812, 1902 and 1979), together with destructive hurricanes such as the one which destroyed the church in Kingstown in 1780, and others which arrived during the closing decades of the twentieth century.

PEOPLE

• Seventeenth century proprietors of St Vincent were James Hay, Earl of Carlisle (1627-1636) and William, Lord Willougby of Parham (1672-1673); the first Lieutenant-Governor was George Maddison (1763-1764); the first Governor was Valentine Morris (1776-1779); the first Administrator was Robert Llewellyn (1886-1889); the first Governor-General was Sir Sidney Gun-Munro (1979-1985).

• The first Governor, Valentine Morris, from Piercefield, Monmouthshire, found to his dismay that the authorities in England dishonoured bills which he had drawn on the Treasury; he was prosecuted, had to sell his considerable estates in England and the West Indies, and was thrown into the King's Bench Prison. He died in September, 1789.

• Captain William Bligh, having survived the famous *Bounty* mutiny, arrived in St Vincent in 1792 aboard the *Providence*, bringing with him the breadfruit from Tahiti which the St Vincent planters had first desired him to collect.

- Early Wesleyan Methodist missionaries in St Vincent include Revs Clarke, Gamble, Werrill and Baxter, followed by Rev Matthew Lumb, who was gaoled in the 1790s for preaching to the black population there. In 1794 he was succeeded by Thomas Owens.

- 'The Spotted Boy'. During the eighteenth century, a poor orphan boy from St Vincent with an unusual skin pigmentation (vitiligo) was hawked around the macabre freak-show circuit in England before being adopted by John Richardson of Marlow, Bucks, who named him George Alexander Gratton. When the boy died prematurely in 1813, Richardson arranged for him to be buried in a plot in All Saints Church, Marlow, which he had earmarked for himself.

RECORDS (UK REPOSITORIES)

The National Archives, London. Colonial Office correspondence (from 1668), sessional papers, gazettes, etc., land and plantation records.

Treasury: T71 includes records generated by the Slave Compensation Commission, 1817-1834, and claims are indexed in T71/938.

Further relevant records may be found in archives relating to the Windward Islands (from 1873) and to the West Indies, general (from 1951).

RECORDS (LOCALLY-HELD)

E C Baker's *A guide to records in the Windward Islands* (1968) provides a useful overview of records relating to the Windward Islands as a whole, and summarises the situation regarding St Vincent in particular, listing an impressive range of public and private records, then held (in 1968) in a range of separate record repositories, These include: acts and ordinances, deed record books, manumissions, land grants, probate records (from 1799), court records, church records, correspondence and dispatches, blue books, and school and hospital records. He also lists registers held by individual Anglican, Methodist and Roman Catholic churches.

This paints a rosy picture, but over the years horror stories have abounded about the condition and poor storage condition of archive material on St Vincent, much of which was said at one time to have been lying in a heap on a porous limestone floor. One report even said that some record books were in such a fragile condition that they could only be accessed in a special room which required researchers to wear a respirator!

Considerable efforts to improve matters have been made in more recent times by the Archives Department (Cotton Ginnery Compound, Frenches, Kingstown). which was established in 1990, and it is hoped that these will go some way to improving matters. Family historians with an interest in records held by St Vincent Archives will need either to pay a personal visit, or employ a locally-based researcher to carry out work on their behalf.

Church records are held by individual churches.

The Cathedral, King's Town, St Vincent. Photograph by John Titford.

Left: A gravestone, Cathedral churchyard, King's Town, St Vincent. A man from Stafford has died of sunstroke. Photograph by John Titford. Right: A memorial plaque inside the Cathedral, King's Town, St Vincent. Henry Arrindell Hazell had been a member of the island's legislative council. Photograph by John Titford.

Civil registration. The Registrar General's Office, Government Buildings, Kingstown, has records of birth, marriage and death from 1863.

GENEALOGICAL SOURCES HELD ELSEWHERE

Records relating to St Vincent before 1783 are held in French repositories. Methodist baptisms for the Windward Islands, 1914-54, are held at the Methodist Headquarters, Nassau, Bahamas.

SECONDARY SOURCES: PRINTED WORKS, etc.

Tracing your West Indian ancestors: sources in the Public Record Office (1995) by Guy Grannum: figure 3 (page 10) shows a list of voters on St Vincent (1868) and figure 4 (page 11) a St Vincent tax return (1870). These two illustrations do not appear in the same author's enlarged work, *Tracing your West Indian ancestors* (2002).

V L Oliver's *Caribbeana* (1910-1920) has lists of wills proved and administrations granted in the Prerogative Court of Canterbury which feature residents of St Vincent, 1776-1799, 1801-1811, 1813-1816.

FURTHER READING

Aleong, J Chin *The picture postcards of St Vincent and the Grenadines*. 2003. An excellent illustrated survey.

Fraser, A and K Joseph *Our country: St Vincent and the Grenadines*. 1998.

Potter, R B *St Vincent and the Grenadines*. 1992.

Ross, R A and L J *Parish records of St George parish, St Vincent*. N.D. (c 1980s) Extracts from 18th and 19th century baptisms, marriages and burials. Available as a book and on microfilm: see LDS Church Family History Library Catalog.

St Vincent handbook, directory and almanack. 2nd edition, 1909.

Shephard, C *An historical account of the Island of St Vincent*. 1831. Reprinted 1971, 1997. Some general history of the islands, much detailed information on the armed struggles of the 1790s, and useful appendices which include statistical information and the many names of individuals: a late eighteenth-century apportionment of Carib lands [names of original occupants and their present estates - including one called 'God save the King']; compensation of £25,000 granted to the sufferers by the volcanic eruption (1812-1813) [names of individuals, estimated loss, amount paid]; militia commissions [names, 1787-1828] and references to John Byres' plan of the island (1776) [surnames (only) of original purchasers, and present estates]. The text of the book itself includes the names of various individuals killed during the armed struggles of the 1790s, a list (page 85) of the officers appointed to the Corps of Rangers and details of two notorious murders (Charles Warner, a planter, murdered by two of his own slaves in 1797, and Major Champion of the 21st Regiment, shot dead by a private named Ballasty in 1824).

Sutty, L *St Vincent and the Grenadines: an introduction and guide*. 1997.

WEBSITES

www.rootsweb.com/~vctwgw/
St Vincent and the Grenadines SVG GenWeb. Includes a number of transcripts of records from the St. Vincent and the Grenadines Genealogy Research website (see below).

www.cousinconnect.com/p/a/147/
CousinConnect.com St Vincent and the Grenadines genealogy enquiries.

http://sv.usaroots.com/
St Vincent and the Grenadines genealogy research. An excellent wide-ranging guide to research, featuring on-line name-lists and much else, which includes records of births, deaths, baptisms, wills, government officials, newspapers, land and property records, estate and plantation records, a history of the island, a time-line, etc.

www.familysearch.org/eng/Library/FHLC/frameset_fhlc.asp
The LDS Family History Library catalog. Search on 'Saint Vincent' for a limited collection of records on microfilm: French censuses, extracts of parish records, St George parish 1765-1870.

The International Genealogical Index (now within FamilySearch) and related records should also be searched for individuals from St Vincent.

CHAPTER TWENTY
Tobago

See also: **TRINIDAD.** Alternative name: **NEW WALCHEREN.**

LOCATION

Tobago, said to be the island from which Daniel Defoe drew his inspiration for the setting of *Robinson Crusoe*, has for long been associated with neighbouring Trinidad. A small cigar-shaped island lying east-west, only twenty-six miles long and nine miles wide, it has a central forested range of hills in the north but is flat and undulating in the south-west. The population is generally concentrated in the west of the island around Scarborough (formerly called 'St Louis'), which is the capital. Inhabitants of the island are referred to as 'Tobagonians' (not 'Toboggans'...).

HISTORY

Tobago has changed hands more often than any other island in the West Indies - almost thirty times, by some reckonings. It was sighted by Christopher Columbus in 1498, at the same time that he first came across Trinidad. The island was then inhabited by Carib Indians, who grew tobacco there (hence the name 'Tobago'), and they successfully put an end to the attempts of a party of English settlers from Barbados to make their home there in 1625.

The title-page of the second edition of a 56-page book on Tobago written by Captain John Poyntz, 1695.

Thereafter the English, the Spanish and the Dutch fought for control, until the island was declared neutral under the terms of the Treaty of Aix-la-Chapelle in 1748. For all that, Britain and France went to war over Tobago in 1756, until eventually, following further bouts of armed conflict between the two nations, it was officially ceded to Britain in 1814.

A particularly virulent hurricane struck the island in 1847, and in general its economy began to suffer as a result of a general depression in the West Indies sugar industry. It became part of the Windward Islands group and later, in 1899, was declared to be a ward of the new colony of Trinidad and Tobago. These islands became a dominion within the British Commonwealth in 1962, and adopted a republican form of government in 1976. Tobago has its own House of Assembly with limited control over internal affairs.

Fort George, Tobago, from Morne Grace, drawn by Captain Frederick Maitland, 1793.

ECONOMY

The island has fertile soil, in which a variety of tropical products can be grown. Sugar, once the staple industry, was eventually replaced by the cultivation of cocoa, coconuts, coffee and nutmegs. In more recent times tourism has proved to be a significant money-earner, though in general Tobago is dependent on Trinidad for a great deal of economic support.

PEOPLE

• One of the earliest visitors to the island from England was Sir Robert Dudley.

• The first British Governor of Tobago was Alexander Brown (1764-1766); the first Administrator was Augustus Frederick Gore (1877-1880); the first Commissioner was Loraine Gedded Hay (1889-1892) and the first Governor of Trinidad and Tobago was Sir Hubert Edward Henry Jerningham (1899-1900).

• Early missionaries from the London Missionary Society serving on the island included Richard Elliott (1808) and Isaac Purkis (1809).

• The first Wesleyan missionary appointed in Tobago was Rev J Rayner (1817). He was succeeded by Revs Smedly, Larcum, Nelson, Stephenson, Powell, Wood, Blackwell, Ranyell, Bickford, Hurd and others.

• In 1790 the Moravian mission on Tobago was in the hands of a planter called Hamilton. The first Moravian missionary appointed there was John Montgomery, father of the hymn writer and poet, James Montgomery.

RECORDS (UK REPOSITORIES)

The National Archives, London. Colonial Office: correspondence (from 1700), sessional papers, gazettes, etc; nominal census 1770 (CO101/14, ff.126-127); eighteenth century land grants. Treasury: T71 includes records generated by the Slave Compensation Commission, 1819-1834, and claims are indexed in T71/937. Further records relating to Tobago are held in TNA with those of Barbados and Grenada, and also under 'France', 'Windward Islands' and 'West Indies General'. For the period after 1888, see Trinidad.

RECORDS (LOCALLY-HELD)

Most archive material relevant to Tobago, including land records, deeds and decennial censuses for 1851, 1861 and 1891, are held by the National Archives in Trinidad, though in 1903 the government building in Port of Spain was destroyed by fire, and administrative and other records were lost, including many relating to Tobago. Records still held in Tobago consist mainly of minutes and documents relating to the Assembly and the Legislative Council. The archives have been closed to the public since an earthquake in the mid 1990s virtually destroyed the public library building in which they were housed.

Churches

Anglican: there are twenty Anglican churches and four Anglican parishes on Tobago. Original records of Anglican baptism, marriage and burial (1818-1873; 1873-1899; 1900 onwards), all in fair condition, are in the custody of St Andrew's Rectory, Bacolet Street, Scarborough, Tobago. The oldest church in Tobago, St Patrick's at Mount Pleasant, currently holds registers of baptism (from 1844), marriage (from 1846) and burial (from 1857). The Diocesan Office of the Anglican Church at 21 Maraval Road, Hayes Court, Port of Spain, Trinidad, is able to offer a certain amount of assistance to anyone researching Anglican records in Trinidad or Tobago.

Methodist: there are ten Methodist churches and one Methodist circuit on Tobago. Original registers of Methodist baptisms (from 1877), marriages (from 1839) and burials (from 1939) are held by the office of the Methodist Church, Bacolet Street, Scarborough, Tobago. Methodist burial records for Tobago have not been destroyed, unlike those for Trinidad. There are no Baptist or Church of Scotland churches in Tobago.

Roman Catholic: there are six Roman Catholic churches on Tobago, and two Roman Catholic parishes. Enquiries regarding records of baptism (from 1891), marriage (from 1920) and burial (dates not established) should be addressed to PO Box 290, Scarborough, Tobago.

Moravian: the Moravians have been active in Tobago since 1790; only later did they turn their attentions to Trinidad. The church has a policy of centralizing its archives, and early records of Moravian baptism, marriage and burial on Tobago have been transferred to the Moravian Theological Seminary, Market Street, Bethlehem, Pennsylvania, USA. It is intended to relocate these registers in the Caribbean area at some stage - possibly on Antigua - once appropriate storage facilities have been found. Requests regarding later records - of baptism from 1877, of marriage from 1863 and of burial from 1878 - should be addressed to the Montgomery Moravian Manse, Bethel, Tobago.

Civil registration

Civil registration on Tobago became compulsory on 30 January 1868. Records from then onwards are held at the Registrar General's Department, Registration House, 72-74 South Quay, Port-of-Spain, Trinidad. An unknown number of records were destroyed during the Water Riots of 1903, and many of those which survive are in poor condition, though some have been removed for conservation. The Registrar General's Office of Tobago is at Jerningham Street, Scarborough.

Cemeteries.
There was no public cemetery in Tobago until after the Second World War; all burial records prior to that time would form part of the archives of the relevant churches.

Other useful addresses for research in Tobago are:
Tobago Warden's Office, Scarborough.
Trinidad and Tobago National Library and Information Systems Authority, St Vincent Street, Port of Spain, Trinidad.

SECONDARY SOURCES: PRINTED WORKS, etc.

Parish registers

A book entitled *English Protestant Church of Tobago: Register of baptisms, marriages, deaths, from 1781 to 1817*, published by the government printer in Port of Spain in 1936, includes registers kept by the Garrison Chaplain. Scots are very much in evidence throughout these registers: *Burial. 15 Sept.1801. Alex^r McCulloch, a native of Rosshire (Scot^d) res$^{d.}$ at Tobago for about two years, Clerk at M.M. Straikland and Clark, aged about 23. Died on the 15th 7 in the morning after an illness of about three weeks at Mount William, near Scarboro, buried there at 6 o'cl. P.M. the same day*. Natives of other countries also died in Tobago: William Gilmour, carried off by fever on 16th September 1801 at the age of twenty one and buried in ground belonging to his uncle, Mr McNeil of Scarboro, was a native of Exeter; eleven days later fever also proved fatal to John Germaine, aged about thirty, a Lieutenant in the 2nd Battalion, 60th Regiment of Foot. He had come originally from Canada. William Bills, from London, aged nine years, a passenger aboard the *Adventure* en route to Antigua to see an uncle of his, died of fever on 1st May 1802. On 31 October 1812 Frantz Petre, a Corsican who had deserted from the 60th Regiment and who had murdered Lieutenant Watson, was pursued by Major Crook and the Island Rangers, who shot him dead. The register is very careful to distinguish 'White Protestants' from 'Coloured Protestant people', but there is much evidence of racial mixing: *Susannah, a mulatto Girl, born the 12th Jany 1796, daughter of [blank] Wightman Esq. by a black (slave) woman named Kitty was publickly christened at Concordia in the parish of St George in the Island of Tobago by me Rev$^{d.}$ Antony Keighley Thomas A.B. Protestant Rector of Tobago aforesaid*. Copies of this invaluable but scarce book may be consulted at the Society of Genealogists in London and at the National Heritage Library and at the National Archives in Trinidad.

Monumental inscriptions

Oliver, V L *The monumental inscriptions of the British West Indies* (1927) has details of four monumental inscriptions from Government House, Scarborough, Tobago.

Probate records

Oliver, V L *Caribbeana* (1910-1920). Tobago wills proved in the Prerogative Court of Canterbury, 1766-1816, are listed in volumes 2, 3 and 5.

Deeds

Oliver, V L *Caribbeana* (1910-1920). Transcripts of deeds relating to Tobago can be found in volume 3, pages 294-295.

FURTHER READING. See also **Trinidad**.

Alford, C E R *The island of Tobago*. 1949.
Archibald, D *Tobago, Melancholy Isle*. 2 volumes (1498-1771; 1770-1814), 1987 and 1995. Volume two contains a transcript of ten very detailed burial entries from a parish register of people who died from yellow fever, 1801-1802.
Ottley, C R *The story of Tobago*. 1973. A general narrative, one of several books by this prolific author.
Woodcock, H I *A History of Tobago*. 1867, reprinted 1971. Contains, *inter alia*, an extensive list of those who were original grantees of land in 1763, together with the names of 'Present possessors' (as at 1867), arranged by parish. Also a list of estates under cultivation in 1832 and in 1862, with the names of owners (many of the surnames featured being clearly Scottish), and a transcript of the will of Betty Creighton (1815), written in rhymed verse.

WEBSITES. See **Trinidad**.

CHAPTER TWENTY ONE
Trinidad

See also: **TOBAGO**.

LOCATION

Trinidad, the most southern of the Caribbean islands and one which is commonly associated with Tobago, lies only seven miles off the coast of Venezuela. The second largest island in the British West Indies, it is approximately the same size as the English county of Lancashire. The island, which is divided into eight counties, is generally flat, though two ranges of hills cross it from east to west, and one runs diagonally across its centre. Roughly half the population lives in the east-west section of the island, which is urbanised; the central flatlands are used for the cultivation of sugarcane, and there are large areas of swamp on the east and west coasts. Port of Spain in the county of St George, which had been burned to the ground in a fire of 1808 and rebuilt, is the capital. Other settlements of a significant size are at San Fernando and Arima.

Trinidad in the Caribbean should not be confused with an island of the same name in the South Atlantic.

HISTORY

Christopher Columbus came across Trinidad in the year 1498; he had specifically invoked the protection of the Holy Trinity for his third voyage of discovery, and when he also noted the fact that three mountains could be seen together as he approached the island, he named it 'La Trinidad'. Spaniards who shared an optimistic belief that they might one day find the fabled 'El Dorado' were the first settlers; during the seventeenth century the Dutch, the French and the British sought to wrest control of what was becoming a prosperous island, but a blight which practically destroyed the cocoa industry in 1727 resulted in a significant exodus of the population (there being only 162 adult males, excluding slaves, recorded as living there in a census of 1733), and a smallpox epidemic of 1741 killed many inhabitants.

A significant number of French immigrants (white and mixed race) and enslaved Africans arrived in the 1780s and 1790s, and following a struggle between the British, the French and the Spanish, Trinidad became a British possession in 1797, being formerly ceded by the Treaty of Amiens in 1802, and remained so until Trinidad and Tobago, which had been united in 1899, became a dominion within the British Commonwealth in 1962. The islands adopted a republican form of government in 1976. Spain had imported West African slaves to work the plantations from 1702 onwards, and a number of East Indian immigrants from Calcutta were introduced annually under a system of indenture between the years 1845 and 1917.

ECONOMY

Trinidad is blessed with fertile soil, in which every kind of tropical produce can be grown. Exports have included sugar, cocoa, coconuts, copra, coffee, rubber, bitters and timber, though Asphalt and petroleum have proved to be the most important money-earners. The tourist industry in the region is mainly centred on Tobago.

PEOPLE

- Early visitors to the island from England included Sir Walter Raleigh and Sir Robert Dudley, who were both there in the year 1595.

- The first Governor of Trinidad was Sir Ralph Abercromby (1797); the first Governor of Trinidad and Tobago was Sir Hubert Edward Henry Jerningham (1899-1900).

- Early missionaries from the London Missionary Society serving on the island included Thomas Adam (1809), James Mercer (1818) and Thomas Dexter (1823).

- The Wesleyan mission to Trinidad originated in the work of Rev Thomas Talboys, who arrived in 1809 from St Vincent. He was succeeded by the Revs Thomas Blackburn, George Poole, S P Wooley, Edmondson, Stephenson, Fletcher, Fidler, Wood, Beard and others.

The splendidly-named Inspector Uailean Hamish McUistean Gooden-Chisholm of the Trinidad Constabulary in the driving seat of his official car, alongside another officer. This picture was taken in about 1900. Mr Gooden-Chisholm, son of a plantation owner, died in Inverness, Scotland, in 1929, aged 35.

RECORDS (UK REPOSITORIES)

The National Archives, London. Colonial Office: correspondence (from 1783), sessional papers, gazettes, etc; land grants 1814; list of people allowed to remain in Trinidad 1814-1815; list of freeborn men 1824, and various other records which list names.

Treasury: T71 includes records generated by the Slave Compensation Commission, 1813-1834, and claims are indexed in T71/939.

TNA also holds army garrison records of births, baptisms, marriages and burials for Trinidad, 1812-1816, originally held by the General Register Office. Microfiche copies of the relevant indexes are available for consultation.

Further records relating to Trinidad are held in TNA under 'Spain' (before 1797) and 'West Indies General' (after 1951), and also in Spanish, Venezuelan and French archives.

Between 1932 (the year of its foundation) and 1941 the Historical Society of Trinidad and Tobago transcribed something in excess of one thousand documents from the then Public Record Office in London relating to the history of both Trinidad and Tobago from the sixteenth to the mid-nineteenth centuries, many translated from Spanish or French, and including Parliamentary Papers. It distributed copies to relevant repositories, and today they may be seen at the National Archives in Trinidad and at the University Libraries, University of the West Indies, St Augustine, Trinidad and Tobago.

London Metropolitan Archives. Births and baptisms (1851-2) and marriages (1850) for Trinidad may be found in the Bishop of London's Registry records known as 'International Memoranda'.

RECORDS (LOCALLY-HELD)

In 1808 Port of Spain was destroyed by fire, and the public records lost. In 1903 insurgents who were opposed to a recently-imposed water ordinance stormed the Red House and set fire to the government offices; most administrative and other records were lost, including many relating to Tobago.

When Herbert C Bell and David W Parker visited Trinidad in the 1920s, they were able to report that various records, including those of the *cabildo* (and of its successor, the City Council) from 1813 were housed in the Port of Spain Town Hall. Bridget Brereton, reporting in the 1980s for *Research guide to Central America and the Caribbean* (edited by K J Grieb, 1985), confirmed the existence of such records, together with rate books and other records. She also found various letter books, rate books and the like in the Town Hall in San Fernando, the island's second town.

Surviving records relating to the history and administration of Trinidad, some of which will be of interest to family historians, may now be found at The National Archives of Trinidad and Tobago, 105 St Vincent Street (PO Box 763), Port of Spain, Trinidad, which has much manuscript material and a very good and well-maintained collection of Trinidad and Tobago newspapers (some also on microfilm) dating from 1821 onwards.

Churches

Anglican
The office of the Anglican Trinity Cathedral is at 30A St Vincent Street, Port of

214

Spain. There are twenty-eight Anglican parishes or circuits on Trinidad; their bound record books are in excellent condition and organised for ease of use. Baptism and marriage records exist from 1801 and burial records from 1802. The Diocesan Office of the Anglican Church at 21 Maraval Road, Hayes Court, Port of Spain, is able to offer a certain amount of assistance to anyone researching Anglican records in Trinidad or Tobago.

Roman Catholic

The principal Roman Catholic place of worship in Trinidad is the Cathedral of the Immaculate Conception, Independence Square, Port of Spain. There are sixty-two Roman Catholic parishes or circuits on the island; their records are well organised, but many are in very poor condition, the later paper ones having suffered more than the earlier vellum records. Baptism records exist from 1744 and marriages from 1851. The starting date for burial records could not be determined. The archivist for Roman Catholic Church records is not able to offer assistance to researchers, but the office at Archbishop's House, 27 Maraval Road, Port of Spain, can provide useful information on parishes.

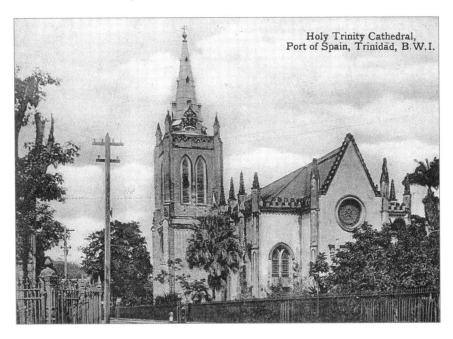

Holy Trinity Cathedral, Port of Spain, Trinidad.

Methodist

Methodist Church records are kept at the Methodist Superintendent Minister's Office at 1 Victoria Avenue, Port of Spain. The bound record books relating to the

21 Methodist circuits are generally in fair condition. Baptism records exist from 1817 and marriages from 1848. There are no burial records, and it is the church's policy to destroy these after a given period has elapsed.

Baptist
The Baptist Church has been in Trinidad since 1854. Its records from 1908 onwards have been lodged with the National Archives in order to save them from further deterioration, but no information is available on the existence or location of any records before this date.

Church of Scotland
There are three Church of Scotland churches. Their records are in fair condition and are kept at Greyfriars Church, 50 Frederick Street, Port of Spain. Baptism and marriage records exist from 1837, and burial records from 1839.

Moravian
The church has a policy of centralizing its archives, and early records of Moravian baptism, marriage and burial on Trinidad have been transferred to the Moravian Theological Seminary, Market Street, Bethlehem, Pennsylvania, USA, where enquiries may be addressed. It is intended to relocate these registers in the Caribbean area at some stage - possibly on Antigua - once appropriate storage facilities have been found. Requests regarding later records - of baptism from 1890 and of burial from 1892 - should be addressed to the Moravian Church Office, 129 Laventille Road, Port of Spain, Trinidad. The marriage records from 1890 are being housed temporarily at the National Archives in Port of Spain while restoration is being undertaken. It is planned to return them to the church in due course.

Trinidad has been home to a number of Quakers, Jews and other believers over the years, but any relevant institutional records of birth, marriage and death are not known to be in existence.

Civil registration.
The Registrar General's Department, Registration House, 72-74 South Quay, Port-of-Spain, which also houses the companies' registry and the land registry, has various deeds, land and legal records (some from the late eighteenth century, but principally from 1865), generally in poor condition. Civil registration on Trinidad became compulsory on 1 January 1848, though some records exist for the years 1844 and 1846. An unknown number of records were destroyed during the water riots of 1903. Many of the records which survive are in poor condition, and those worst affected have been removed for conservation. The Registrar General has sub-offices in Arima and San Fernando, which also issue certificates.

Census
Returns for decennial censuses for Trinidad from 1851 onwards are kept at the National Archives.

Probate records, etc.
The Supreme Court of Judicature, Hall of Justice, Knox Street, Port of Spain, together with the National Archives, holds all-island probate and Port of Spain court records from 1905 onwards. All such material of an earlier date was destroyed during the riots of 1903, except for records relating to courts held at the city of San Fernando, which date from about the year 1846, the year in which English law was introduced to the island.

Monumental inscriptions
When V L Oliver visited Trinidad in the 1920s, he reported that he had no time to copy any of the 'many hundreds' of inscriptions from memorial stones (the earliest he noticed being dated 1838) in the Lapeyrouse Cemetery in Port of Spain. Records relating to Lapeyrouse from 1865 onwards are now held at the cemetery itself, where conditions are not favourable and some deterioration is taking place. Researchers with an interest in these records should contact the Port of Spain Corporation, City Hall, Knox Street, Port of Spain.

Other useful addresses for research in Trinidad, particularly for printed and microform material, are:

National Heritage Library, 8 Knox Street, Port of Spain.
The University Libraries, University of the West Indies, St Augustine, Trinidad and Tobago.
Trinidad and Tobago National Library and Information Systems Authority, Hart and Abercromby Streets, Port of Spain.

SECONDARY SOURCES: PRINTED WORKS, etc.

Probate records

Some Trinidad wills proved in the Prerogative Court of Canterbury are listed in volumes 2, 3 and 5 of V L Oliver's *Caribbeana* (1910-1920).

Monumental inscriptions

Oliver, V L *The monumental inscriptions of the British West Indies* (1927) has details of monumental inscriptions from the Cathedral and from the Peschier Burial ground (private), both in Port of Spain.

FURTHER READING

Anthony, M *Historical dictionary of Trinidad and Tobago.* 1997.

Anthony, M *Profile Trinidad: a historical survey from the discovery to 1900.* 1975.

Brereton, B *A history of modern Trinidad 1783-1962.* 1981.

Brereton, B *Dictionary of Caribbean biography. Vol 1. Trinidad and Tobago.* 1998.

Carmichael, G *History of the West Indian islands of Trinidad and Tobago 1498-1900.* 1961. A book devoted in the main to the period 1797-1846.

Chambers, F *Trinidad and Tobago* (World bibliographical series, vol 74). 1986.

De Verteuil, L A A *Trinidad: its geography, natural resources, administration, present condition and prospects.* 1858.

Fraser, L M *History of Trinidad (1781-1839).* Two volumes, 1891 and 1896, reprinted 1971. Immensely detailed on political and constitutional history, and makes use of the early minutes of the Cabildo (1733-1813) which are now lost, having possibly been destroyed in the fire of 1903, along with a planned third volume of Fraser's work, covering the years 1840-1865, which was never published.

Handbook of Trinidad and Tobago. 1924.

Joseph, E *History of Trinidad.* 1838, reprinted 1970. Contains extracts from Cabildo records, many of which have since been destroyed.

Mount, G S and J E *Historical resources in Trinidad.* A paper presented to the Conference of Latin American Historians, Washington DC (December 1976).

Sewlal, E 'List of archives of Trinidad and Tobago' in *Report of the Caribbean Archives Conference 1965.*

The Trinidad review. Second year of issue, London, 1899. Includes commercial directories and a substantial biographical section ('Cyclopaedic record of public officers, etc') giving birth dates, education, employment, etc..

Williams, E *History of the people of Trinidad and Tobago.* 1962. The author founded the *Caribbean Historical Review*, which he also edited during its short life, 1950-1954.

WEBSITES

www.rootsweb.com/~ttowgw/
Trinidad and Tobago GenWeb page.

www.rootsweb.ancestry.com/~caribgw/cgw_archive/archive.htm
Links to: A Handbook of the Island of Tobago, 1899; list of Governors of Tobago; selections from Colonial Offices of Tobago; selections from Trinidad Colonial Handbooks; selected Cemetery Inscriptions; Governors of Trinidad; Trinidad Civil Service Officers.

http://natt.gov.tt
National Archives of Trinidad and Tobago. Includes a collections listing.

www.nalis.gov.tt
Trinidad and Tobago National Library and Information Systems Authority.

www.mainlib.uwi.tt
Library of the University of the West Indies, St Augustine.

http://genforum.genealogy.com/trinidad/
Trinidad Family Genealogy Forum.

www.cousinconnect.com/p/a/175/
CousinConnect.com Trinidad and Tobago genealogy queries.

http://boards.ancestry.co.uk/localities.caribbean.trinidad/mb.ashx
Ancestry.co.uk Trinidad and Tobago Message Board.

http://lists.rootsweb.ancestry.com/index/intl/TTO/
Rootsweb Trinidad and Tobago Mailing Lists.

www.familysearch.org/eng/Library/FHLC/frameset_fhlc.asp
The LDS Family History Library catalog. Search on 'Trinidad and Tobago' for a limited amount of material on microfilm, including: lists from the *San Fernando Gazette*, Trinidad (1865-1896), manumissions and indentures, c1780-1840 (arranged by name of master or slaveholder).

The International Genealogical Index (now within FamilySearch) and related records should also be searched for individuals from Trinidad and Tobago.

Trinidad Constabulary guard of honour.

CHAPTER TWENTY TWO
Turks and Caicos Islands

LOCATION

The Turks and Caicos islands, consisting of over thirty cays, are an archipelago lying at the south-east end of the Bahamas. The Turks (named after a local variety of cactus which resembles a Turkish fez) consist of eight islands, of which only Grand Turk and Salt Cay are regularly inhabited; there are six main islands in the Caicos, of which the most important are South and North Caicos. Cockburn Town on Grand Turk is the capital. Native-born individuals are known as 'belongers'. In a recent United Nations survey, the Turks and Caicos Islands scored the lowest name recognition of any nation on the planet, way behind Bhutan or Vanuatu...

HISTORY

The Turks Islands were first occupied by English settlers from Bermuda in 1678, and the Caicos Islands were settled by Loyalists from America in the 1780s, following the War of Independence. The Turks and Caicos were fought over by the French and the Spanish during the eighteenth century, but became part of the British empire in 1766, when they were placed under an administrative agent.

Having been part of the Bahamas from 1799 to 1848, at which time the Turks and Caicos Islands constituted the Bahamian parishes of St Thomas and St George respectively (Salt Cay becoming the parish of St John's later), they were transferred to Jamaica in 1874. Between 1958 and 1962 the islands were a member of the Federation of the West Indies, eventually becoming a Crown Colony with a British Governor and an elected executive and legislative council. They remain a British Overseas Territory, though the influence of the USA is very much in evidence, and the economy is calculated in US dollars. A particularly devastating hurricane struck the islands in 1866.

ECONOMY

Salt collectors, Turks and Caicos.

The collection of salt, sponges and conches and the cultivation of cotton and hemp were once the mainstay of the islands' economy, but in recent times tourism, financial services and a modest amount of fishing and agriculture have been the chief source of wealth. The investment of a great deal of foreign capital has made the formerly-remote island of Providenciales ('Provo') a successful centre of development.

PEOPLE

- The first known English visitor to the Turks Islands was Captain John Hawkins, who called there on his way home from Hispaniola in 1563.

- The first individuals to hold various senior posts in the islands were: Frederick Forth (Council President 1848-1854); Daniel Smith (Commissioner 1874-1878); Geoffrey Guy (Administrator 1959-1965).

- Notable Loyalist settlers on Caicos include William Wylly, Wade Stubbs, Colonel Thomas Brown, William Gamble, John Barclay, John McIntosh, Thomas Ingham, John Petty, Peter Dean, and John Lorimer, after whom the village of Lorimers on Middle Caicos was named.

- James Misick, a young planter who was granted lands on North Caicos, enlisted in the Royal Navy during the Anglo-American War of 1812; captured by the Americans, he was eventually released and became a leading member of the Turks Islands legislature.

- A Methodist missionary named William Dowson was detained on the Turks Islands whilst en route to New Providence in 1812, and saw the potential for a Christian presence there; nine years later Roger Moore became the first Methodist missionary to serve in the Turks, to be followed in later years by Theophilus Pugh (1829-1832) and others.

- The forerunner of the Baptist missionary presence on the islands was Rev Ebenezer Grant, who arrived from England in 1836. The first Baptist church was built in 1838, and the most noteworthy Baptist missionary who served there was Rev William Rycroft, who arrived with his wife in 1847.

- One of the earliest Anglican ministers on the islands was Rev Henry Jenkins, who arrived in Caicos in 1797, having thrown all his personal papers overboard when the ship in which he was sailing seemed to be in imminent danger of an attack by a French vessel. Later Anglican pastors include Rev M M Dillon, born in Jamaica, who had served as Captain of the guards in Canada, and who died in Toronto in 1884, and Rev H F Crofton (1886-1899).

RECORDS (UK REPOSITORIES)

The National Archives, London. Colonial Office: correspondence (from 1799), sessional papers, gazettes, etc. Records of the slave registry and Slave Compensation Commission for the Turks and Caicos Islands are with records for the Bahamas.

RECORDS (LOCALLY-HELD)

Michael Craton, writing for the UNESCO *General history of the Caribbean* (1999) is brutally frank when it comes to Turks and Caicos: 'Separate records for the Turks and Caicos Islands were as scanty and scattered as the population itself and there are still no adequate archive facilities. A small museum was established in 1992, but there is no local historical society, nor, in a society where literacy has never had much value, even a daily newspaper, proper bookstore, or more than two deficient libraries'.

Various records relating to the islands (many in a parlous condition) have been held at Waterloo, Grand Turk, at the government archives, the Governor's office and the judicial department. Very few original records survive in the islands, and a number were destroyed during disturbances there in the early 1970s. In 1997 the archives were moved from the Post Office, where they had been subject to flooding, to the prison, and later many were relocated at the National Museum at Guinep House (PO Box 188), Front Street, Grand Turk. About 20% of the surviving records were in such poor condition that they had to be destroyed. Microfilm copies of parish registers from the late eighteenth century and other material relating to the archives, from Jamaica and TNA, are held at the museum, and further records relating to the islands may survive in Jamaica, the Bahamas, or in The National Archives in London, under Jamaica and the Bahamas. The Museum recently issued the following statement: 'One of the commonest forms of requests for help in research comes from family historians. Unfortunately, even though the Museum does hold a wealth of information, such as the Parish Records for St Thomas' Church, we are unable to provide staff time to carry out this research for individuals. We are of course happy to accommodate visiting researchers and will give as much assistance as possible during their visit'.

Churches
Anglican parish records, 1799 to 1929, have been kept at the parish of St Thomas (one of two parishes on Grand Turk, the other being St Mary's), but would now appear to be at the Museum.

Civil registration.
Registers of births, marriages and deaths from 1863 onwards are at the Registrar General's Office, Front Street, Grand Turk.

FURTHER READING

Boultbee, P G *Turks and Caicos Islands* (World bibliographical series, vol 137). 1991.
Davies, J and P *The Turks and Caicos Islands: beautiful by nature*. 2000.
Hutchings, C D *History of the Turks and Caicos islands*. 1975.
Kozy, C J *A history of the Georgia Loyalists and the plantation period in the Turks and Caicos Islands*. 1983.
Pusey, J H *The handbook of the Turks and Caicos Islands*. 1897.
Sadler, H E ('Bertie') *Turks Island landfall*. Originally published in eight volumes. New edition edited by M Sadler and K Collins, 1997. A fascinating compendium of historical material, including, *inter alia*, details of ships which have been wrecked around the islands, with the names of their captains.
Smithers, A *The Turks and Caicos Islands: lands of discovery*. Second edition, 1995.

Turks and Caicos, historically the most marginalised of all Caribbean territories, has scarcely any historiography whatever. Given its history, passing references to the Islands can be found in books dealing with the Bahamas and Jamaica.

WEBSITES

www.tcmuseum.org
Turks and Caicos National Museum.

http://boards.ancestry.co.uk/localities.caribbean.turks-caicos/mb.ashx
Ancestry.co.uk Turks and Caicos Message Board.

www.cousinconnect.com/p/a/1156/
CousinConnect.com Turks and Caicos genealogy queries.

www.britishislesgenweb.org/turkscaicos/
CaribbeanGenWeb: Turks and Caicos Genealogy Project. Links to bulletin boards and a mailing list.

www.turksandcaicos.tc/government/
Government of the Turks & Caicos Islands Website.

www.rootsweb.ancestry.com/~tcawgw/
Rootsweb/Ancestry.com Turks & Caicos GenWeb.

www.familysearch.org/eng/Library/FHLC/frameset_fhlc.asp
The LDS Family History Library catalog. Search on 'Turks and Caicos' for a collection of material, some of it on microfilm: registers of births, baptisms, marriages, deaths and burials, from civil and parish records 1864-1991; public records 1849-1954; probate records 1849-1954.

The International Genealogical Index (now within FamilySearch) and related records should also be searched for individuals from the Turks and Caicos Islands.

INDEXES

Compiled by Nicholas Newington-Irving FSG

SUBJECT INDEX

INDEX TO PLACES IN THE WEST INDIES

229

Beef island 106
Broken Jerusalem 106
Dead Man's Chest 106
Dutchman's Cap 106
Fat Hog Bay 108
Jost Van Dyke 105, 108
Little Jost Van Dyke 109
Peter Island 105
Prickly Pear 106
Rum Island 106
Saint George's 110
Saint Mary's 110
Saint Paul's 110
Salt Island 105
Tortola 105, 107-109, 111-113
Road Town 105, 110-112
Virgin Gorda 105
Virgin Islands, Danish: *see* Virgin Islands, US
Virgin Islands, US 106-107
Charlotte Amalia 111
Saint Croix 14, 106, 109, 181
Saint John 106
Saint Thomas 106, 112
Windward Islands (The): *see* Saint Lucia, Dominica, Grenadines (The), Saint Vincent and Grenada

NOMINAL INDEX

The spelling of some names have been rationalised for ease of reference. This index includes all authors mentioned in the text

BLAKE Martin 161
BLAKE Richard 162
BLAKE family 14, 161
BLEBY (Rev) 54
BLIGH William (Capt) 200
BLOCK family 111
BLOWAR John 62
BLUNDER family 111
BLYDEN Christopher 31
BOCOCK Joseph (Rev) 123
BODDEN Elizabeth 117
BODDEN Isaac 116
BODDEN Mary 116
BODDEN family 117, 119
BOLLER Mary 91
BOLLERS Henry 91
BOLTMAN William 63
BONAPARTE Napoleon: *see* NAPOLEON (Emperor)
BONNET Stede (Maj) alias Capt THOMAS alias EDWARDS 23
BONNY Anne 24
BONNY Thomas 161
BOOKER McConnel & Co 92
BOOTH Andrew or Anthony (Capt) 160
BOOTHBY Jeremiah 63
BOOY: *see* DE BOOY
BORKE David 161
BOULTBEE P. G. 224
BOURNANO or DE BERNANOS (a buccaneer) 20
BOURNE John 6, 176
BOURNE Margaret 176
BOURNE Nehemiah 7
BOWDON: *see* BODDEN
BOWEN Anne 82
BOWREY James 90
BRABSTON family 111
BRACE Francis 192
BRADLEY William 161
BRADLEY family 111
BRADNACK Isaac 63
BRAE Thomas 130
BRANDOW James C. 9, 73
BRANSBY (Ensign) 162
BRANSFORD Charles 144
BRAYNE William 143
BREBNER James 7
BREEN H. H. 197
BRERETON Bridget 214, 218
BRIANT Daniel 29
BRIDGEMAN (Capt): *see* AVERY John (Capt)

BRIDGES G. W. (Rev) 151
BRIGHT John 23
BRINKLEY James 24
BRISKET Anthony 158, 161
BRITNOR L. E. 166
BRITT family 111
BRIZAN George 130, 137
BRODIE David 95
BRODIE Margaret Elizabeth 95
BROKE (Surgent) 62
BROKER William 62
BROOKEHAVEN Christian 8
BROOKS Joseph 22
BROOKSHAW Benjamin 63
BROWINING family 143
BROWN Alexander 207
BROWN Hugh 144
BROWN John 24, 144
BROWN Thomas (Col) 222
BROWN family 111
BROWNE (a gold finer) 192
BROWNE George 192
BROWNE William 62
BROWNELL (Rev) 109
BROWNELL John 181
BROWNING Elizabeth Barrett: *see* MOULTON BARRETT Elizabeth
BROWNING Robert 143
BRUCE Charles (Sir) 196
BRUNT M. A. 118
BRYAN Peter 161
BRYANT John 29
BUCHNER J. H. 151
BUDGE (an Olive Branch member) 192
BUISSERET D. 153
BULCOCK Samuel 90
BULL Dixey (Capt) 23
BURBE Samuel 62
BURDON John (Sir) 103
BURDON K. J. (Lady) 177, 186
BURGAN W. G. L. 136
BURK Redmond 161
BURKE Bernard (Sir) 14
BURKE John 158
BURKE Richard 161
BURNABY William (Adm Sir) 102
BURNETT Joseph 30
BURNS A. 10
BURNS Robert 143
BURRELL Susannah 102
BUSE Anna Christina 14
BUSH family 119

BUSHELL family   14
BUTLER James   130
BUTLER Moyse   7
BUTLER Thomas   192
BYAM family   44
BYNN Francis   161
BYRES John   122
BYRES John   203
BYRON E.   176
CADBURY H. J.   74
CADMANE John   62
CADMORE John   62
CADWALLADER John   108
CAESAR (a pirate)   22
CAHOSY Edmond   161
CAIGER S. L.   103
CALLWOOD family   111
CALVERT (Mrs)   32
CAMP Anthony   2
CAMPBELL Alexander (Hon)   130
CAMPBELL Daniel   116
CAMPBELL James   8
CAMPBELL M.   151
CAMPBELL Mary   116
CAMPBELL P. F.   74
CANNIGETER (a sugar planter)   31
CANTELLY Luke   161
CANZONERI A.   58
CARDIN (Mrs)   37
CARIES George   144
CARLISLE (Earls of): *see* HAY
CARLISLE Francis   38
CARLISLE family   44
CARMAN Thomas   23
CARMICHAEL G.   218
CARMICHEAL H. L. (Maj Gen)   90
CARRELAM Patrick   161
CARROLL (Capt)   162
CARROLL Francis   90-91
CARROLL Roger   161
CARRUTHERS Francis Donald   130
CARSON E. A.   56-57
CART B.   30-33
CARTEACHE Mary   91
CARTER Christopher   80
CARTER Thomas   90
CARTWRIGHT William   117
CARTY Darby   29
CARTY Florence   161
CASH P.   57
CASSE: *see* DU CASSE
CATLIN (Capt)   192

CAVANAN William (Sgt)   161
CAYLER Christian Frederick   91
CELCARTE John   62
CERNY J.   4
CHALIVELL William   29
CHALKLEY Thomas (Capt)   108
CHALWILL family   111
CHAMBARD (Mrs)   32
CHAMBERS Arthur (Capt)   192
CHAMBERS F.   218
CHAMBERS J.   85
CHAMPION (Maj)   204
CHANDER Henry alias RISE Rammetham   23
CHANDLER Michael J.   135
CHAPIN J.   85
CHAPMAN E.   151
CHAPMAN John   29
CHARD (Mr)   80
CHEESBROUGH (Rev)   54
CHEESWRIGHT (Rev)   89
CHISHOLM (a mariner)   116
CHISHOLM family   119
CHISHOLM: *see* GOODEN-CHISHOLM
CHITTICK (Dr)   32
CHREW (Mrs)   37
CHURCH Charles   23
CHURCH Sam Fred   144
CHURCH Samuel   144
CHURCHILL Else   vii
CHURCHILL Nicholas   22
CLANDANIEL family   111
CLARK Thomas Henry   144
CLARK W.   47
CLARK family   111
CLARK: *see* also STRAIKLAND and CLARK
CLARKE (Rev)   201
CLARKE C. G.   151
CLARKE family   119
CLEMENT Peter   90
CLIFETE Thomas   62
CLOUGH William   181
COAKLEY Caesar (Sir)   108
COAKLEY Edward   29, 31
COAKLEY Thomas   29
COBHAM (Capt)   24
COBHAM Maria   24
COCHRANE Andrew James (Hon)   123
COCHRANE Thomas (8th Earl of Dundonald)   123
COCHRANE-JOHNSTONE: *see* COCHRANE
CODRINGTON Christopher (Sir)   37 -69, 47, 63,107, 181

EVANS (an Olive Branch member)   192
EVANS (Rev)   109
EVELYN family   176
EVERETT family   111
EVERY John: *see* AVERY John (Capt)   22
EWARNER family   44
EWING Alexander (Rev)   83
EZRATTY   H. A.   11
FAIRWEATHER D. N.   103
FARIS J. T.   112
FARQUHAR James   130
FARRINGTON John   31
FARRINGTON William   29-30
FEARON Peter   108
FÉDON Julien   130, 132
FERGUS H. A.   167
FERGUSON S.   11
FERGUSON Tom   191
FERRELL Catherine   102
FEURTADO Walter Augustus   151
FIDLER (Rev)   213
FIELD John (Rev)   38
FIELDING Joshua   107
FILBY P. William   6
FINCENT Samuel   29
FINNY John   161
FISH William   144
FISHER E. F. S.   11
FISHLOCK W. C.   112
FITZGERALD John   24
FITZMORRIS James   161
FITZROY family   44
FLANDERS (sugar planter)   31
FLANDERS Thomas   29
FLAT David   8
FLEMIG John   192
FLEMMING family   111
FLEMMING Jonathan   31
FLETCHER (Rev)   213
FLETCHER Duncan   144
FLIGHT Alice   29
FLOID Samuel   29
FOREMAN John (Rev)   90
FORTH Frederick   222
FORTINE Henry   62
FORWARD Giles   89
FOSTER William   116
FOSTER family   119
FOTHRINGHAM Patrick   130
FOTT Isaac   62
FOWLE Dawe   62
FOX Lewis   91

FOZZARD John   63
FRANCE Christina   90
FRANKLIN Benjamin   144
FRANKS Moses   55
FRARE Peter   29
FRASER A.   203
FRASER Henry   74
FRASER K.   203
FRASER L. M.   218
FREEMAN family   44
FRENCH WEST INDIA COMPANY   190
FRITH M. K. S. (Rev)   82
FROBISHER Richard   80
GACHET Charles   194
GAINER John   63
GALENSON D.   47
GALLOWAY David   161
GALLWAY (Maj)   160
GALWAY David   162
GAMBLE (Rev)   201
GAMBLE William   222
GANAN Mosett   161
GANAN Thomas   161
GANDY Michael   10
GANDY W.   9, 85
GARBIN Johanna Rebecca   90
GARDINER Jeanne   82
GARDNER William James A.   144, 152
GARFIELD G.   11
GARNETT (Rev)   65
GARRAT Richard   192
GARRAWAY D. G.   138
GARRAWAY E. G.   197
GARRET James   192
GARTSIDE Benjamin   163
GATES Thomas   22
GAWTHROP Thomas   108
GEORGE family   111
GERMAINE John (Lt)   209
GERRALD James   161
GERRALD Redmond   161
GIBBES Mary   31
GIBBON W. L. (Rev)   82
GIBBONS Garret   22
GIBBS A. R.   101
GIBBS Sarah   91
GIBSON John (Rev)   144
GILBERT Nathaniel (Hon)   38
GILBERT William   62
GILCHRIST Williams   130
GILES James   90
GILGRASS (a Methodist missionary)   181

MONTAGUE (Duke of) 190
MONTEFIORE family 73
MONTGOMERY James 207
MONTGOMERY John 207
MOORE Alice 82
MOORE J. M. 97
MOORE J. R. (Rev) 97
MOORE John (Rev) 83
MOORE Richard 80
MOORE Roger 223
MOORE William 22
MORE William 161
MORGAN Edward (Col) 21, 143
MORGAN Henry (Sir) 21, 116, 142-143, 153
MORGAN John 29
MORGAN Robert 21, 143
MORIS family 125
MORRIS Elise 177
MORRIS John 89, 130
MORRIS Valentine 200
MORRIS family 112
MORRISON J. H. 186
MORTIER (Rev) 89
MORTON Philip 21-22
MORTON family 119
MOSELY M. 57
MOTTET Mauritz Johan Jacobus 91
MOULTON BARRETT Elizabeth 143
MOULTON Charles 143
MOULTON Elizabeth 143
MOUNT G. S. 218
MOUNT Joan E. 136, 165, 195, 218
MUIR J. (Rev) 97
MUIR William 130
MULLET alias MILLET James 23
MULLINS Darby 22
MULLOON family 112
MULLREAN Thomas 161
MUNDON Stephen 24
MUNRO James Wright 90
MUNRO: see also GUN-MUNRO
MURDOCK (Rev) 109
MURKLAND Sidney Smith 89
MURPHY Daniel 161
MURPHY Dennis 161
MURPHY John 161
MURPHY Nathan W. vii, 16, 75
MURRAY Andrew 38
MURRAY John (Maj Gen) 90
MUSGRAVE Eliza 45
MUSGRAVE William 45
MYERS A. C. 75

NARDIN J. C. (M) 135
NASH family 112
NEDESE William 62
NEISCHER John Anthony 90
NELSON (Rev) 207
NELSON Frances Herbert (Viscountess): *see* NISBET Frances Herbert
NELSON Horatio (Vice Admiral Viscount) x, 37, 172, 181
NELSON Prince 97
NEWBY Joseph 38
NEWMAN Henry 62
NEWTON Joshuah 29
NEWTON M. 74
NICHOLAS Thomas: *see* NICHOLLS alias NICHOLAS Thomas
NICHOLL John 192
NICHOLLS alias NICHOLAS Thomas 23
NICHOLLS: *see* ALFORD NICHOLLS
NICHOLSON D. V. 48
NICHOLSON Robert (Lt Col) 89
NEWINGTON-IRVING, Nicholas vii, 266
NISBET Frances Herbert 172
NISBETT family 176
NORTH Goody 82
NORTH Roger (Capt) 89
NORWOOD Richard 82
NOTTINGHAM Mary: *see* HUNT Mary
NOTTINGHAM Samuel (Rev) 108
NOTTINGHAM family 112
NURSE Mary Jane 90
O'REILLY Philip 31
OASTERMAN Thomas 45
ODEL Samuel 22
ODLUM R. W. 97
OKE (a missionary) 48
OKELL William 144
OLIVER Vere Langford 3, 5-6, 16, 29, 33, 40, 42-43, 45-47, 57, 71, 73, 85, 96, 103, 112, 125, 136, 149, 160, 164-166, 170, 173-175, 177, 183-185, 187, 196, 203, 210, 217-218
OLIVER family 46
ORDE (Governor) 123
OSBORNE F. J. 153
OTTLET C. R. 210
OUCKAMA Paul Augustus 91
OUDKIRK G. 97
OUGHT Samuel 130
OUTERBRIDGE Thomas 82
OUTERBRIDGE family 82
OWEN (an Olive Branch member) 192
OWENS Abel 22

PROWSE Lawrence (Capt) 23
PRYSEN John 62
PUGH Theophilus 223
PULSIPHER L. M. 167
PURKIS Isaac 207
PYLE Howard 20, 36
QUIGLY Teige 161
QUOSSEY Rosanna 14
RABY James 181
RADCLIFFE Virginia 19
RADFORD D. A. 75
RADFORD Robert 62
RAGATZ L. J. 5
RAIN Thomas 89-90
RALEIGH Walter (Sir) 212
RALEIGH family 112
RANKIN Andrew 13
RANYELL (Rev) 89, 207
RAPSOT family 112
RASPUTIN Grigory Yefimovich 21
RATTRAY Charles 89
RAVENS Henry 81
RAWLEIGH: see RALEIGH
RAYNER (Rev) 89
RAYNER J. (Rev) 207
READ Mary 24
READ William 24
REAN Teige 161
REAN William 161
RED Catharine 30
RED Samuel 30-31
REDFERN William (Rev) 117
REDWOOD Phillip 6
REGAN Morgan 161
REGATZ L. J. 12
REID John 130
REID Mary Jane 196
REID Robert 196
RENED Edmund 161
RENNY John 161
RERFIGGS Dermond 161
REYNOLDS family 112
RHODES John 62
RICARDS Robert 90
RICE Jenkin 130
RICE Owen 24
RICHARDS John 8, 29
RICHARDSON (a stock farmer) 32
RICHARDSON (a sugar planter) 31
RICHARDSON Alexander (Rev) 83
RICHARDSON Anne 31
RICHARDSON Anthony 123

RICHARDSON Anthony Bacon 123
RICHARDSON Benjamin 31
RICHARDSON James 29
RICHARDSON Jeremiah 29
RICHARDSON Joan 30
RICHARDSON John 29-31, 201
RICHARDSON Mary 31
RICHARDSON Nehemiah 29
RICHARDSON R. 31
RICHARDSON Richard 29
RICHARDSON Thomas (Rev) 123
RICHARDSON William 30
RICHARDSON family 112
RICHMOND John 8
RIDGE John 23
RILEY S. 57
RINGE Roger 161
RINGROOME Thomas 63
RINGROSE Basil 20
RISE Rammetham: see CHANDER Henry
RISON Thomas 161
RIVERS family 119
ROACH Thomas 161
ROACH William M. 90
ROBARTS Richard 29
ROBBINS James 22-23
ROBERT Bartholomew (Capt) 22
ROBERTS Edward 144
ROBERTS Owen 22
ROBERTS W. A. 153
ROBERTS William 29
ROBERTSON George 13
ROBERTSON James 14
ROBERTSON, mapmaker 148
ROBINSON (a London Adventurer) 128, 130
ROBINSON Edward 23
ROBINSON John 63
ROBRYAN Daniel 161
ROBY John 150, 153
ROCK Nicholas 161
RODNEY George Brydges (Adm - 1st Baron Rodney) 122, 181
RODWAY J. 96
ROGERS Barll 29
ROGERS Benjamin 29
ROGERS Berell 29
ROGERS John 29, 62, 192
ROGERS Peter 29
ROGERS Thomas 29
ROGERS Woodes (Capt) 53
ROGOZINKI J. 24
ROOME James 89

SINCKLER E. G. 75
SINCLAIR Norma 138
SLATYER William 144
SLIFFORD George (3rd Earl of Cumberland) 122
SLINGSLEY Henry 62
SMEDLEY (Rev) 207
SMITH Anthony 31-32
SMITH Bradley 172
SMITH Daniel 222
SMITH John 89, 161
SMITH John: *see* GOW John
SMITH Margaret 91
SMITH Michael 90
SMITH R. C. 119
SMITH Vernona T. C. (Mrs) 3, 5, 44, 145
SMITH William 95
SMITH William (Rev) 54
SMITH family 112
SMITHERS A. 224
SOLLY William Henry 119
SOMERBY H. J. 186
SOMERS George (Adm Sir) 79-81
SOMERS Matthew 81
SOMERVILLE D. 167
SOUND Joseph 24
SOUZA: *see* DeSOUZA
SPENCER Aubrey George (Ven) 83
SPENCER Jeremiah 29
SPOFFORTH Sam 116
STAMPER Ann 91
STANFORD C. J. 75
STANFORD William (Rev) 101
STAPLETON William 159
STAPLETON William (Col Sir) 105, 107, 160, 163
STAUNTON Kitty 91
STEPHENS James Thomas 90
STEPHENSON (Rev) 207, 213
STEPHENSON John (Rev) 82
STERN M. 177
STEVENSON Christian (Mrs) 82
STEVENSON Robert Louis 106
STEWART J. 12
STEWART MACKENZIE Francis Pelham 136
STEWART MACKENZIE James Alexander 136
STILES Richard 22
STOKELY (an Olive Branch member) 192
STOKES Luke 170
STOKES Mark 62
STOLL Sophia Elizabeth 91
STRACHAN W. G. (Rev) 90
STRAIKLAND and CLARK 209

STRITCH John (Fr) 158
STRODE H. 85
STRONG Leonard 89
STRONG Peter 63
STRONG family 112
STUBBS Wade 222
STURGE Joseph 160, 162
STURGEON William (Rev) 131
SUCKLING G. 113
SULLIVAN Daniel (Ensign) 161
SULLIVAN Dermond 161
SULLIVAN John 161
SUTCLIFFE Abraham 108
SUTTY L. 204
SYMONETTE M. C. 58
TALBOYS Thomas (Rev) 89, 213
TATUM family 119
TAYLOR (Mrs) 37
TAYLOR Ann 90
TAYLOR David 144
TAYLOR John 181
TAYLOR Robert Barry 89
TEACH Edward (Capt) 21
TEAGUE Robert 23
TELLIES Andrew 29
TEMPLER Philip Arthur 122
TENCH (an Olive Branch member) 192
TERRELL Michelle 177
TEW Thomas 22
THIBOUE Isaac 29
THOILL John 161
THOMAS (Capt): *see* BONNET Stede (Maj)
THOMAS Antony Keighley 209
THOMAS Charles 9
THOMAS John 23, 29
THOMAS family 44, 112
THOMPSON Gilbert 108
THOMPSON Janette Elizabeth 91
THOMPSON John 130
THOMPSON Peter 130
THOMPSON Peter Henry 91
THOMPSON Richard 89
THOMPSON Rob vii
THORNTON Dorcas: *see* DOWNING Dorcas
THORNTON Jane 108
THORNTON Mary 108
THORNTON William (Dr) 108
THORNTON William 108
THORNTON family 112
THURSTON A. 5
THURSTON William 103
TILLY: *see* DE GRASSE

About the SOCIETY OF GENEALOGISTS

Founded in 1911 the Society of Genealogists (SoG) is Britain's premier family history organisation. The Society maintains a splendid genealogical library and education centre in Clerkenwell.

The Society's collections are particularly valuable for research before the start of civil registration of births marriages and deaths in 1837 but there is plenty for the beginner too. Anyone starting their family history can use the online census indexes or look for entries in birth, death and marriage online indexes in the free open community access area.

The Library contains Britain's largest collection of parish register copies, indexes and transcripts and many nonconformist registers. Most cover the period from the sixteenth century to 1837. Along with registers, the library holds local histories, copies of churchyard gravestone inscriptions, poll books, trade directories, census indexes and a wealth of information about the parishes where our ancestors lived.

Unique indexes include Boyd's Marriage Index with more than 7 million names compiled from 4300 churches between 1538-1837 and the Bernau Index with references to 4.5 million names in Chancery and other court proceedings. Also available are indexes of wills and marriage licences, and of apprentices and masters (1710-1774). Over the years the Society has rescued and made available records discarded by government departments and institutions but of great interest to family historians. These include records from the Bank of England, Trinity House and information on Teachers and Civil Servants.

Boyd's and other unique databases are published on line on **www.findmypast.com** and on the Society's own website **www.sog.org.uk**. There is free access to these and many other genealogical sites within the Library's Internet suite.

The Society is the ideal place to discover if a family history has already been researched with its huge collection of unique manuscript notes, extensive collections of past research and printed and unpublished family histories. If you expect to be carrying out family history research in the British Isles then membership is very worthwhile although non-members can use the library for a small search fee.

www.sog.org.uk

The Society of Genealogists is an educational charity. It holds study days, lectures, tutorials and evening classes and speakers from the Society regularly speak to groups around the country. The SoG runs workshops demonstrating computer programs of use to family historians. A diary of events and booking forms are available from the Society on 020 7553 3290 or on the website **www.sog.org.uk** .

Members enjoy free access to the Library, certain borrowing rights, free copies of the quarterly *Genealogists Magazine* and various discounts of publications, courses, postal searches along with free access to data on the members' area of our website.

More details about the Society can be found on its extensive website at **www.sog.org.uk**

For a free Membership Pack contact the Society at:

14 Charterhouse Buildings,
Goswell Road,
London EC1M 7BA.
Telephone: 020 7553 3291
Fax: 020 7250 1800

The Society is always happy to help with enquiries and the following contacts may be of assistance.

Library & shop hours:

Monday	Closed
Tuesday	10am - 6pm
Wednesday	10am - 6pm
Thursday	10am - 8pm
Friday	Closed
Saturday	10am - 6pm
Sunday	Closed

Contacts:

Membership
Tel: 020 7553 3291
Email: membership@sog.org.uk

Lectures & courses
Tel: 020 7553 3290
Email: events@sog.org.uk

Family history advice line
Tel: 020 7490 8911
See website for availability

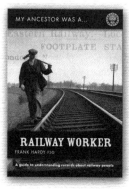
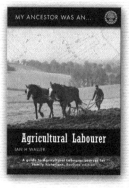